HEARTENING

HERITAGE

ON A

CAROLINA CRESCENT

BY J. M. M. HOLDEN

Library of Congress Catalog Number
89-91160

Printed in the United States of America
for LHG Research Associates

Printed by
New Hanover Printing and Publishing Company
Wilmington, North Carolina

Contents

Illustrated with maps, charts, photographs and drawings

Acknowledgements

I am happy to acknowledge several individuals who have contributed in various ways to this study. First, I am indebted to Herbert Hucks, Jr., Archivist at Wofford College and Curator for the Historical Society of the South Carolina Conference of the United Methodist Church. Mr. Hucks patiently located sources and guided me through the minutes, maps, and other pertinent records of 1773 to 1850.

William Erwin, Jr., gave generous assistance in the Manuscript Room of Perkins Library at Duke University. For other assistance at Duke, I am indebted to the staff in the Divinity School Library and to the curator of the Rare Book Room.

I was graciously and efficiently assisted by the staff in the North Carolina Room of Wilson Library at the University of North Carolina at Chapel Hill.

Brooks Little and Frances Hart gave encouragement and help in the Heritage Center at Lake Junaluska, North Carolina.

Numerous other helpers I found in the North Carolina Archives and Library; in the colleges of Louisburg, North Carolina Wesleyan, Methodist, and Lees-McRae; also, in the public libraries of Brunswick and New Hanover Counties.

To "The Scribblers", a local writers group, I give thanks for hearing some chapters, giving encouragement, and prodding me to publish.

I owe a special debt to Mary Wyche Mintz, who patiently read my manuscript, offered some suggestions, and helped me decide that publication of this arrangement of scarce and scattered information may assist local church historians and give to other people a view of our HEARTENING HERITAGE.

Preface

Fostering a personal interest in a local congregation, the author discovered by studious inquiry that the history of Concord United Methodist Church and her neighboring sister churches generated from the days of exploration and colonization of the Carolinas' Coastal Crescent between Cape Fear and Winyah Point. This region shares a common background in many aspects, especially in its religious heritage, beginning with the efforts of the established Church of England to propagate itself in the New World and continuing with early Methodist missionaries and circuit riders.

After reading journals and letters of some circuit riders who, in all-weather efforts to reach their appointments, forded rivers and waded swamps, I felt impelled to make an effort toward revelation of their devotion and determination to "spread the word" while facing travel hazards and long absences from their families.

No attempt has here been made to compile individual church histories; but the common heritage of all the churches in the area seems worthy of discovery, preservation, and dissemination.

From notes taken during several years of research, I have chosen to present information that may be helpful to church historians in the Cape Fear-Long Bay area and to individuals with interest in the general history of this area. This presentation offers information on the five historical decades in which the Church of England was the Established Church; on the appearance, growth, and influence of Methodist societies before the Civil War; a chronology of related historical events up to the Reconstruction; a two-century list of appointed Methodist ministers who served in Brunswick County and environs from 1787 to 1988.

These I believe to be the heart of our heritage; and since with them "my cup runneth over," I make this offering for your HEARTENING HERITAGE.

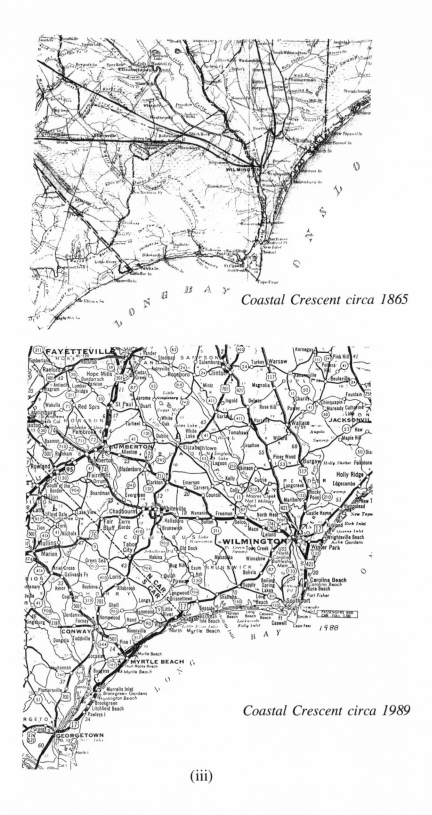

Coastal Crescent circa 1865

Coastal Crescent circa 1989

(iii)

Chapter I

The Coastal Crescent

The Coastal Crescent of the Carolinas is an appropriate designation for the curving land that extends from Cape Fear in North Carolina to Winyah Point in South Carolina. This crescent-shaped shore is one of several facing the Atlantic Ocean, but with its own singular pattern. This picturesque formation has evolved through centuries of artistry by storms and calms, spring tides and neap tides, flood tides and ebb tides; and in *each* of the innumerable days gone by, *two high tides* and *two low tides* moving in harmony with the moon's schedule.

The area's existence had for millions of years remained unknown, except to a few aborigines. Then in the 1500's some brave Europeans ventured to cross the Atlantic Ocean and attempted settlement on what is now Long Bay Shores.

Behind this scenic shoreline lay an area later to be colonized, largely by Anglo-Saxons who brought their own culture, including a religion which has had a continuing influence on the life style of people living today in this Coastal Crescent. The sixteenth-century failure at attempted settlement was later overshadowed by early eighteenth-century successes in colonization and Christianization.

The Native Americans living near Long Bay could not understand the passing ships or the varied colors of strangers landing on their shores.

Their first mysterious visitors arrived in Giovanni de Verrazzano's French-sponsored vessel in 1524 when his ship stopped briefly and then continued westward. Later it returned, passed the first landing place, and continued northward toward Newfoundland.[1]

The mission of this Florentine was to explore and afterwards to relate his findings, to "see and tell." His report a few months later acclaimed Nature's beauty in the sand dunes, palms, and high cypresses; he also mentioned pleasant weather and abundant game for hunting. He described the natives as russet-colored, tall, broadbreasted; with strong arms and legs and black hair that hung like tails over the necks. Some were partially dressed in skins, leaves, and garlands of fur. They came near the shore, then fled in fear of the newcomers, but returned when attracted by small gifts and food.[2] These natives were later identified as "Cape Fears" and "Waccamaws," two tribes of the Siouan nation.[3]

The Indians seen by Verrazzano had no knowledge or suspicion of a growing threat in traders who, with or without Spanish permits, were gathering natives of Mexico and Florida to sell as slaves in Hispaniola where labor was needed.

Lucas Vásquez de Ayllón, a Spaniard serving as a public official in Hispaniola, was able in 1523 to secure a charter for eight hundred leagues of land north of Florida for the purpose of exploration and colonization. The first ship he sent joined forces with slave traders who, upon arriving on the southern mainland, invited 130 Indians into their boat and immediately transported them toward Hispaniola. The vessel became a scene of grief, fear, suicide and rebellion—a failure for Ayllón. To clear his own record, he freed the surviving slaves, but continued to be interested in settling Chicora.[4]

Ayllón's second venture was carefully planned and directed so as to settle over five hundred persons including whites from Spain and Santo Domingo, Negro slaves, and Indian interpreters with wives and maidens. Over eighty horses were loaded along with supplies for all. To transport these people, livestock, and supplies required the use of the flagship, a big *nef* called *La Bretona*; two smaller vessels, *Santa Catalina* and *Charruch*; a *bergantin* (a light craft for shoal waters); one *garbarra*, (a lighter barge or tender.[5]

Near the mainland a sudden wreck of the flagship made necessary their landing by a river to which they gave the name "Rio Jordan." A unique assemblage of men and horses came ashore on the west side of this river which would at later times bear these different names: the Charles, the Clarendon, the Hanover; and presently, the Cape Fear River.

Among those who came ashore at this location were three Dominican friars who held mass, the usual thanksgiving service after safe passage on sea. This is considered to have been the first

2

Christian service in the territory that is now North Carolina.[6]

The settlers brought by Ayllón did not remain here on the northern shore of Long Bay. After their growing discontent they moved westward and then to the southern shore of Long Bay, still in Indian "Chicora", later called the "Land of Ayllón". Most of the five hundred would-be settlers went by boat, but some traveled by land, riding or leading horses, walking on beaches or Indian trails, and at times cutting a way through brush and trees. Some Indian interpreters, to escape the hated Spaniards, fled inland before reaching the second settlement by Winyah Bay, the confluence of the Waccamaw and Pee Dee Rivers.

Those who completed the trip became the settlers of San Miguel de Gualdape. At this location, Ayllón lived only a few months. The others existed amid suffering, disease, strife, and rebellion against the Spanish leaders. Many died, and some joined Indians in order to escape through woods and waters. About one-fourth of the original settlers attempted to return to Santo Domingo, but death claimed many souls, and the ocean received many bodies, including the remains of Ayllón.[7]

The shores of Long Bay and Cape Fear were again given back to the Indians, but this time the natives had been joined by some black slaves and other escapees from the ill-fated colony. It is not certain to what extent the races may have mixed, or where they found sanctuary away from the dreaded Spaniards. Some historians believe that from this attempted settlement, Carolina received the first African slaves and that some of them remained on the southern shores of the Gualdape, now the Waccamaw River. Others that survived may have joined friendly Indians and fled inland by way of the present Pee Dee and Lumber rivers, near which have been discovered some early settlements described as the *melanges* or *mixty-maxty* settlers.

After various studies based on translations of Friar Montessimo's report to historian Gonzales Fernández de Oviedo, it is generally accepted that Carolina in 1526 witnessed its first shipwreck and shipbuilding, its first Christian service, and the arrival of the first black slaves, some of whom stayed near the shore and others who moved inland. Though little of the scattered evidence remains, "The Land of Ayllón" did remain on official maps for half a century.[8]

More Attempts at Settlement

The natives of the Cape Fear area were free to use the lands and waters for the 136 years between the Spaniards' visit and the next settlement in 1663 by a group from a New England colony. Leading the new settlers was William Hilton who purchased from the natives the river and adjacent lands; but this group stayed only three months at their Clarendon settlement. Their departing gifts were their cattle and, on a post, a discouraging notice for future would-be settlers. Their departure took place just before the Lords Proprietors issued a declaration which would have given better opportunities, including "freedom and liberty of conscience in all spiritual and religious things."

Believing that prospects would improve in the Cape Fear area, some residents and local merchants of Barbados formed a corporation of Barbadian adventurers and engaged William Hilton to help them find a suitable place for their settlement. When Hilton returned, he explored farther up the same river and renamed it "Cape Fear." With two of the company's agents, he purchased the river and adjacent lands—again.[9]

With the arrival of colonists from Barbados, plans were made for County Clarendon and its governor from Barbados, Sir John Yeamons. Charles Town was laid out and organized on the west side of the Cape Fear River, below the forks; but it was not sufficiently supported by London. The Indians became revengeful after some of the children were sold into slavery instead of being taught as had been promised. Indian raids on cattle threatened the survival of the new settlers, who then began to leave. Soon the governor was unable to keep a dozen men with him. As homes were deserted to decay, the gardens and fields grew wild again. Here ended the prospect for a leading port and community. The Cape Fear area, years later to become Brunswick County, reverted to its wilderness scene and Indian usage. The decayed and buried Charles Town left only a name for the creek by which it had stood: *Town Creek.*[10]

Lockwood's Loss and Legacy

A few years after the abandonment of Charles Town on the Cape Fear River, another river provided the site for a new settlement started by a Barbadian leader named Lockwood. It is believed by some that he intended to enter the Cape Fear River but by error entered a smaller river west of it. Here he and those accompanying him encountered unexpected hazards, the first of which was the loss of his vessel. Afterwards, by mistreating the natives, he incurred their wrath and was driven away.

4

This Barbadian's errors and his uncontrollable temper branded him as a man of folly never to be forgotten. His name, his nature, and his failure to establish his "folly" were combined in giving this river the distinctive name, *Lockwood's Folly*. Unlike the Cape Fear, this river has continuously been known by *one name only*, and has for over three hundred years appeared as "Lockwood's Folly' on maps of the Cape Fear environs.[11]

The James Settlement Destroyed

Nearly fifty years passed without foreign intruders in the areas surrounding the Cape Fear and Lockwood's Folly Rivers. For a period around 1700, these areas south of the Cape Fear River were considered part of South Carolina; north of the Cape Fear was North Carolina. South Carolina was granting lands south and west of the Cape Fear River. One grant on August 17, 1714, was to Thomas James for more than a thousand acres on the west side of that river. The grantee had only one year to build and plant there; he was the following year found by Maurice Moore, presumably killed by Indians. Hugh Meredith reported ten years later that dangers from Indians were then less than when "Thomas James and his family were murdered and the settlement plundered and burnt." In a few years the Indian threat was overcome and the Cape Fear area welcomed newcomers who were planning a town.[12]

First Grant of Cape Fear Land

Some land claims were made when the Cape Fear area was part of the Proprietary Albemarle, and some later when it was part of Bath and also of Archdale; but with cancellations and failures to settle, no permanent grants were completed here until the years of the Craven Precinct, 1712-1729.

The oldest continuing grant in the Cape Fear area was made May 8, 1713, to Thomas Smith II for Cedar Island, previously called Cape Island or Barren Island; later it became known as Smith Island and Baldhead.

Thomas Smith had claimed the island since 1690 and is believed to have planned to use it for continuing his Indian trading after this activity became strictly regulated in South Carolina. He probably never resided on the island, but others inhabited it as indicated by the Indian family sites and relics that have been found there. Settling the mainland was for a while discouraged by hardship and possible dangers from pirates and Indians. Although the Cape Fear area was not a major sanctuary for pirates, in 1718 Stede Bonnet was captured here and taken to Charleston for hanging.[13]

Attitudes toward the Anglican Church

The English settlers desiring to reproduce in the New World the same institutions familiar to them emphasized their desire that the church of the mother country become the church of Carolina. The first requests for ministers were made by the governors and sent to the Bishop of London. Governor Sayle wrote to Lord Ashley that the colony needed a godly and orthodox minister: "Pray send us a minister qualified according to the Church of England."[14]

Quakers, who had even before 1700 provided their own church needs, felt no inclination to import English preachers and to pay more taxes. It was in the Quaker settlements north of the Cape Fear that the Anglican church met its earliest and strongest opposition in Carolina. In the Cape Fear area, few Quakers had settled and most of them moved farther inland.[15]

The Church of England was strengthened by Henderson Walker, who became governor in 1699. A leader in the Anglican church, he was determined to to work for legislation to support it in the colony.[16] He informed the Bishop of London that for twenty-one years the colony had been "without priest or altar."

Royal Governor Walker is credited with the passage of the Vestry Act of 1701, which organized parishes, established churches and provided support by poll tax; however, this Vestry Act was not permanent. The governor had been disappointed in 1700 and complained to the bishop of "trouble and grief brought to us who have great veneration for the church that the first minister sent to us should prove so ill as to give Dissenters so much occasion to charge us with him."[17] In 1703 an act was passed creating a commission of twenty to dismiss ministers for misconduct.

The Society for the Propogation of the Gospel

The locating of ministers for the colony proved to be a problem almost insurmountable. The Church of England did not have enough ministers qualified and willing to go to a foreign land. An assisting organization appeared in 1701 when the Reverend Thomas Bray and his associates received from King William III a charter giving them authority as The Society for the Propagation of the Gospel with the purpose of sending gospel messengers to offer divine worship and education to His Majesty's subjects throughout the British Empire.

6

It was to this society that early governors appealed for help in locating missionaries and in providing financial assistance. In England this society was considered the missionary arm of the church; but to many colonists it was looked upon as an "ally of monarchs."[18]

For missionaries to America the Society (hereinafter, SPG) agreed to pay fifty pounds a year in addition to the initial twenty pounds offered by the Crown. As discontent persisted in the colonies, John Blair was sent in 1703 to survey the North Carolina religious scene. Blair was discouraged with attitudes of the Quakers, "the most powerful enemies of church government"; also, he deplored his finding many people with *no* religion, some religions with no manner of order, and only a small group really zealous for the interest of the Anglican Church. He finally concluded this to be "the most barbarous place in the continent" and departed.[19]

For four years after Reverend Blair's abrupt departure in 1704, no missionary from the SPG came to the Carolina Province, perhaps because of Blair's derogatory reports. The SPG did, however, send literature to the colony in 1705 to combat the despised doctrines of the "Anabaptists", for word had reached headquarters that North Carolina "swarmed with Baptists." More than thirty parish libraries were sent by the SPG to North America; one of these came to Bath in North Carolina.

The Province of North Carolina continued to be "the most arduous and deadly of missionary fields." As arriving missionaries were introduced to the swamps, forests, and rivers without bridges, they thought the settlers were the most backward and illiterate of all the colonies.[20]

Opposition to English governors and imported preachers continued, but by 1711 less stringent laws were enacted and the Anglican Church became more acceptable for a time.

The Legislated Church

In 1715 an act was passed officially establishing the Church of England in North Carolina. Nine parishes were created; vestrymen were selected and given the duty of "procuring an able and godly minister, qualified according to the Ecclesiastical Laws of England." Even after this law was passed, no ministers arrived; only a few missionaries came during the first seventeen years. Legislation in 1715 to regulate morals was intended to prevent the grievous sins of cursing and swearing, to check drunkeness, to enforce Sunday observance, and in other ways to improve public morality.[21]

After three decades, the Church of England and the SPG practically failed to place ministers. In the period of 1708-1723 the SPG sent six missionaries, but only one remained longer than two years. Dissenters appeared at various places, and living conditions were not attracting Anglican ministers.[22]

The last Proprietary Governor, Richard Everard, left office in 1731. He had seen the colony expand southward and westward, but he was unable to work satisfactorily with the colonists. Political turmoil blotted out church progress—except in the town of Brunswick where the Reverend John LaPierre had arrived and had already begun his ministry.[23]

The First Permanent Settlement in Cape Fear Area

After the many failures of attempted settlement during the proprietary, the Cape Fear development began just four years before Carolina was purchased by the Crown of Britain in 1729. To the south of this area was Charleston, already progressing in business, culture, and growth of an Episcopal church established in 1681. The Charleston area would later share its culture with the Cape Fear area; from there would come the founder of the first town, and also the first Christian minister in the Cape Fear area.[24]

During the efforts to remove Indian dangers, Maurice Moore was traveling toward South Carolina and crossed the Cape Fear River about twelve miles from its mouth. After that experience in 1715, his interests were directed toward this attractive area for a settlement of his own. Encouraged by a legislative act concerning courthouses and local officials, he started planning his own venture, a town by the Cape Fear River.[25]

It was Maurice Moore's foresight, planning and executive skill that brought to the Cape Fear area its first permanent settlement and the first resident Christian minister. Moore donated land and planned for the first church, first courthouse, a burial ground, a market house and other public buildings. These plans were in place before the state boundary line was established, before New Hanover Precinct was formed, and before Carolina was transferred from the Proprietors to the Crown of England.

Meanwhile George Burrington visited the Cape Fear area in 1723 and reported no residents. From that time, he was interested in attracting reliable settlers. When he became governor in 1724, he encouraged the building of a road from New Bern and the granting of available land on both sides of the Cape Fear River.[26]

Maurice Moore was among the first four grantees, all of whom were from South Carolina. The site of his river crossing was chosen to become a center of trade, a collecting point for produce, and a place of disembarkation for settlers. Moore made carefully detailed plans for business, for residences and for sale of lots. With these plans, the town of Brunswick was established in 1726 on the west bank of Hanover River, "otherwise called the Cape Fear."

With the growth of this first permanent settlement and port on the Cape Fear, land granting for the surrounding area increased. In addition to Maurice Moore's 7,000 acres, large grants were made to his relatives from South Carolina until 1731 when a total of 115,000 acres of Cape Fear land was in the hands of "the family." Thus the best lands went to a few upper-class South Carolinians. By the new road from New Bern there soon came some families from Albemarle to take up lands along the tributaries of the Cape Fear River.[27]

After overcoming the threatening power of Indians and establishing a promising town, the Moores did not forget that their original plan provided a church location. Here, two hundred years after the Catholic service held by friars in Ayllón's shipwrecked settlers, a church was being planned and a minister being sought. This was the Episcopal beginning in the Cape Fear area, and Long Bay shores would never again be the *churchless crescent*.

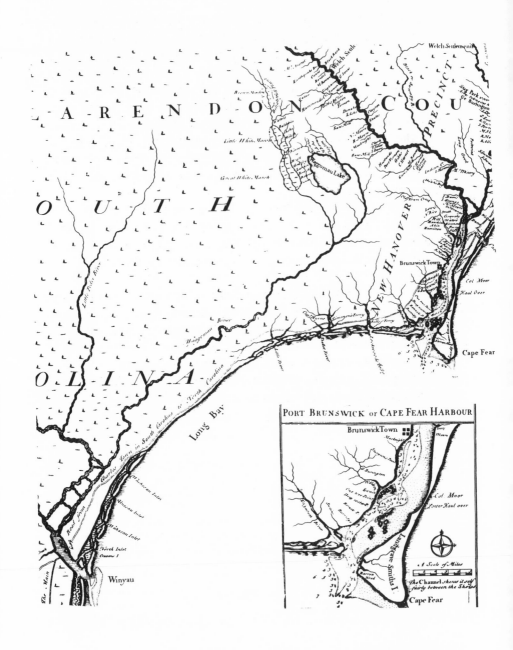

Moseley Map - 1733
Department of Cultural Resources, Division of Archives and History

10

Chapter II

The Anglican Church Parish
of St. James

Three years after the establishment of the town of Brunswick, legislation was passed creating a new precinct to include lands from Haulover and Little Inlet to the southernmost bounds of the North Carolina Province. Provision was made for courts and elections of New Hanover Precinct to be held, and for the courthouse and jail to be built in the town of Brunswick.[1]

The bounds of the precinct of New Hanover simultaneously became also the bounds of St. James Parish, the first organized parish in southeastern North Carolina; and the St. James Parish Church was ordered to be built at "a place called Brunswick."[2]

The formation of this new precinct and parish took place in 1729, the same year that the English Crown bought the North Carolina Province from the Lords Proprietors. The results of this purchase were for a while uncertain in Brunswick Town and St. James Parish.

Richard Everard, the last proprietary governor, was in office still trying to deal with disruptive factors that were adding to his unenviable reputation as governor. His numerous confusing problems became part of the legacy of the Proprietary. He was followed by George Burrington in a *second* term as governor, but his first term under the Crown.[3]

The Crown and Governor Burrington

As did every other royal governor, George Burrington received from the king a long list of detailed instructions for governing North Carolina. Included were religious guidelines and regulations for the established church. The following are a selected few of the instructions dated December 14, 1730:

74. You are to permit a liberty of conscience to all persons (except papists) so as they be contented with a quiet and peaceable enjoyment of the same not giving offence or scandal to the government.

75. You shall take especial care that God Almighty be devoutly and duly served throughout your Government, the Book of Common Prayer as by law established to be read each Sunday and Holiday, and to the blessed sacrament administered according to the rites of the Church of England.

76. You shall take care that the Churches already built there be well and orderly kept and that more be built as the Province shall by God's blessing be improved.

. . . .

82. And we do further direct that no schoolmaster be henceforth permitted to come from this Kingdom and keep school in that our said Province without the license of the Lord Bishop of London and that no other persons now there or that shall come from other parts shall be permitted to keep school in North Carolina without your license first obtained.

. . . .

88. You shall also cause an exact account to be kept of all persons born, christened, and buried, and send yearly fair abstracts thereof to us.[4]

Among other guidelines received by the governor was an act for the better observation and keeping of the Lord's Day and the suppression of vice and immorality. This required that all persons on the Lord's Day apply themselves to duty of religion and piety. There was to be no business or work, no hunting game, no fishing, sport, or play. Penalties included: for swearing, cursing - 2 shillings, 6 pence (*public officials* would pay 5 shillings for each and every oath or curse); for drunkenness on the Lord's Day - 5 shillings, on other days, 2 shillings.

The fines collected were to be divided, giving one half to the informer and one half to the parish.[5]

The Reverend John LaPierre

Among the earliest ministers to serve in the American colonies was the Reverend John LaPierre. He was *the first* to arrive and serve in the Cape Fear area, which was soon after his arrival called New Hanover Precinct and St. James Parish.

LaPierre, a French Huguenot, had been ordained in 1707 by the Bishop of London and by 1708 was serving in St. Thomas Parish

12

of South Carolina among old French settlers who did not understand the English language. He was still there in 1723 and for some time afterwards served French refugees conforming to the Church of England. There he received from the treasury a salary equal to those in other county parishes. Reverend Gideon Johnson, however, did not classify LaPierre as a "missionary" when the report on South Carolina parishes was made in 1723.

Early in the planning and settling of the town of Brunswick, John LaPierre was invited in 1728 and arrived in 1729 at this colonial town by the Cape Fear River. He was already located at this place and was conducting church services when St. James Parish and New Hanover Precinct were created in 1729. The Provincial Assembly Act creating the parish and the precinct directed that New Hanover church be built at Brunswick; but it was not built in time for this minister to serve in it.

The Reverend LaPierre thus began his ministry without a church building. While plans progressed slowly toward building, the minister labored in St. James Parish under discouraging circumstances. His letters to the Bishop of London revealed his disappointments and his concern for prospective clergymen who would find here a "lawless place, a scattered people, no glebe, no parsonage." In 1734 he wrote the Bishop that his salary had never been paid in full and that he was "forced to work in the fields to help maintain my family."

The minister continued to be concerned about the "children to be instructed," the distribution of leaflets sent by the SPG, and the needed encouragement for parishioners in the Carolinas to build churches.[6]

The newborn town of Brunswick was unable to keep the Reverend LaPierre. He moved to New Bern in 1735 and continued to organize churches, which finally numbered twenty. This discouraged minister was not able in his time to recognize the value of his work or to foresee its future fruits in the Carolinas.

Many of LaPierre's descendants now reside in the Carolinas and Virginia. The family was well represented at the unveiling of the LaPierre Historical Marker which was placed in the Brunswick Town State Historic Site November 24, 1968.[7]

Unveiling the LaPierre Marker is Miss Mary Grady Koonce of Raleigh, an eleventh generation descendant.

New Hanover Precinct Church of St. James at Brunswick Town

Gabriel Johnston became governor in 1734 and, just as his predecessor, received instructions from England to see that laws were passed for the support of the Anglican Church. Political pressures also built up problem details. The tasks became more difficult as various groups of "dissenters" asserted themselves.[8]

Governor Johnston tried to persuade the assembly to support efforts of the Anglican Church and the SPG. In 1739 he presented to the governing body the fact that only two churches in the province had regular services: Bath, in the oldest town; and Edenton, in the political center. He emphasized the fact that religious conditions were "really scandalous" and that there was a "deplorable and almost total want of divine worship throughout the province."

The assembly passed the Vestry Act of 1741, but this act was disallowed by the king because it would give to local church governing bodies the privilege of choosing ministers, a right reserved for the king and the Anglican bishop.

14

After the Reverend LaPierre left Brunswick, Governor Gabriel Johnston became more aware of the distressing condition of religion. The governor saw the town of Brunswick without an approved minister, as it relied on a business man of New Hanover Precinct to fill in for absent or unavailable qualified ministers.[9]

Richard Marsden attended the small chapel on Lot 36 in Brunswick. He was mentioned as a minister of the SPG in Cape Fear Parish and reference was made concerning his record of baptisms. Apparently Marsden served several years unofficially. The SPG records show for Marsden an appointment in 1738, but also a cancellation of it for misconduct before he began serving.[10]

St. James Parish Divided

There was a new up-river town started in 1733; it was first called New Town and later named Newton. This town began efforts toward acquiring port facilities and also being made the seat of precinct government. Becoming the town of Wilmington and "county seat" was not easily accomplished.

In 1740 the assembly was presented with a bill providing for the courts and the election of vestrymen for the Parish of St. James to be held in Wilmington only, "*not* in the village called Brunswick."[11] By a strongly contested passage of this bill, the assembly repealed the previous act that would have provided a church at Brunswick, and the courts were moved from Brunswick Town to Wilmington.[12]

This bill was opposed by residents of Brunswick Town, but they were unable to prevent its passage. From that time, the Brunswick Town leaders concentrated on plans they considered best for their west side of the Cape Fear River, the area which in 1741 became St. Philip's Parish.

New Hanover Precinct was still young, in its fifth year, when Gabriel Johnston began serving as governor for an eighteen-year period, the longest term of any governor's officialdom. He was a man of great learning—a physician, writer, and professor of languages.

Upon his appointment in 1734, he moved to Brunswick Town. Here in Carolina he observed and deplored what he considered moral laxity, disregard of law, inadequate educational facilities, and oppression of the poor. For correction of these, his efforts were directed without special consideration or encouragement of the established church, which had never been strong.

15

Governor Johnston saw in 1735 the departure of Cape Fear's first Church of England minister. The Reverend LaPierre had served seven years in Brunswick without a building for his church services. In 1736 the governor saw a small St. James Chapel built at Brunswick where there was then *no minister* to serve.[13]

In 1741 New Hanover Precinct was divided and became two parishes, St. James and St. Philip's. Neither parish had "a minister qualified according to the Church of England."[14]

Besides New Hanover Precinct's St. James and St. Philip's Parishes, there were in 1741 fourteen other North Carolina parishes located in the precincts of Chowan, Perquimons, Pasquotank, Currituck, Bertie, Tyrell, Beaufort, Hyde, Craven, Onslow, Bladen, and Edgecombe.[15]

Colonial families, recognizing the danger of loss by fire, provided for their homes a "desk" box or "Bible" box which could easily be carried out in case of fire. The "desk" box usually had a flat top and contained valuable personal papers such as deeds, wills, and military records. In a home of means and literacy, there was usually a "Bible" box for the family copy of the Holy Word. These had steeply slanted tops, carved sides, and a lock. Some were more elaborately decorated than others; most of the extant examples today are handsomely carved, often with the owners' initials.

16

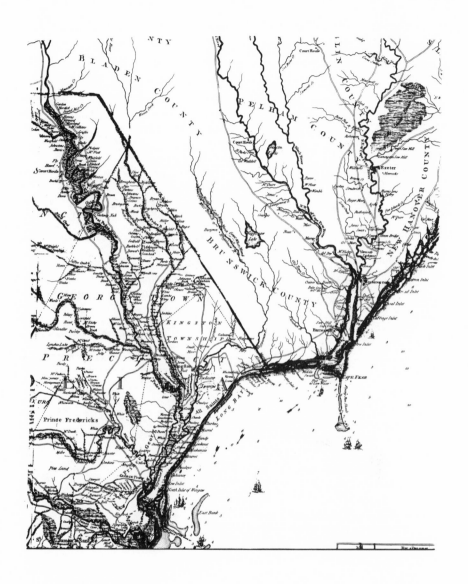

St. Philip's Parish was between the Cape Fear River and the South Carolina line, shown here as Brunswick County.
Mouzon Map - 1775
Department of Cultural Resources, Division of Archives and History

17

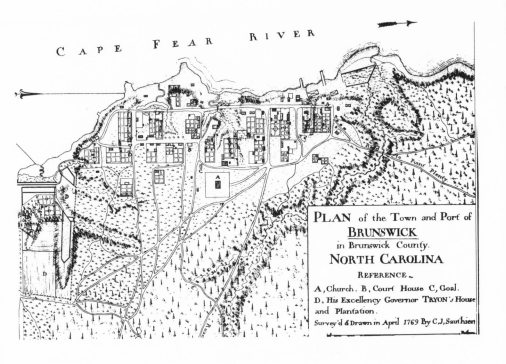

PLAN of the Town and Port of
BRUNSWICK
in Brunswick County.
NORTH CAROLINA
REFERENCE .
A , Church. B , Court House C, Goal.
D , His Excellency Governor TRYON 's House
and Plantation .
Survey'd & Drawn in April 1769 By C.J, Sauthier

Survey Plan of Town of Brunswick drawn in April, 1769

18

Chapter III

His Majesty's Chapel
St. Philip's Parish Under the Royal Governors

After the proprietary period, as noted in the previous chapter, the royal governors actively supported the Anglican Church in America. Richard Everard had bridged the transition by serving under both the Lords Proprietors and the Crown until George Burrington arrived. Although Burrington served only three years, the foundation for the Anglican Church was strengthened, largely through the efforts of Reverend John LaPierre. It remained for the next three strong-minded governors to foster the church and to invigorate the area in general. These representatives of the Crown were Gabriel Johnston (1734-1752), Arthur Dobbs (1754-1765), and William Tryon (1765-1771), each of whom influenced the progress of Saint Philip's Parish.

Governor Gabriel Johnston

After Governor Johnston's success in promoting Newton to become Wilmington, the town became the seat for all legislation, the principal port of entry, and the site for St. James Parish Church.

The churchmen at Brunswick continued to use the small chapel. In 1741 they were able to persuade the assembly to create St. Philip's Parish on the west side of Cape Fear River and also to persuade the St. James missionary to divide his time between the two New Hanover parishes. By the Brunswick Act of 1745 the St. Philip's parishioners were promised that their church "shall be built in Brunswick." *Six years later* a committee was appointed to collect subscriptions for financing the building.[1]

Governor Johnston was in office eleven years after the creation of St. Philip's Parish. During that time Brunswick Town's first school was started in the house that served also for church services on

Sunday. Settlers continued to move up the Cape Fear River, and some were arriving around upper Town Creek and on both sides of Lockwood's Folly River. For protection of the whole area, Fort Johnston was begun at the mouth of the Cape Fear River.

Before the fort was completed, Spaniards attempted to capture slaves that were working there. The next year, Spaniards came to Brunswick and pillaged where the fearful residents had left their homes. Surprised by some local forces, the intruders fled to their large ship, the *Fortuna*, and tried to fire from there; but the powder keg blew up. There they lost their largest ship and half their men. In a hasty departure, the Spaniards left the damaged ship, and its valuables which later were sold for the benefit of the church.[2]

Governor Johnston saw the mission work of John LaPierre, Richard Marsden, James Moir, and Christopher Bevis; but he died in 1752 before construction of the large brick chapel of St. Philip was begun.

Reverend James Moir

A missionary named James Moir came to New Hanover at a time when the precinct was being divided into two parishes. The town of Wilmington urged construction of a St. James church there. The people of Brunswick Town wished to continue building in their town the chapel that had been authorized in 1729. Challenging Mr. Moir were New Hanover's *two* parishes, neither of which had a church building.

In 1742 Mr. Moir reported for New Hanover 3,000 inhabitants, two-thirds of them black. He estimated that half of the white inhabitants were "dissenters" of various denominations. Further, he stated that there were "no churches, no glebes, no parsonage houses, nothing so far as I can see that discovers in the people the least intention of providing even the necessary travel charges."

Mr. Moir resided in Wilmington and at first preached in the courthouse there. He was made uneasy by demands of St. James Parish where communicants objected to his going to lead services at St. Philip's. He left Wilmington and went to Brunswick Town, continuing to observe discord between the two vestries and reporting his work with "neither church nor chapel."

In Brunswick Mr. Moir had quarters in the garret of a small building that was used for Sunday services. He took his meals at taverns and public houses, which he considered "the very worst on

20

the face of the earth." He also had a school in the house that served for services on Sunday.[3]

After leaving Brunswick, James Moir had some difficulty obtaining certificates of good conduct. Several years later Governor Dobbs referred to "neglects of his mission."[4] Mr. Moir's representation of his situation in 1742 is shown in his letter to the secretary of the SPG:

Brunswick Sept 4, 1742

REVEREND SIR [TO THE SECRETARY]

This County of New Hanover where I reside was last year divided into two Parishes Viz^t the Parish of St. James on the North side of Cape Fear River, and that of St. Philip on the South. The Vestry of St. James immediately after division agreed to pay me annually 50 pounds sterling upon my consenting to be their Minister. The year before, they allowed me only 16 pounds sterling of which not one farthing is paid as yet. The Vestrys are chosen in this Province every other year & are empowered to fix the Parish charges & Tax the People accordingly; they make a new agreement with or reject their Minister yearly according to pleasure; and the Parishes being very large it happens that sometimes there is a majority of the Vestry in one Quarter & sometimes in another, which renders it difficult for the Minister to know in what places he shall officiate next year or whether he is to officiate at all, in that very Parish where he was elected the preceding year.

The new vestry of St. James in May last thought their predecessors had been too generous to me & insisted on my officiating twice a month in two different places about the distance of 20 miles from Wilmington each, and once in 3 months in two other places, one at the distance of 36 miles, the other of 60, all in the Parish and where I had officiated formerly; signifying to me at the same time, that they would allow me one Month in the year to visit the other parishes within the bound of my Mission; the remainder of the year was to be spent at Wilmington—with which I promised to comply upon the condition they would continue the 50 pounds S^{tr} p^r ann^m according to my agreement with the last Vestry. This they refused and would promise me no more than 37 pounds, 10 shillings, which was the least they were permitted to give by law. I immediately took my leave of them, being fully convinced from the experience of the two former years, that this allowance together with the Bounty of the Venerable Society would not defray the necessary charges of my office.

Some time after, they sent for me, pretended the Parish was poor and they had some thoughts of getting me 12 pounds, 10 shillings by Subscription—this I could not consent to because of the uncertainty of the very payments that are to be made as the Law directs.

21

Several of the Gentlemen belonging to the Vestry of the Parish of St. Philips being in town at the time; and hearing what had passed in one Vestry gave me to know they would gladly accept the offer I made to the other Vestry. I took some time to consider this. And upon recollecting how the Venerable Society had recommended me to Brunswick and Wilmington (formerly called Newton) while they made but one Parish ordering me at the same time to be directed by the Governour, who allows me to chuse for myself, and after reading the 22nd of the New Orders relating to the Missionaries; I thought I could not in justice refuse the Gentlemen who presently agreed to give me 10 pounds ster: more than I desired of the other Vestry.

A Missionary in this River has a most difficult part to act, for by obliging one of the Towns he must of course disoblige the other, each of them opposing the other to the utmost of their power. Notwithstanding the majority of the present Vestry at Wilmington are professed Dissenters & endeavored by all ways & means to provoke me to leave that place yet they cannot endure my settlement at Brunswick— while I was their minister they were offended at my officiating sometimes in St. Philips & now to exasperate that Vestry against me, they insist on my officiating frequently among them—I lived two years & upwards in St. James Parish & baptized many, but could never prevail with them to give me an opportunity of baptising one in the Court house, which is their place of Public Worship, and now that I live in another Parish they still want me to Baptize when & wheresoever they please, which I cannot comply with, and therefore offered to do it at stated times in their Parish; but this would not satisfy them—Some of them seemed resolved to complain against me at any rate, and actually threatened to do it upon my refusing to baptize any child in their Parish when desired—I shall always be ready to perform any part of my Function at proper seasons and in proper places, & indeed upon any occasion if a just reason can be assigned—Though I cannot help condemning myself for having baptized many children here in corners, who might have been brought to the Public Service, with very little inconvenience—the better sort of People where I now live need no persuasion (thank God) to bring their children to be Baptized on Sundays; whereas at Wilmington the meanest of them reckoned it an affront to desire them.

No Province in America, as far as I can learn, has more need of Missionaries & none can deserve them less—As we are subject to the humours and caprices of Vestrys here, I cannot think it would be amiss to permit us to settle in such Parishes as are most willing to contribute towards our Maintenance; and must confess I have no prospect at all of bettering our condition here unless the Venerable Society oblige every one of our Parishes that applys to them for a

Missionary to make some certain provision for him before he is sent over—And so soon as I can hear that the Venerable Society is disposed to send over any, I shall not fail to let them know the particular Parishes where they are likely to be most serviceable.

I hope my letter of April last is come to hand before this time, together with the copy of it I left to be transmitted when I set out for the Northern parts of my Mission, and now beg leave to acquaint you that since that time I have baptized 74 white children and one slave & administered the Sacrament of the Holy Supper to 56 persons—from the Boundary Line of the S° Carolina to the S° West Branch of Neuse River. We have five Countys—as to the County of New Hanover, I have mentioned it already—The other four countys make but five Parishes—and the number of the Inhabitants Male and Female from 16 to 60 amounts to 7,000 and upwards. They have but few Negroes among them in comparison to what we have in this county. I propose to travel twice a year betwixt South Carolina and the Neuse till another Missionary come in but shall not be able to do so above once after this Fall—For no parish here will consent to any more, and if we have no Parish we can not live—There are no Fees in this Province but for Marriages, and the Justices of the Peace take all of those fees where there is no settled minister in the Parish— undergo toil and fatigue as I have done heretofore. Moreover my health won't permit me to undergo toil and fatigue as I have done heretofore. Many are the inconveniences Missionarys are exposed to in this country, as I could easily prove were it not I hate dwelling on such a subject, and should not have tired your patience with such hints but that too many here want to make slaves and drudges of us and yet won't allow us any reasonable satisfaction for our pain.

I am Rev. Sir, yours
James Moir

Letter from the *North Carolina Letter Book* of SPG Quoted in *Colonial Records IV, 606-608*

Christopher Bevis at Brunswick

Christopher Bevis was a resident in St. Philip's Parish after his being granted 640 acres of land next to Roger Moore. Governor Johnston recommended Mr. Bevis as minister, stating that he had been a satisfactory layman for two years.

In Mr. Bevis' account to the SPG Secretary, he stated that he was born in Northamptonshire and attended Emmanuel College at Cambridge. He stated also that he took priest orders in 1711 and served several years—until an excessive nosebleeding made him weak and melancholy.

At Brunswick he was again failing in health and was not an active leader of St. Philip's Parish. After serving the one year of 1747, he died. After his death, the Lower Cape Fear was without a minister for several years.[5]

Construction of St. Philip's Chapel

In St. Philip's Parish, construction of the large brick chapel was begun in 1752, after Governor Johnston died earlier in that year.

The administration of Johnston's successor, Nathaniel Rice, lasted only six months. Rice was a resident of the Town Creek area, a vestryman of St. Philip's, and had served on the committee to erect Fort Johnston.

Matthew Rowan succeeded Rice as the colony's governor and served only one year. He had previously been a church warden in Bath and had served in the assembly.

These two short administrations of Rice and Rowan did not effect much progress toward construction, membership, or missionaries for St. Philip's Parish. This situation stood as a challenge for the next governor, who was a zealous churchman, composer of hymns, political and financial supporter of the Established Church. He was interested in St. Philip's Church progress even before he moved to Brunswick Town.[6]

Governor Arthur Dobbs

Governor Arthur Dobbs was a descendant from an old English family who had settled in Antrim, Ireland, about 1599. He was born in Scotland where his mother had been sent for safety against possible invasion by English forces.

As a young man, Arthur became recognized as a classical scholar and scientist. In Scotland he served with a regiment of Dragoons. Upon his return to Ireland in 1714, he became master of Castle Dobbs and received a good income from the estate. He served as high sheriff of County Antrim and later was mayor of Carrickfergus.

Not content with being an eighteenth-century landlord, he became acquainted with influential people and by 1727 was in the Irish Parliament. There he served on various important committees and became interested in the American colonies, and in the possibility of a northwest passage across this continent to the Pacific Ocean.

In 1735 he approached English government officials and London merchants with a scheme to settle distressed Protestant families from Ireland to North Carolina. With the support of Governor Gabriel Johnston of North Carolina, he received a grant from the Board of Trade for a tract of one and one-fourth million acres of land at the headwaters of the Pee Dee, Cape Fear and Neuse rivers. Ten years later, he and Colonel John Selwyn purchased 400,000 acres in Mecklenburg and Cabarrus counties. About five hundred people from Ireland had settled on his lands before he became governor. His venture in the Ohio Valley helped that region to become British rather than French.

By 1751, Arthur Dobbs was interested in becoming governor and began settling his Irish estate on his elder son. Upon receiving his appointment as governor, he came to New Bern, where he was enthusiastically received by people hopeful of better direction, more money, and protection from the French.

At the beginning of the Dobbs administration, the legislators appropriated large sums of money to pursue the war against France; raised troops for the protection of Virginia; regulated quitrents; improved the court system; passed the Vestry Act which divided the colony into parishes and led to a stronger Established Church. The Governor initiated a plan for the seat of government to be at Kinston, but the appropriation was disallowed in England. This discouraging event and his recognition that New Bern was too humid for his rheumatism led Dobbs to purchase a residence at Brunswick Town to which he moved in 1758.

In 1759 there was some dissatisfaction with British rule. The Governor tried to uphold the royal prerogative; the Assembly tried to maintain its rights and privileges as an elective body whose powers they thought should be equal to those of the Parliament.

In 1760 George III began his reign in England and the following year Governor Dobbs ordered in Brunswick Town a celebration and proclamation honoring their new king.

After this period of numerous concerns and general confusion, there was a brief quiet time—until the seventy-three-year-old governor married a fifteen-year-old girl, Justina Davis. Then he was subjected to an avalanche of ridicule; yet the young wife appeared happy, and she was a solace to him in his later years.

Without major political unheavals Dobbs carried on his duties, even after being partly paralyzed by a stroke. He requested and was granted a leave of absence to visit England, but before the departure date, he had a severe seizure and died two days later, March 28, 1765.

Governor Dobbs was buried inside the unfinished St. Philip's Church in the Town of Brunswick in the one-year-old County of Brunswick.[7]

Governor Dobbs and St. Philip's Church

From the beginning of Governor Dobbs' administration and his residence in New Bern, he encouraged the building of St. Philip's Church, the construction of which was under way in 1754 when he took office.

In 1758 the Governor purchased "Russelboro" at Brunswick Town and moved there. His interest and efforts increased to build a magnificent structure which he designated as "His Majesty's Chapel in the Province." For this purpose, Dobbs had the support of some local gentlemen, including William Dry, collector for the Port of Brunswick, and Richard Quince, a prominent merchant there.[8]

Five years after construction began, the brick chapel was still not finished. The poll tax had not brought in sufficient finances.

A lottery was authorized in 1759 to raise funds, though the Governor had misgivings about this method. In 1760 another lottery was necessary; also, some funds were raised by the sale of items saved from the destroyed Spanish ship.[9]

It was necessary that same year to increase efforts for securing funds for the minister. Reverend John McDowell was expressing dissatisfaction with the pay he had been receiving, so a letter on his behalf was sent by the church wardens to the SPG. With this letter was sent Governor Dobbs' sanction of the request for more funds.[10]

The Church wardens and Vestry of St. Philip's Church had assured the SPG in 1760 that the "very large brick Church" was "near done." In 1762 the "near-done" building was struck by lightning and the roof went down. With this severe setback, it was necessary to repair the small old chapel and to postpone work on the new brick structure.[11]

The next year, 1763, the Parish lost the Reverend John McDowell.

This minister's letter of June 15, 1762, gave to the SPG secretary an account of the situation in St. Philip's Parish at that time:[12]

Brunswick June 15, 1762

My parish of St. Philips runs from the mouth of Cape Fear River along the seaside about 40 miles to Little River which divides this from South Carolina; then about 45 miles along the south line then joining Bladen County; runs about 45 miles to the north west Branch of Cape Fear River; then down said north west branch to the ferry opposite Wilmington, about twenty miles, and from the down to the river's mouth about thirty miles. Brunswick is situated on the West Bank of the River, about halfway between Wilmington and the river's mouth, where we have a fort. Wilmington stands on the East Bank of the River, But I intend to send a map of my Parish which will give a better idea of it than this description; we have about 800 taxables in this parish. Taxables here are males, white and black and mixed blood, from 12 years of age and upward, and female blacks or mixed blood from the same age. We have but few families in the Parish, but of the best in the Province, viz His Excellency the Governor, his honor the President, some of the honorable the council, Col. Dry, the Collector, and about 20 other good families who have each of them great gangs of slaves. We have in all about 200 families; and are about to have our Parish made into a County. We have no dissenters of any sort excepting a few poor families of fishermen who came from Cape May at the mouth of the River Delaware and are settled by the seaside between the mouth of the River Lockwood's Folly and Shallot, they call themselves new light Anabaptists; but we hope this frolic will soon dwindle away and disappear among them as it has already done in many places in this and neighboring provinces. We have this spring repaired our old chapel at Brunswick in a decent manner and the timber for the roof of our new church is provided • • • I have but 15 actual communicants as yet, whereof 2 are black, but I hope the number will soon increase. • • • I am with profoundest submission and their most devoted humble servant.

John McDowell

St. Phillip's Parish
1763
Head of Household Listing

Allen, Drury
Bell, James
Bennett, William
Benson, Nathan
Bradley, William
Cains, Christopher
Campbell, John
Caulkins, Jonathan
Dalrymple, John
Danford, John
Daniel, John, Sr.
Davis, Elizabeth
Davis, Jehu
Davis, John, Sr.
Davis, Roger
Davis, Thomas
Dick, Thomas
Doane, Nehemiah
Dobbs, Arthur (Governor)
Dry, William, Sr.
DuPree, Josiah
Egan, Darby
Eagle, Richard (Estate)
Ellis, Robert
Espy, Usher
Fergus, John
Furnel, Algernon
Gause, William
Generatt, Elias (Estate)
Gibbs, John
Gibbs, John
Grissette, George
Grissette, William
Grooms, John
Hall, William
Harnage, Jacob
Harrison, Joseph
Hasell, James
Hasell, James, Jr.
Hewett, Ebenezer
Hewett, Richard
Hewit, Joseph
Hewit, Randolph
Hickman, John
Hill, George
Hill, William
Holden, Benjamin
Holland, John
Howe, Robert
Keeter, Charles

Lay, Enus (Lea)
Lay, John (Lea)
Leonard, Henry
Leonard, Samuel, Sr.
Leonard, Samuel, Jr.
Lord, William
Ludlum, Isaac (Sr)
Ludlum, Jeremiah
Ludlum, John
Marlow, James, Sr.
Mitchell, Joseph
Moore, Schenkling
Morgan, John
Morris, William
Munro, Revel
Nanson, Richard
Neale, Thomas
Neale, William
Newton, Joseph
Paine, John
Perison, Thomas
Porter, Edward
Potter, Miles
Quince, Richard, Sr.
Ready, Thomas
Richinard, George
Riley, Richard
Rowan, John
Sampson, Jeremiah
Sellers, Elisha
Simmons, Isaac, Sr.
Simmons, Isaac, Jr.
Simmons, John
Simpson, William
Smeeth, David
Snow, Robert
Spears, William
Sturges, Jonathan
Swain, David
Thomas, John
Vernon, Nancy
Waldron, Jacob
Watters, Samuel
Wilkinson, John
Willets, Hope
Willetts, Samuel
Wingate, Edward
Wingate, John
Wotton, Christopher[14]

The Reverend John McDowell

The Reverend John McDowell on August 8, 1753, was listed among emigrating ministers to America. As one of these ministers, he would receive from the King of England twenty pounds toward expenses, and the SPG would pay him fifty pounds a year.

Mr. McDowell first served the St. James church in Wilmington for a period of four years. In June of 1758 he went to St. Philip's and there served the remainder of his life's ministry. He was appointed chaplain to the Dobbs Family and for this was paid twenty pounds a year. At Brunswick Town he was minister of the largest Carolina church and lived among the leading families.

McDowell resided in a rented house furnished by the St. Philip's Vestry. After two years there, his wife died in childbirth and left an infant son. Subsequently, his pay was reduced because he had fewer mouths to feed.

Added to these grievous events was his disappointment in not being granted a permanent mission, which would have increased his pay and given him some assurance of support in the future of his son.

After lingering health problems, he died in November of 1763 and was buried beside his wife in St. Philip's Cemetery. He had earlier requested that his son be in care of the Moravians and The Society for the Propogation of the Gospel.[13]

Governor William Tryon

William Tryon was born in County Surry, England, in 1729. His parents were Charles and Lady Mary Tryon, who arranged for his education and early military training. He married Margaret Wake, an heiress and a relative of Lord Hillsboro, president of the Board of Trade.

At age thirty-six, with wealth, position and influential connections, the young Lieutenant Governor arrived in North Carolina October 11, 1764, accompanied by his wife, four-year-old daughter, Lady Tryon's cousin, a servant, and a master builder, John Hawks.

The Tryons were disappointed to learn that Governor Dobbs did not intend to relinquish his office until the following spring. They were offered hospitality at the Dobbs home, but they rented a house in Wilmington and also a villa near New Bern.

After Governor Dobbs died March 28, 1765, William Tryon took the oath of office in Wilmington and promised to preserve the liberties already enjoyed by the colonists, but to uphold the authority of the Crown.

He purchased "Castle Dobbs" and renamed the house "Castle Tryon". From Brunswick Town he made excursions in Eastern North Carolina and inland to Halifax. Later he and his wife traveled to the areas that are now Fayetteville, Hillsboro, Salisbury, Charlotte and Winston-Salem. Afterwards he decided to place the state capital at New Bern.[15]

Before Tryon's first year as governor was completed, the Stamp Act complicated his problems in the colony. There were demonstrations in Brunswick, Wilmington, New Bern, Edenton and Cross Creek.

Twice during Governor Tryon's residence at Brunswick Town his house was surrounded by armed citizens. Officials at the Court House were compelled to sign a statement that they would not execute any stamped paper in their various offices.

Tryon brought on another crisis by building a mansion in New Bern. The cost of this building and the symbolization of royal authority were not acceptable to the colonists. Piedmont and mountain residents were particularly resentful and rebellious.[16]

Another kind of storm was described in the Governor's letter to the Earl of Hillsboro September 15, 1769:

> On the 7th instant we had a tremendous gale of wind here. It began about 10 in the morning at northeast and blew and rained hard till the close of the evening when both wind and rain increased. The wind shifted before midnight to the northwest. The gale became a perfect hurricane between twelve and two o' clock on Friday morning the 8 instant. The fury of its influence was so violent as to throw down homes and I believe from report, hundreds of thousands of the most vigorous trees in the county, tearing some up by the roots, others snapping short in the middle; many houses blown down with the Court House of Brunswick County. All the Indian corn and rice leveled to the ground and fences thrown down, add to this upwards of twenty saw mill Dams carried away with many of the timberworks of the mills and lastly scarce a ship in the river that was not drove from her anchor and many received damage. This, my Lord, is but the relation of what happened within fifty miles of this town. We are therefore in hourly expectation of receiving as melancholy accounts from other parts of the Province, it is imagined that as the corn was within 6 weeks of its maturity the planters may save but half a crop, but they have no hopes for recovering the rice lying at this pond of water from the freshes that this gust occasioned.

> This county will I fear be greatly distressed this winter for provisions as far as this gale has extended, for the people not only will be short of corn, but the hogs which are the support of many families will lose the acorns and nuts in the woods which used to fat them

for market, the wind having stripped every acorn from the tree, before they were ripe. In short, my lord, the inhabitants never knew so violent a storm; every herbage in their gardens had their leaves cut off. This hurricane is attributed to the effect of a blazing planet or star that was seen both from New Bern and here, rising in the east for several nights between the 26 and 31st of August, its stream was very long and stretched upwards toward the southwest.

I am my lord with greatest respt.

Wm Tryon[17]

Early in Governor Tryon's adminsitration he began efforts to complete the St. Phillip's Church building. He donated considerably to the expenses and requested the House of Assembly to establish one clergyman for each parish, at the general expense of the public. Also, he worked more closely with the Bishop of London and the SPG.[18]

In 1766 Tryon joined the Society for the Propagation of the Gospel and continued to encourage that organization's support of missionaries to the colonies. He gave more emphasis to these efforts after he had witnessed the burial of Governor Dobbs when there was no clergyman within a hundred miles of Brunswick Town. There a magistrate had officiated when the aged and respected Governor Dobbs was laid to rest.[19]

Governor Tryon's effective interest in the Established Church made possible an increase in the number of ministers from five to eighteen. One of these was John Barnett.[20]

Reverend John Barnett

The Reverend John Barnett arrived October 26, 1765, after a period in which St. Philip's Parish was without an Anglican minister. He was received into the family of Tryons, and the Governor reported, "His conduct is a credit to both his function and to the mission." Also, the Governor requested this minister *for Brunswick only.*[21]

After one year at Brunswick Town Mr. Barnett wrote, "Since my arrival in Carolina I have heard from no one friend," and he expressed regrets that he could not expect visitors from England because of the requirements of three months for the trip. He mentioned that the New Lights had offered him their meeting house for his services and that he would consider occasional services there at Lockwood's Folly.[22]

31

This minister complained of sickness and was conscious of unfriendly pressure building up against all symbols of British rule. To the SPG he wrote, "The people of this parish do still so violently oppose the presentation of the Crown to the Living, that I believe it will be found necessary for me to remove to another part of the Province as my settling here, contrary to the inclination of the people, must render my situation very disagreeable, and also prevent my being any longer useful here."[23]

The following is another letter of Mr. Barnett:

Brunswick 22^d Augt 1767

Revd Sir [Dr. Burton]

In my last to the Venerable Society (dated February last) I mentioned my fears of the Church in Brunswick remaining in the condition it then was for a long time to come—

His Excellency our very worthy Governor has been pleased to give all the sashes completed; the expence of which amounted I think to upwards of Thirty Guineas—This seemed to give some life to the design of finishing the Church; and large subscriptions were talked of. A few workmen were employed who erected a small belfry, made and hung the doors and fixed up the arches for the ceiling—It is now about two months since they shut up the Church and I see little prospect of their setting about it again this year.

From 24th June 1766 to 24th June 1767 I baptized One hundred and forty nine White Children and nine Adults and of negroes eighteen Children and twelve Adults.

In the course of the year I ride near fourteen hundred miles to the outposts of my parishes to preach and Baptize on week days—The poverty of these places prevents any views of pecuniary advantages arrising from the labor.

But conscious that the duty of a Missionary is more extensive than a mere parochial cure I trust I do it from principle.

Nine times in the year I preach at the Boundary House situated on the line between the two Carolinas—

Here a large congregation meets—at my first coming they were so unacquainted with the Liturgy that I was obliged to make every response myself, but I for many Sundays afterwards spent about half an hour before divine service in explaining every part of the Liturgy and I have now the pleasure of seeing it as well performed there as in most Country Churches.

In my last letter Sir I mentioned my long and dangerous illness in this very unhealthy place, the heats are now very violent and sickness greatly prevails—

I have been lately attacked with the bilious fever but I thank God I am much better—But as I have not recovered my former state of health since my great illness I am very doubtful of the Event of this Summer and fall.

But I pray I may submit to the will of the Almighty disposer of all events with due humility.

I have been much pressed by the physicians here to go to Bermuda or to New England for the recovery of my health. But as I have not had permission from the Venerable Society I shall not leave my mission this summer.

I most humbly beg leave of the Board to return to London next Spring on some very earnest business I ask so short a stay there as only while the Ship I come in is ready to return which is commonly seven weeks I believe.

Be pleased Reverend Sir to present my most dutiful respects to the Venerable Board.

Yours & c.

John Barnett[24]

The Completed Chapel

After his many years of enthusiastic support for the building of St. Philip's Chapel, Governor Dobbs was silent during its completion. He lay in his grave near the altar inside the church while a new governor took charge for the finish; and a new minister planned its dedication as the "Chapel of His Majesty" honoring King George III, the legally constituted head of the Established Church.

Reverend John Barnett found no helpful precedent as he planned for an appropriate program for the dedication, but he was able to secure the assistance of the Reverend John Wills of Wilmington for the ceremony on May 24, 1768.[25]

The completed edifice after the thirty years of planning and construction was Carolina's largest church and one of America's finest. It's construction was made possible by the efforts of professional planners and by common and slave labor; its finance by donations and lotteries. The structure was 76' 6" long and 53' 3" wide; the walls were almost three feet thick and were 24' 4" high. There were eight large footings supporting the roof and thirty-four smaller ones for the floor. The aisles were paved with brick tiles one foot square.[26]

A short time after St. Philip's Chapel was dedicated, Reverend Barnett resigned in disappointment and poor health.

33

The Last Anglican Ministers
of the Cape Fear Area

After Governor Tryon's departure, James Hasell was governor for about a month in 1771. He was a resident of Belgrange plantation on the Cape Fear River. He had served in various capacities of government and had been recommended by Governor Tryon.

In his brief time in office Hasell made no progress toward replacing Mr. Crump who had served St. Philip's Parish one year and had left in 1770, a few months after the hurricane that devastated Brunswick Town the preceding September.[27]

St. Philip's Parish had no minister until 1774 when Nicholas Christian served one year only. He was disappointed by attendance at his services: fourteen for Whitsuntide, eighteen for Easter. In a letter of July 27, 1774, he stated that he held services at five places in the county, including Lockwood's Folly. He recalled roads that were "exceedingly bad, especially to Waccamah." On this route he found twelve swamps to cross, some so deep that his horses were in water up to the saddle.[28]

The departure of Reverend Christian in 1774 left a vacancy that never again was filled at St. Philip's.

The Reverend John Wills stayed at St. James in Wilmington until 1777. He was the *last* Anglican minister in the Cape Fear area.

The Last Royal Governor
of North Carolina

Josiah Martin, the last royal governor, claimed ancestry dating back to a soldier who arrived in England in 1066 with William the Conqueror. His grandfather left England and settled on Antigua in the West Indies. It was on this island that Josiah Martin was born in 1737 and grew up with twenty-two brothers and sisters. He was in military service at an early age and married a cousin on Long Island, New York.[29]

Upon receiving his commission granted by King George III, the new governor of North Carolina conferred with William Tryon, then governor of New York. After nineteen days' travel he arrived at the Governor's Palace at New Bern. There he took the oath of office August 12, 1771, in the new residence, "The Palace."

Martin soon understood that he was expected to emphasize the power of the Crown above the power of the Assembly. He had inherited disagreements and soon faced new problems between the mother country and the colonies. The Assembly would not vote support for emergency criminal courts, and the judicial system was in jeopardy; active women were refusing to buy English tea. These and other acts of defiance of British authority soon led to the Provincial Congress and the naming of delegates to the Continental Congress.[30]

Martin watched the crumbling royal government and the diminishing chance for continued British domination.[31]

The Provincial Congress and the Continental Congress worked through safety committees, which Martin called "motley mobs"; but he could not check them.

The Governor sent his family back to New York, and he fled by night to Fort Johnston, below Brunswick Town on the Cape Fear River. Later he went off shore on the *Cruizer*, a British sloop of war. From there he saw the burning of Fort Johnton and learned that rebellion was spreading over Brunswick County.

Field guns were sent from Wilmington for James Moore to erect a battery at Brunswick Town. Supplies were ordered for William Gause and the people at Lockwood's Folly.

Upon hearing that Captain Collet was determined to burn Brunswick Town in retaliation for the burning of Fort Johnston, the Brunswick Town residents fled.[32] The Wilmington Safety Committee established values on buildings likely to be burned. Brunswick town *was burned*, and also Bellfont, the home of William Dry, who was once on Martin's Council. His house had formerly been the home of Governor Dobbs and also of Governor Tryon. It's burning was reported in a Virginia newspaper: "The elegant house was burned by Capt. Collet, destroying therein all the valuable furniture, liquors, etc."[33]

The Hillsboro Convention began preparation for war. On the *Cruizer* just off shore Martin laid his scheme for the reconquest of North Carolina and the other southern states. By the time British forces arrived at Cape Fear the Governor was disspirited. He joined the British fleet when it departed for Charleston, leaving North Carolina without a governor. He assisted in British efforts, but the tempers and determination of the colonists were never quelled, and the long War for Independence continued, with former governors Martin and Tryon in the British forces.

In failing health, Martin returned to England and died there in 1786.[34]

The Changing of the Church

The finest church building in the North Carolina Province had survived its bolt of lightning, the attack by Spanish forces, and the disastrous hurricane of 1769; but after its burning in 1776 by the British, only the brick walls remained.

The same disasters that tested the strength of the church building had sent the Brunswick Town residents seeking more secure locations. Before the exodus, the town had sixty families and was one of eight towns of this size in the province. It had been the home of royal governors, two of whom had contributed generously toward the construction of St. Philip's Church. It was the burial place of Governor Dobbs, Governor Tryon's son and other colonial leaders.[35]

It is notable that after his residence at Brunswick and his support for St. Philip's Church, Governor Tryon was in British military service in New York and New England. For his outstanding leadership of *Loyalists* against American colonists, he was promoted to the rank of "Major General in America."[36]

The great brick walls of St. Philip's continued to stand after the Anglican lamp was extinguished in the conflict. But more tapers were being lighted; more missionaries were volunteering to carry them. Methodist circuit riders were appearing in Brunswick County as the old parish passed away.

The envisioned transplantation of the Anglican Church for America had the English king's instructions, the Bishop of London's official blessing, the royal governors' efforts in the colonies, the missionaries' labors in the parishes; but the church established by law had never grown strong.

To the colonists, this church represented foreign authority and would lead to unending taxation. In her role subordinate to politics, "The Mother Church was enslaved and her daughter bound with her".[37]

Of the scarce and scattered ministers, most returned to England. One in Tyrell County thought differently. He, who owned two plantations and thirty slaves, decided, after taking a drink, to stay with his amassed immovable properties and to pledge his allegiance there.[38] In later years he was in touch with the Methodists and cooperated with them.

Anglican chapels were left bare; some received new denominations. St. Philip's church walls remained deserted. To Malcolm Ross they were "not a monument to piety there in use, but to the New

World's triumph in breaking bonds binding worship of God to secular power."[39]

Successors to the
Disestablished Anglican Church

A group of families came from Cape May, New Jersey, about 1750 and bought many tracts of land, the total of which comprised most of the area between Lockwood's Folly River and Charlotte River, later Shallotte River. Most of these families lived by fishing and farming.

These settlers were known to Reverend John McDowell, the Anglican minister of St. Philip's Parish, as "New Light Anabaptists." He considered them to be "dissenters" of little consequence.[40]

In 1766 St. Philip's minister John Barnett reported numerous "new light Baptists" in the southern part of his parish. He considered them "poor fishermen" and illiterate churchmen. But this minister was not aware of their numerous purchases of land from the Crown or of court records concerning their property and their wills; nor could he foresee their near-at-hand service as officers and soldiers in the war to lift the British yoke. He did in 1766 record the offer of their New Light "meeting house" at Lockwood's Folly for his every-other-month Anglican services. This record establishes the existence of one dissenter meeting house, the birthplace of Brunswick County "separate Baptists," before St. Philip's Church was completed and consecrated in 1768.[41]

The New Lights had grown out of the religious awakening following George Whitefield's revivals aimed at combatting the "soft" attitude and the falling away from the churches. He emphasized conversion, claims of the Holy Ghost, and free enthusiasm in proclaiming salvation. His methods were different from the Anglican forms which allowed him less freedom than what his enthusiasm required.[42]

Following the widespread revivals in the colonies, a dispute arose among the Baptists, dividing them into the "Old Lights" or "Regulars" who distrusted revivals and emotionalism, and the "New Lights" or "Separates" who demanded a reborn membership in their churches.[43]

Baptist historians George Paschal and M. A. Huggins referred to the Lockwood's Folly Baptists as "Separates" who had in 1712 been connected with the Philadelphia Association. Once residing in

37

Brunswick County, they corresponded with the Sandy Creek Association requesting assistance in securing a minister. These Baptists organized in 1762 and were served by Ezekiel Hunter until 1773. For some time afterwards, there were periods in which no preacher was available, and no regular schedule was in place until after the Revolution. Later with purpose, push, and perseverance they effected growth and expansion in Brunswick County.[44]

Photograph courtesy of Brunswick Town State Historical Site
Ruins of St. Philip's Anglican Chapel

Chapter IV

Birth of Methodism in England—
Advance to America

While the Anglican Church was becoming established in America, Susanna and Samuel Wesley were preparing their sons for study at Oxford University. Both parents found joy in seeing their sons' progress, especially with Charles's "serious thinking" developing into the Holy Club, and with John's decision to assume holy orders.

As students at Oxford, the brothers added to their regular curriculum a serious search for personal holiness and for opportunities to contribute to the comfort and education of less fortunate people. Their methodical study was followed by methodical feeding and teaching.

In humanitarian concerns the young Wesleys were joined by other young preachers who wanted to see their Anglican Church purified and participating in Christian outreach toward the needy, the neglected, the illiterate, and the hopeless. They felt an urgency to devise an exact plan for carrying out their duties as teachers of a full, free, and present salvation as the privilege of *every man* through his *faith*. Their goal was greater than their grasp in the established church. The young preachers' activities were at first limited, but their efforts were continued and soon were directed to more distant goals in America. John Wesley provided *another method*: ask for volunteers to go.

For an understanding of America's early Methodism, it is necessary to consider the work of these early preachers: John and Charles Wesley, Thomas Coke, George Whitefield, Joseph Pilmoor and others.

The Wesley Family

Samuel and Susanna were reared in homes of nonconforming clergymen, both of whom were ejected from their pulpits in 1662.

Samuel Wesley became a Tory, a High-Church Anglican, and a writer of poems.

Susanna Annesley married Samuel and became the mother of nineteen children, all of whom were provided with a portion of their mother's time for individual teaching while they were young. Her Christian teaching and guidance continued until they were adults.

Samuel, Junior, and Charles became Kings scholars at Westminster School in London. Charles had the distinction of becoming captain of the school in 1725. The following year he headed the list of Westminster scholars elected to Oxford University and later was ordained a priest in the Anglican Church.

John became a foundation scholar at Charterhouse School and later a student in Christ Church College at Oxford where he was maintained by a donated allowance. In 1726 he was elected Fellow of Lincoln College of Oxford. In addition to regular school classes, he studied languages that gave him mastery of the original texts of the Bible; read "Imitation of Christ" by Thomas à Kempis and Taylor's "Holy Living and Dying" in which he "found a spur to holiness of living"; and he found further inspiration in William Law's "Serious Call to a Devout and Holy Life" and "Christian Perfection." Both John and Charles cherished a book recommended by their mother Susanna; it was Songal's *Life of God in the Soul of Man.*[1]

Charles Wesley — from the painting by Frank O. Salisbury in the World Methodist Building at Lake Junaluska, North Carolina.

40

After a period of preaching and assisting his father in two parishes, John Wesley returned to Oxford where he was chosen Greek lecturer and moderator of the classes. When he took his M.A. Degree in 1727, his three lectures were in the fields of natural philosophy, moral philosophy and religion.

After another period of assisting his infirm father, John resumed his academic teaching and studies at Oxford. Upon returning there, he learned that his brother Charles had founded the Holy Club, which methodized the study of the Bible, the classics and the needs of the poor people. Club members were derisively called "Bible moths," "Sacramentarians" and "Methodists." The club was best described by its founder: "My first year at college I lost in diversions; the next I set myself to study. Diligence led me to serious thinking; I went to the weekly sacrament, persuaded two or three young students to accompany me and to observe the method of study prescribed by the statutes of the University. This gave me the harmless name of 'Methodist.' In half a year after this, my brother left his curacy at Epworth and came to our assistance. We then proceeded regularly in our studies and in doing what good we could to the bodies and souls of men." Sunday evenings were set aside for Greek New Testament reading; other evenings for Greek and Latin classics.[2]

John's concentration on the necessity of having the mind which was in Christ "in all things" led him to join the Holy Club; his organizational ability soon made him the leader of it. At first, the Wesley brothers had only William Morgan and Robert Kirkman meeting with them; later, George Whitefield and others made a total of fourteen.

Morgan suggested visiting prisons and the poor where permission had been received. The group started a school, paid the mistress when necessary, clothed some of the children, and supervised their work. Teaching was provided for children in the workhouse, and books were read to the old people. Against these works of charity ridicule was directed by other students.

Soon after the death of his father, John Wesley felt a need for closer communion with God and accepted a chaplaincy in the colony of Georgia "to learn the true sense of the gospel of Christ by preaching to the heathen." In 1735 he left England to become a missionary to the Indians. Charles Wesley also went on the mission to Georgia, there to become secretary to Oglethorpe and secretary of Indian affairs. Accompanying the brothers Wesley were Benjamin Ingham of the Holy Club, Charles Morgan, William Morgan and James Hutton. George Whitefield went later.

41

In the third ch. of Job at y[e] 17th v. are these Words,
There y[e] Wicked cease from troubling, there y[e] Weary
are at rest.

The Miseries of Life have been so copiously described, and the Inconsistency of perfect Happiness
with this State of Probation so clearly evinc'd by many Writers; that Reason alone is easily induced us to
give Sentence on their side. This is confirm'd by y[e] Testimony of daily Experience; too great an assurance of
so melancholy a Truth. The words of Jacob, Few & evil
have been y[e] days of the years of thy Servant (Gen. 47.9)
may be justly applied to the whole race of Mankind.
Such is the inheritance, which the Sin of our first Father
has intail'd on his whole Posterity. We meet with a far
greater multitude of Objects that excite in a painful,
than is raise in us a pleasing Reflection: The Number
of our Faculties being in this Respect, a great Inconvenience; since they afford us so many more Capacities of
Suffering: Every Sense being an inlet to bodily Pain, it

Portion of John Wesley's First Sermon

42

The Wesleys' service in Georgia was brief. Both met unforeseen difficulties and left discouraged. But both had been impressed by the faith of Moravians sailing to Georgia. After returning to England, the brothers found themselves on the receiving end of missionary efforts; the Moravians shared their message of *salvation by faith alone*. Following conversations with Charles Bohler and William Holland May 21, 1738, John "found a deeper rest for his soul" and on May 23 said "I waked up under the protection of Christ and gave myself up, soul and body to him."[3]

John Wesley — Portrait by John Jackson, R.A. (1778-1831), in the World Methodist Building, Lake Junaluska, North Carolina, U.S.A.

The next day, John attended a meeting where his heart was "strangely warmed." Immediately afterwards he returned to Charles's sick room and cried out "I believe." The two brothers sang together the hymn Charles had just composed. The Wesleyan revival had begun![4]

The awakened brothers' evangelistic preaching met opposition from Anglican church wardens who did not like the plain and fervent sermons. Charles Wesley was forcibly kept out of the pulpit, but he preached in the church yard until his brief pastorate ended. Afterwards for twenty years he preached in fields and public places, sometimes facing persecution and mob violence. He continued writing hymns; he is said to have written more than 6,500.[5]

New Faith, Greater Goals

The new faith of John Wesley brought forth a new emphasis; the new voice and attitude caused uneasiness among leaders at Oxford University, especially when Wesley agreed to fill George Whitefield's place in field preaching. One criticism of Whitefield after his first field sermon had been "Having already learned to pray without form, and to preach without notes, he now ventured another step and preached without a church."[6]

Young John Wesley and his preachers were attacked by churchmen who disapproved outdoor sermons and who feared the emotional excess that a few converts displayed. But the combination of literary attacks and physical attacks served to give the Wesleys nationwide publicity. It also built up strength for outdoor evangelism, which had been started in 1738 by Whitefield, and afterwards was taken up by the Wesleys.

Whitefield extended his evangelism to America but not officially representing the Anglican Church or the Methodist societies. In America he was considered the first great evangelist. In England he founded the Calvinistic Methodist Church. He left no long-lasting organization in either country, but his evangelistic appeal in America gave rise to the Great Awakening in a new country.[7]

With the Anglican church doors closed against them, the Wesleys could not carry out their initial purpose: to purify their church and give it outreach to the poor and neglected people. They began to acquire places for schools and preaching, but they carefully planned a schedule not conflicting with regular church services.

The first chapel was erected in Bristol. In 1739 a vacant foundry was purchased and used for a school. This was the site of the first Methodist conference.

The minutes of this conference in June of 1744 included the statement that all Methodists regarded themselves as members of the Church of England, but as members led by a vision of purification and greater outreach ministry.[8]

By this time Methodist societies were being organized throughout England. These were groups of people who met to worship and hear preaching. Soon there evolved within these societies the smaller groups called "classes." These met weekly with a dedicated leader for testimony and discipline; they contributed financially; they committed themselves to help each other to live and grow in the Christian faith and to reach out to the needy. A little later the class members were issued individual tickets for admission, proof of good standing in the class.[9]

It is believed by some that if John Wesley had been permitted to work within the Anglican church where his loyalty was, he would have led the Oxford-educated preachers in purifying and strengthening the old church. He set Methodist meetings for times not conflicting with services of the mother church. Also he encouraged Anglican preachers to double their efforts within their churches rather than to defect and rebel. When Dr. Thomas Coke was attracted to Methodism and had thoughts of leaving his Anglican pulpit, John Wesley told him to return to his own parish and establish prayer meetings "doing all the good he could, omitting no part of his clerical duty, and avoiding every reasonable ground for offense." This Dr. Coke did, and with new zeal in his sermons he urged the congregations to sing hymns; and he began to substitute extemporaneous prayers for the Prayer Book.[10]

For these innovations he was rewarded with dismissal and insults. The following Sunday Dr. Coke returned to preach but used the village square for his sermon. A mob gathered with clubs and stones, but a riot was prevented by a sister and brother who stood at their minister's side. Later he told John Wesley "I have no parish, no church! What shall I do?" The founder of Methodism is supposed to have answered "Why, go out and preach to all the world!" Here Dr. Coke "bade adieu to his honorable name and determined to cast his lot with other outcasts—the Methodists." He was later invited back to South Petherton and there was able to organize a Methodist society.

Dr. Coke was a popular and capable preacher. With his help, John Wesley added Ireland and America to the Methodist parish. Coke became "the foreign minister of Methodism".[11]

John Wesley led Methodism wherever schools were needed, wherever orphans had no homes, and wherever laboring adults seemed to hunger for the Methodist message. The first chapels soon had lay preachers to "pray and expound the scriptures"; these laymen proved to be potent instruments for the spread of Methodism.

The increase of societies and Methodist classes made necessary further organization. This took place in 1774 at the Foundry in London and was called the "Conference." In the minutes of that meeting the preachers were declared members of the Church of England, "defending it in preaching and in life." By 1766 ninety-seven preachers were appointed to forty circuits. In 1767 there were 25,911 Methodist society members.

In 1784 John Wesley signed the Deed of Declaration making the Annual Conference through the "Legal Hundred" preachers the heir of Wesley and establishing the principle of itineracy. The Conference of preachers inherited the plans and the power to proceed in the Wesleyan tradition, sending out each *traveling preacher* to a designated circuit for a specified time.

By the provisions signed by Wesley the Methodists would, after his death, be a distinct church, apart from the Anglican Church which gave it birth. The new church would continue its invitation to an abundant life through faith, in a parish that was and is the World.[12]

Methodist Lay Preachers
for America

Besides George Whitefield, there were other volunteer Methodist preachers arriving in America before the Revolution.

In 1764 Philip Embury and Captain Thomas Webb came to New York. Robert Strawbridge arrived the same year and worked independently in Maryland, where at Sam's Creek one of the first Methodist societies in America was organized. Robert Williams came of his own accord in 1768, and John King came unofficially in 1769.[13]

At the Conference of 1769 a new circuit was added: *Circuit No. 50, America*. To this new circuit the first of the missionaries sent by John Wesley were Richard Boardman, designated as "Assistant" with authority to station the preachers; and Joseph Pilmoor who preached in the eastern states from Pennsylvania to Georgia. In 1771 Francis Asbury and Richard Wright arrived; two years later, Thomas Rankin and George Shadford began their mission work.

Before the Revolution, Methodism was represented in America by these *volunteer lay preachers*. A few Episcopalian ministers aided the cause. Devreux Jarratt, day or night in private homes or chapels, testified to the gospel of the Grace of God in a conversational manner and answered questions. He visited North Carolina in 1775. In New York and Maryland there were clusters of Methodists.[14]

The Cape Fear area was visited in 1739 by George Whitefield when he was on his way to start an orphan house in Georgia.

Joseph Pilmoor

Another outstanding visitor to the Cape Fear area was one of the first two accredited missionaries appointed by Wesley for America. Joseph Pilmoor crossed coastal North Carolina as he was going south in December of 1772 and January of 1773. His approach to Wilmington caused him great distress on the road, with excessive rain and a crossing where the bridge had been washed away. There he "loosed the horse from the chaise, placed planks for the wheels, and drew it over myself."

Pilmoor attended some Episcopal services and sometimes preached. At St. Philip's Anglican Church in Brunswick Town, he preached the first Friday in Janaury of 1773 and again the following February 23 and 24.[15]

Returning from Georgia, Pilmoor enjoyed hospitality at the Allston Plantation on Waccamaw Neck, South Carolina. His next five days are best described in the preacher's own words written in his *Journal* for February 19 through February 25, 1773:

"Two Exciting Adventures"

Friday 19. Took leave of my hospitable friend, and went on toward Long Bay. I had not gone far before I saw how wonderfully I had been preserved by staying all night with the planter. They were building a Saw-mill by the road side and have made it almost impossible, so that if I had gone in the night as I intended, I should have been in the utmost danger of my life. After much difficulty, I got safe over, and hastened on to the Bay. As the tide just suited, I pushed along in hopes of reaching the ford at the eastern end of it before the flowing of the tide, but was too late. As I was a stranger to the nature of the *Shifting sands*, I did not know what was best for me to do. There was no house on the beach; to return fifteen miles over the Bay was very discouraging; to stay all night upon the shore, without anyone to speak to, very disagreeable, and to ford the water very dangerous. However, I ventured in, but had not gone far before I was at a full stop. The horse stood still and would not move one way nor another, so that I was in the greatest danger of being lost. The Spring-tide came in very rapidly, the waves rolled against the sides of the horse and presently flowed over his back. In this situation I did not know what I must do; the sea was flowing in so violently that I must in a very short time have been swallowed up of the waves. In my distress I lifted up my heart unto God and cried to him for deliverance, and immediately it was impressed upon my mind as distinctly as if I had heard a voice saying to me *"Jump down into the water—go along by the side of the horse—take hold of the reins— wade through the water, and pull the horse after you"*. The impression was so powerful, that I plunged into the Sea immediately, and soon found the horse had got into quicksand, as the water did not reach up to my breast; I kept close to the shaft, got onto his head, took hold of the reins, and pulling him forward, he plunged with all his might to get out of the sand, and I drew him along and escaped

47

safe to the shore. This was one of the most remarkable deliverances of my life. In all my travels in Europe and America, I never was in such distress before, yet the Lord redeemed my life from destruction and saved me in the trying hour. After I had travelled about a mile through the Wood, I found a little cottage belonging to a French Refugee who had left all for the sake of his Conscience—where I was glad to take up my abode for that night. I was thoroughly wet from head to foot, and had nothing dry to put on, for all my linen, cloaths and books in the chaise box had been under water a considerable time. But the honest Frenchman was remarkably kind; he lent me a shirt, and his own cloaths to put on till mine could be dried. They made up a large fire, and hung all my cloaths and Linen around, and sat up most of the night to get them properly dried. Then next day, when I had gotten my things a little in order, I took leave of my kind friends & set forward in hopes of reaching Lockwood's Folly, and called at the Boundary House to bait [to eat—obsolete use of the word]. As I was detained much longer than I expected, I wanted to hire another horse to help me forward, but could not obtain one, so I was obliged to stay all night. This house stands exactly on the Line between the two Carolinas; It was built by twenty-four Gentlemen, twelve in each Province, as a place of rendevous, the accommodations are remarkably good. The next morning Mr. Merion would not take anything of me, but sent a Negroe with two horses fifteen miles to help me along my journey towards Mrs. Moors. Here I met with a kind reception indeed; Mr. Moor is a sincere lover of all good men, and rejoices in the prosperity of Zion. The day following I found he had sent word to all his neighbors that he had a minister at his house, and there would be a Sermon about twelve o Clock. At the time appointed, a fine company assembled to whom I preached Christ Jesus the Lord, as the only Savior of lost and ruined sinners, and called them to look unto Him for pardon of sin, salvation & eternal life.

Tues. 23. I had a comfortable opportunity with the familiy in solemn calling upon God, and afterwards hastened to Brunswick. Immediately on my arrival, I engaged a person to go around the town to publish preaching for me at five o Clock, when we had a good congregation of most attentive hearers, who all behaved as if they really felt that God was there. *Wednesday* a large congregation assembled in the Church, and the chief Shepherd and bishop of souls, gave me much light and liberty to preach and pray, that I found the work of the Lord truely pleasant, and his service perfect freedom. About one o Clock I set forward for Wilmington, and got over the first Ferry and long causeway pretty well, but before I could reach the other, the wind rose so high and blew right up the river, it was impracticable to get over. This was the more distressing, as there was no house and I was likely to be detained on the Island all night. Presently the dreadful lightenings flashed all around me in a most terrible manner, the rolling thunder burst over my head, the wind blew tempestuously and brought a very high tide which flowed all around me. As I had no other shelter, I put up the head of the chaise and expected I must stay there all night; but being a stranger to the place I was very uneasy on account of the tide as I did not know how high it might rise. When the wind and the thunder abated, I shouted for the boat which presently arrived and took me over to the town... This day has been trying indeed; I have been in perils by land, and in perils by water; the heavens bursting with thunder over my head and forked lightning flying all around me while I was detained on a desolate Island, yet the Lord has kept me so that not an hair on my head has been injured![16]

Pilmoor preached at Wilmington Court House and traveled northward. With his preaching he was encouraging reforms in the Anglican Church, which he hoped would be freed from political domination; and he continued hoping to hold the Colonies within the Mother Church.

*Joseph Pilmoor, one of Wesley's
first two accredited missionaries.*

George Whitefield

George Whitefield was one of the volunteers who preached in America before the Revolution; but he came independently, first in 1737. He worked to raise money for an orphan house in Georgia where the Wesley brothers had been. On six other trips to America he preached in several provinces displaying his unique strong voice which Benjamin Franklin believed was capable of reaching 30,000, though the congregations in America were never that large. His preaching distinguished him as the greatest single factor in the Awakening of the 1740's. He visited twenty-nine counties in Virginia and North Carolina.

By touching every denomination, he became a great unifying agency, generally; but within each denomination the "revival" or "awakened" members began to separate themselves. The "separate" Baptists left the "Regulars"; "new side" (evangelical) Presbyterians left the "Old Sides." Reverend Joseph Travis in his autobiography referred to Brunswick County's "New Lights" as the "disciples of the great and good Mr. Whitefield."[17]

In America Whitefield could disregard Anglican forms and sweep aside old customs. Here he considered himself serving his Creator "who had a mountain for a pulpit, and the heavens for a sounding board; and who, when his gospel was refused by the Jews, sent his servants into the highways and hedges."[18] In part of North Carolina Whitefield commented, "Jesus makes the barren wilderness to smile." Of the Cape Fear area he wrote, "Two churches were begun . . . but neither finished. There are several dancing masters but scarcely one regular settled minister; so that in most places they have readers, who read a sermon every Sunday to the people, for which they pay five shillings a quarter of their currency, which is ten shillings *sterling* for one."[19]

Just south of the state line between North Carolina and South Carolina is an historical marker commemorating Whitefield's visit to a tavern there. It was during a New Year party that the distinguished preacher arrived and surprised the merrymakers; he talked with the people, baptized a baby, led prayer, spent the night and continued his journey the next day, January 1, 1741.

America Calls

John Wesley's organization and supervision of Methodist Societies in England, Ireland, Scotland and Wales brought significant growth in the number of preachers and members. By 1770 he recognized the need to assist the few preachers in America.

At the conference in Bristol, August 17, 1771, Mr. Wesley made his request, "Our brethren in America call aloud for help. Who are willing to go over and help them?" Young Francis Asbury was one of five who volunteered and was one of the two who were chosen. Within a month young and penniless Asbury was given some clothing and ten pounds in cash; with these he was ready to sail from Bristol to America.[20]

Francis Asbury was not an Oxford graduate as were the Wesley brothers and George Whitefield. This only son of Joseph and Elizabeth Asbury must have had excellent early teaching at home for he could read the Bible before age seven. Discouraged by a cruel schoolmaster, he left school and went to work for a wealthy, but ungodly, family. At thirteen he was an apprentice in the "Old Forge" and was a friend to the son of the owner, a Methodist.[21]

Asbury was converted at an early age while praying in the old barn by the Asbury home. He had opportunities to hear many notable preachers of that area and time. His attendance at Methodist meetings gave him a view of the groups' struggles against persecution, and of their growth in outreach ministry. Impressed by the singing and the spontaneity of the services, he became a member. When he accompanied his mother to women's meetings, he read scripture and announced hymns. He preached his first sermon while he stood behind a chair in a cottage at Manwoods near his home. He was a local preacher at age eighteen.[22]

After substituting for an ailing itinerant, he entered the Methodist Conference on trial. In 1768 he was admitted to full connection and began a three-year itineracy, during which he became an esteemed young preacher. Even with his limited preparation, he was accepted

Francis Asbury was a young missionary to America. When he viewed the American challenge and risk, he said "The work of God puts new life into me, and why despond? The land is before us, and nothing can hurt us but division among ourselves."

by the Oxford graduates when the call was made to "go over and help in America"—to become a missionary outside his native land.

After five years of preaching, Asbury had learned some of Wesley's views and methods for encouraging workers and improving organization. During the rugged fifty-three days on the Atlantic Ocean, he seriously examined his own direction and purpose, and preached to the ship's crew. He remembered that John Wesley kept good records, so on the tossing ship, he started his own now famous and treasured *Journal.*[23]

On October 27, 1771, the twenty-six-year-old Francis Asbury landed at Philadelphia, and the next day preached his first sermon in America at St. George's Chapel, which still functions as the oldest Methodist Church building in use in this country. There is now an active congregation with a full-time minister.[24]

After ten days in Philadelphia and some time in New York, he observed the preachers' preferences for city locations. In contrast to the recommendation of his superiors, his conscience directed his efforts against what he thought could become a dangerous partiality. This was the time to "show them the way" to work beyond the cities. He initiated the era of the circuit rider and established itineracy firmly in American Methodism.[25]

Thomas Rankin, who presided at the first Conference of American Methodism, at Old St. George's, July 14, 15, 1773.

Chapter V

The New Denomination 1784
Southward 1785

Francis Asbury's earliest preaching efforts in America were in Maryland, New York, Pennsylvania, Virginia, and New Jersey. These efforts were rewarded with great success until colonists became suspicious of all Englishmen as the revolutionary spirit built up. Also, he had to face serious opposition after Wesley's *Address* which had been written to discourage colonial efforts to separate from England.

Francis Asbury, first Bishop of American Methodism

After the war, he had the wisdom and practicality to check Dr. Coke's orders, transmitted from John Wesley. He insisted on more democratic participation, saying that the American Methodists needed more preachers than planners. Asbury first declined his appointment by Wesley, and held out for a unanimous vote by the preachers in America. Only in this way could he feel sure that he had sufficient confidence and support among the American Methodists for his superintendency.

When at Baltimore the Christmas Conference ended January 3, 1785, the first Methodist denomination in the world had been organized. The American Methodist Episcopal Church had, in addition to the appointed Superintendent Dr. Thomas Coke, a *unanimously elected* Superintendent, Francis Asbury. There were 104 preachers and 18,000 members in Methodist societies. More than 60 chapels were claimed and occupied, nine of them North Carolina.[1]

Both superintendents traveled in the northern states, but it was Asbury who spent part of his first Episcopal tour time in Brunswick County, North Carolina. This was in mid-March, 1785, two years before any circuit riders were appointed for this area.

Superintendent Asbury had heard of Stephen Daniel, probably from Methodists in South Carolina where the Daniel family had previously lived. Asbury hurried to the Daniel home where he found hospitable friends after having been ''out for six weeks, and ridden near 500 miles among strangers to me, to God, and to the power of religion.''

After this first Episcopal tour which brought the Superintendent to dinner at Lockwood's Folly and to visit with ''Brother Daniel'' at Town Creek, there was born an early Methodist mission in Brunswick County; in 1787 there appeared appointed Methodist circuit riders looking for preaching places. At Lockwood's Folly they found the county Courthouse, newly built and available.

The Great Awakening begun by George Whitefield in the 1740's had some influence in southeastern North Carolina, but it was after the Revolution that the great revival begun by John Wesley was able to take root and flourish in this coastal area. His "strangely warmed" heart generated *awarming*.

Considerable progress had earlier been made by Methodism in New York, Philadelphia and Maryland. When the societies had spread across Virginia, North Carolina was next in line for missionary efforts. By 1779 the circuits of New Hope, Tar River and Roanoke had been formed. The Yadkin Circuit was added in

54

1780 so that before the War for Independence had closed, all the northern half of North Carolina was being visited by circuit riders from Virginia.[2]

Methodism Begins in Wilmington

Preachers from the Virginia Conference were not successful in southeastern North Carolina. During the Revolutionary War Philip Bruce and James O'Kelly started a society near Wilmington, but it was soon broken up.

Beverly Allen and James Hinton were sent in 1784 to form a Wilmington circuit, but no societies were permanent. John Baldwin made similar efforts in 1785, but the feeble societies crumbled away, and the Wilmington circuit as planned by the Virginia Conference was discontinued in 1786.

During the ensuing absence of Virginia Conference preachers, another missionary effort was made by William Meredith, an associate of William Hammet, who had come from the West Indies. Hammet was known to be a seceder from the regular order of Methodism, and his followers were called "Primitive Methodists." Meredith came on his own initiative to Wilmington and began a mission with the black people. He drew great crowds, and authorities tried to limit his preaching time to daylight hours only. Because of disorderliness and lawlessness around his mission, Meredith was jailed at Second and Princess Streets; there he preached from the windows. After his release from jail, he was able to replace the meeting shack by building "the tabernacle and dwelling," which he later signed over to the Methodist Episcopal Church.[3] After the brief time and efforts of the Virginia Conference and nearly ten years of Meredith's mission, Wilmington welcomed circuit riders of the Methodist Episcopal Church which at the same time sent preachers to the areas south of the Cape Fear River.

New View of Brunswick

For Brunswick County the scene had changed. Gone were the Anglican missionaries who had preached in "His Majesty's Chapel" of St. Philip's Parish; arriving on horseback from the south were young Methodist preachers who would stop at any shelter or yard to deliver their messages of hope.

Many changes had taken place in the time between the arrival in 1728 of Reverend John LaPierre at the Anglican parish on the Cape Fear River and the arrival of the first circuit riders. The Anglican

Church had been disestablished and the new Constitution had separated church and state. New churches thereafter would have no financial aid from government or from the SPG.

The former generosity of wealthy resident royal governors had passed. The governor's residence and the state capital had moved, first to New Bern; and later from the "finest government house in America" to seven other locations before being permanently located at Raleigh in 1794.[4]

Brunswick Town had suffered but had survived Spanish attacks and hurricanes, both of which had taken a toll. The "finest church building in the province", St. Philip's, had been lost to fire set by the British. Many of the leading families had moved away from the Town of Brunswick; but more people had come to other parts of Brunswick County, especially to Town Creek and Lockwood's Folly.[5]

Travel was still slow, hard and dangerous—by boats and by barely passable roads. Scattered communities were building small chapels of different denominations. George Whitefield would not have found great evidence of his dreamed-of "nation on fire for God." But Methodist preachers were working elsewhere to spread their warm message of grace, and they would soon find their way by Long Bay to Cape Fear. Young Brunswick County was waiting.

Visit to Southeastern North Carolina

After Superintendent Asbury's visit with Stephen Daniel in 1785, he left Brunswick County by way of the bad causeway over Eagle's Island and the risky crossing of Cape Fear River. He arrived in Wilmington after dark and was disappointed in not getting the accommodation he had expected; but he preached to a large congregation the next day.[6]

From Wilmington he crossed the Cape Fear River again and traveled westward to Lake Waccamaw Chapel where he "found a few hearers." From there he went to Elizabethtown and Swansboro. At Kinston the Superintendent was entertained by Governor Richard Caswell April 11, 1785. He met Dr. Coke at Green Hill's, near Louisburg, the evening of April 19. At this home they found hospitality and peace for the first Conference of the newly formed American Methodist Episcopal Church. Visiting Brunswick County had been part of the prelude to the first Annual Conference in America.

56

Thomas Coke — First Superintendent of American Methodism. Portrait in World Methodist Building, Lake Junaluska, N.C.

The preachers attending this conference represented the area of the Carolinas and Virginia, thirty-one circuits and 9,063 members. The ordinations here were the first in North Carolina. Another significant accomplishment of this conference was the placement of a few ordained elders over groups of circuits, thus creating the new office of "presiding elder."

As the Superintendent continued northward he became ill for a while; but he regained strength and completed his first Episcopal journey. Over long roads and trails he had gone southward through mid-Virginia, mid-North Carolina, and eastern South Carolina to Charleston. Returning northward he visited South Carolina's Georgetown and Kingston; then North Carolina's Lockwood's Folly, Town Creek, Wilmington, Lake Waccamaw, Elizabethtown, Swansboro, Kinston, Louisburg, and Bridge Creek Chapel.[7]

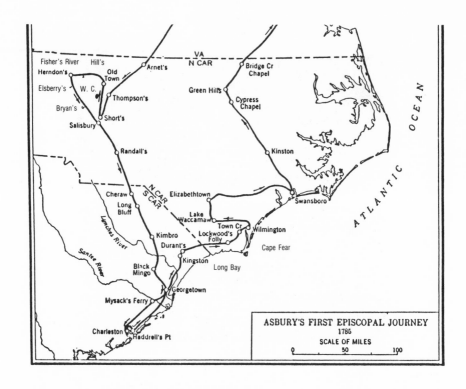

ASBURY'S FIRST EPISCOPAL JOURNEY
1786
SCALE OF MILES
0   50   100

1. Arnet's	12. Randall's	23. Durant's
2. Thompson's	13. Cheraw	24. Lockwood's Folly
3. Short's	14. Long Bluff	25. Town Creek
4. Waggoner's Chapel	15. Kimbro's	26. Wilmington
5. Old Town	16. Black Mingo	27. Lake Waccamaw
6. Hill's	17. Georgetown	28. Elizabethtown
7. Fisher's River	18. Mysack's Ferry	29. Swansboro
8. Herndon's	19. Charleston	30. Kinston
9. Elsberry's	20. Hadrell's Point	31. Cypress Chapel
10. Bryan's	21. Georgetown	32. Green Hill's
11. Salisbury	22. Kingston	33. Bridge Creek Church

This southern tour completed in 1785 had a special historic significance in the area of Long Bay shores and Cape Fear. In this region the Superintendent recognized the people's needs and the Methodists' opportunity to minister south of the reaches of the Virginia Conference circuits. The area south of the Cape Fear River would no longer be ignored. Circuit riders would come on schedule to Brunswick County.[8]

58

Chapter VI

South Carolina District, Bladen Circuit 1787

Two years after his first southern tour Bishop Asbury headed to Charleston for the first conference of Methodists in South Carolina that convened there March 22, 1787, at Cumberland Street Church or "Blue Meeting House." There Dr. Thomas Coke assisted in presiding and organizing to serve and to increase the number of Methodists in South Carolina and Georgia, which together numbered 2,070 whites and 141 blacks. One circuit was planned to reach across the state line and to include some North Carolina counties.[1]

First Circuit in Southeastern North Carolina

Young Daniel Combs, who had just entered the itineracy, was appointed to serve Horry County, South Carolina, and northward through the North Carolina counties that were not then included in the Virginia Conference. Combs is credited with organizing the Bladen Circuit, most of which was in North Carolina between the Cape Fear River and the Pee Dee River. Thus Daniel Combs was preaching throughout Horry County, Brunswick, New Hanover and as far as possible up the rivers of Cape Fear, Waccamaw, and Lumber. He was finding his way and making trails; finding people and making Methodists. This he did for one year and was later sent to Pennsylvania and New Jersey. James O'Kelly was the first elder for the Bladen Circuit.[2]

Annual Conferences and Bladen Circuit

The second session of the South Carolina Conference began in Charleston, March 12, 1788. To arrive there Bishop Asbury

Circuit Rider of the Low Country
by V. Gillispie

traveled by Fayetteville, North Carolina, and crossed the Santee River by ferry. The session was considered successful, but at Sunday preaching there was a riot outside, and the confusion frightened some ladies who left through windows. Some rocks went inside the church and one rested on the pulpit. The service continued when order was restored.[3]

This second conference appointed Thomas Hardy to minister to the large and arduous circuit of Bladen. He served only one year. At the end of the first two years, Bladen Circuit reported only thirty-five members. John Tunnell was the elder this second year of the Bladen Circuit.[4]

At the third South Carolina Conference, which convened March 17, 1789, no minister was appointed for the Bladen Circuit; but preachers from the Little Pee Dee Circuit visited the area during that year. They were able to increase society memberships to 228.[5]

Bishop Asbury was pleased with the growth during the work of the Little Pee Dee preachers, Thomas Humphries and Lemuel Moore.[6]

In 1790 the leadership of the Bladen Circuit was restored with Jonathan Bird as minister and Thomas Ware, Elder. A. M. Chreitzberg noted that Jonathan Bird was "in point of ability above the ordinary." After serving Bladen Circuit, he preached forty-six years; in declining health, he settled in McDowell County, North Carolina, near his father.[7]

On his way to the South Carolina Conference of 1791, Bishop Asbury crossed the Cape Fear River and rode thirty miles to "Sister Turner's." He recorded that the quarterly meeting had a good crowd, but some backsliders had hurt the Methodist cause. After passing Lockwood's Folly, he crossed the Shallotte River and Waccamaw River with the horses ferrying themselves over these streams.

As the Bishop and his companion entered South Carolina, they missed the road and were delayed. By the time they reached Georgetown, the Bishop felt "unwell and very low in spirits," but he preached two sermons; both were met with inattention while "wicked youths were playing without."[8]

In Charleston the "long-looked-for Dr. Coke" arrived; he had been shipwrecked off Edisto Island. Dr. Coke preached to a large crowd and Asbury preached last. The latter had by this time become concerned about disputes between some Georgia Methodist preachers and some preachers of other denominations. There were growing claims among Methodists for a right to choose their own preachers;

also, certain preachers were said to be working toward schisms in early American Methodism.[9]

The good work of Jonathan Bird on the Bladen Circuit was followed by another beginning preacher, John Ahair, assisted by William Bellamy. These two were able to increase membership to 287. John Ahair was a native of North Carolina. After only three years of preaching, he faced failing health and death.

In 1792 the membership of Bladen Circuit societies was 467, and preaching places had increased in number. The circuit included in its regular appointments Kingston, South Carolina; in North Carolina, Lumberton, Elizabethtown, and Wilmington; in Brunswick County the Bladen Circuit preachers had regular appointments at the old Brunswick County Courthouse at Lockwood's Folly. Between these regular appointments, there were many short-notice preaching places, wherever someone was able to give notice and gather listeners.[10]

Samuel Edney, another North Carolinian, was on the Bladen Circuit in 1792, assisted by Joshua Cannon. He had previously served the Virginia Conference in the New Hope Circuit in North Carolina. Later he served at Swannanoa; also in the Hendersonville area where he had appointments as long as he lived. He often stated, "I have served God over fifty years and have never seen the moment when I regretted it." In his honor a town in Henderson County was named Edneyville.[11]

The Eighth South Carolina Conference

The South Carolina conference of 1794 began on New Year's Day at Finch's residence, located at the fork of Saluda and Broad Rivers. Bishop Asbury recorded in his *Journal*, "We were straitened for room, having only twelve feet square to confer, to sleep, and to accommodate those who were sick."[12] The conference was not long in session, partly because medicine was needed for Philip Bruce and Bishop Asbury; but it was a memorable conference for those attending, and was later considered significant for several reasons. This eighth South Carolina conference was the first which officially included representatives of Georgia. Its personnel included two future bishops, William McKendree and Enoch George; also other pioneers: Tobias Gibson, Hope Hull, Reuben Ellis. The group witnessed progress in construction of Bethel Academy, the first Methodist school in South Carolina. The school was not completed at conference time, so worship services were held in the Presbyterian

Church. There James Jenkins was ordained deacon, Asbury remarking "you feel the hands of a bishop very heavy, but the devil's hands will be heavier still."[13]

The next preachers appointed to Bladen Circuit were William Bellamy and Robert Cox.[14]

Rufus Wiley and John Shepperd followed in 1795.[15]

Bishop Asbury did not record for Bladen Circuit a progress report in 1795, but he did write a description of his travel through part of it in December:

> Sat. 19 We crossed the south branch of Black River and came to Elizabethtown, about fifty miles above Wilmington: We had a very cold day, and nothing to eat for thirty miles. Brother McRea met us near the town and took us to his house; and it was well he did, or we might have been lost in the woods. But the kindness of the people in supplying our wants made up for our toil — Lord comfort them who comfort us! Here we had a quiet retreat, and spent the Sabbath in public and private exercises.
>
> Mon 21. We set out by sunrise, and had to work our way through swamps, where I feared being plunged in headforemost. I have lately been much tried several ways; and much comforted. We came down Brunswick County, North Carolina, twenty miles to Norman's within the line of South Carolina. Cross where you will between the states and it is a miserable pass for one hundred miles west. I was much led out on Rev. xxi, 6-8. This country abounds with bays, swamps, and drains; if there were no sinners, I would not go along these roads. I am in want of rest, and should be glad of better fare. O, for patience, faith, courage and every grace! Sometimes I feel as though I could rejoice to die and go home: but at other times the work of God is in my way, and sometimes my own unworthiness."[16]

In 1796 American Methodism was divided into six conferences: Philadelphia, New England, Baltimore, Western, Virginia and South Carolina. That year the South Carolina Conference appointed to the Bladen Circuit Anthony Sale, a preacher with more experience than his predecessors. He had served at Camden, Amherst, and Franklin. While in Bladen Circuit he served alone, supervised by James Meacham, Elder. Over a month was required to travel and preach around the circuit, which included areas of the present North Carolina counties of Brunswick, New Hanover, Columbus, Bladen, Robeson and Cumberland; also the Horry in South Carolina.[17]

Sale found in Bladen Circuit 428 members; during the year of 1796, he increased the membership by 212.[18]

When Bishop Asbury visited the circuit that year, he noted the need for help: "If we had men and money, it would be well to station a preacher in such places as Wilmington."[19] Later, in 1803, when he had left Fayetteville in the rain, ferried over the Cape Fear River, visited Purdy's, Elizabethtown, White Marsh, and Lake Waccamaw, he wrote in his Journal "I feel for this circuit, having ridden through it; they have need of three preachers at least."[20]

During February of 1803 Asbury was accompanied by Nicholas Snethen, who traveled and preached with him in the Bladen Circuit. From Wilmington they made their way toward New Bern. On this trip there was again wind, hail and snow; the Bishop's horse, Little Jane, "had a shoe which clogged and made some difficulty."[21]

Preaching Places and Personnel
of the Bladen Circuit

During the first nine years of the Bladen Circuit, more than half the preachers were beginners, each challenged by the long distances between preaching places, by the hazards and hardships of travel, and by the problems in finding accommodations for preacher and horse.

Only a few settlements had a building usable for a congregation. In most places services were held in shelters built for other purposes. Some homes were available, large or small.

By 1795 a brush arbor was in use at Kingston; later an old Presbyterian meeting house was available there. In Brunswick County the Courthouse at Lockwood's Folly was available for the earliest Methodist preachers, 1787 to 1808.[22]

A workers' camp building was used at Charlotte (now Shallotte). At Town Creek the earliest preaching places were "Daniel's" and "Sullivan's" — house, yard, or barn? Available there later was a small chapel north of the present site of Zion United Methodist Church. At Brunswick Town the old Anglican Chapel visited by Joseph Pilmoor was not usable after the Revolution, so the home of Mrs. Grimshaw was sometimes used by circuit riding Methodist preachers.

Wilmington's Courthouse was for a short time used for Anglican services and for Meredith's congregation, but the Methodists had acquired a large chapel there by 1807. Fayetteville had the State House, the Courthouse, and the early chapel of Henry Evans.

In Lumberton the earliest services were held at Robeson's new Courthouse in 1787 and at an academy which was serving as a church in 1803.

Lake Waccamaw had one of the earlest chapels; Bishop Asbury recorded his visit there in 1785. "Union meeting house" was mentioned in 1801, and the same year "the house" was dedicated in Smithville (now Southport). Between these *regular* preaching locations, other gathering places were used for "public congregations."[23]

Bladen Circuit in 1798 had three preachers: James Jenkins, Moses Wilson, and T. Milligan; Jonathan Jackson was presiding elder of this circuit.

James Jenkins had served seven circuits before coming to Bladen. Afterwards he became Presiding Elder of the Camden District of the South Carolina Conference. Thereafter, he served other circuits, was superannuated in 1805 and located in 1806. He wrote his *Autobiography* which is one of the earliest such records from preachers that served the eastern part of the Carolinas.[24]

James Jenkins's work in Bladen was noted not only for his plain and simple preaching on regular appointments, but also for revivals in which he earned his "Thundering Jimmy" nickname. At Conwayboro (formerly Kingston) his preaching effected the conversion of all the young people but two. In Wilmington Jenkins met with a newly organized Methodist class of white people and also with Meredith's "colored" society. Jenkins raised four new societies on the Cape Fear River, and later, as presiding elder, encouraged and worked in camp meetings. His sincerity, his unique personality and his outstanding results made a great impression on the South Carolina Conference.[25]

Reverend James Jenkins

Conference of 1799

Concerning the South Carolina Conference of January 1, 1799, Bishop Asbury wrote that thirty preachers were present and "kept our seats four days." He noted the generosity of the people of Charleston, not only the accommodations for the preachers, but also a gift of a hundred dollars for those in need.[26]

After the conference the Bishop stayed in Charleston the remainder of January, teaching, preaching and visiting classes. In his account of leaving Charleston on January 30, he mentioned the cold weather. Jesse Lee, who was traveling with the Bishop, told more in his own journal: "Mr. Asbury ran his carriage against a stump, and it turned over and hurt him a little by falling out."

In South Carolina they crossed the Black River, the Waccamaw River, and arrived at Gause's by the sea for the night. On the very cold Sunday of February 10, both Asbury and Lee preached at Shallot (formerly Charlotte).

The Genesis of Concord
United Methodist Church

At Lockwood's Folly, Asbury and Lee stayed with Daniel Bellune, a frequent host for Methodist preachers. The whole Bellune family helped make their guests comfortable and notified neighbors who would come for services at the old Brunswick County Courthouse near the Lockwood's Folly River.

Mr. Bellune told of a revival that took place the previous Christmas Eve. He did not give the name of the "young man" leading the service.[27] (The church now at this location would love to know!)

Jesse Lee did not explain "one of our friends," but we may assume that it was one of the circuit preachers for that year: James Jenkins (most likely), Moses Wilson or T. Milligan.

This quotation is from Jesse Lee's *Journal*, January 10, 1799:

> We then rode to friend Belvieu's [Bellune's].[28] There I received some account of the beginning of the great revival of religion which began at this house. On the 24th of December last, one of our friends was at Mr. Belvieu's house and prayed in the family. The next night, Mr. Belvieu said to a young man "What shall we do about prayer tonight?" The young man said he did not know, he would read and sing a hymn, if the other would pray. The other said he could not pray. However, after supper the young man came out of the other room, and said to Mr. Belvieu, "I feel a desire to pray in the family, and I wish you would call the black people together." Mr. Belvieu told me he felt struck with astonishment, and did not know whether he was in earnest or not; however, he went to the door to call the black people; but before he had time to call them, one of the women in the house began to pray earnestly, and he ran back into the house, and they were soon in a flood of tears. All the people now flocked into the house, and the young man began to pray; and they continued praying till Mr. Belvieu's wife got converted; and the young man who prayed also became a subject of converting grace, and others were

66

deeply distressed on account of their sins. And thus they continued praying and rejoicing, till late in the night; this was the beginning of a revival of religion on Lockwood's Folly; and it has prospered since; many having been born again, and brought into the liberty of the children of God. There is still a blessed prospect of religion in the neighborhood: Lord, increase it.[29]

Soon after this incident Bishop Asbury, also approaching Lockwood's Folly, referred to the prayer meeting saying "Here are several young converts."[30]

This group of converts were forerunners and ancestors of members in the present Concord United Methodist Church now near the site of the Bellune Tavern and the Old Courthouse. So, with James Jenkins's work, Bellune's cooperation, Lee's and Asbury's visits, Methodism at Lockwood's Folly had a good beginning. The Old Courthouse was the earliest regular appointment in Brunswick County.

John Simmons and Moses Wilson assisted on the Bladen Circuit in 1799, but these two young preachers did not return in 1800. Benjamin Blanton stayed for another year as presiding elder and was in charge of the sale of books around Charleston.[31]

Asbury and His Activities at the Turn of the Century

From 1795 to 1800 the South Carolina Conferences were held in Charleston. While preparations were being made for the Conference of January 1, 1800, Charleston received news that George Washington had died December 14. Respectfully the pulpits were clothed in black and the bells were muffled. The city arranged for a parade of soldiers; a public oration was scheduled for January 14; a statue was ordered to be placed in the city.[32]

The solemnity weighed like a burden on the preachers, but they resumed the conference with ordinations and appointments. Nicholas Snethen was appointed to travel with Asbury. The Bishop requested Jesse Lee to visit Georgia, using the bishop's horse and traveling about 600 miles.

The year of 1800 began with a week of snow. The preachers started out in this bad weather toward their new appointments in South Carolina, Georgia and North Carolina. Some had their patience tried by noisy travelers pretending to be drunk and dangerous. Later it was learned that the action was deliberate to disturb the Methodist preachers. This and other incidents were thought to have been encouraged by slave holders who doubted the wisdom of preaching to slaves.[33]

On one occasion, Bishop Asbury was distressed for a wagoner whose horses ran away "at the sight of my carriage" and whirled the wagon among the stumps and trees. The Bishop was traveling toward the western parts of the Carolinas. He had completed the Conference in which a significant step was taken looking to the development of a ministry among the black people, thousands of whom had been won to Christ and had joined local Methodist societies. Approval was given for ordaining black deacons where a house of worship had been built and two thirds of the male members of the society approved a qualified man.

The Conference of 1800 approved Wilmington to become a station church, and appointed Nathan Jarratt as minister.

Appointment in 1800:
Reverend Jeremiah Norman

One of the preachers going out from Charleston in January of 1800 was Jeremiah Norman. He had been admitted to the Virginia Conference in 1792, had served two years beyond the Blue Ridge, and had served the Pamlico Circuit. He taught singing lessons a few years and reentered itinerancy in the South Carolina Conference. In 1800 he was appointed to the Bladen Circuit and was the first preacher to complete two years traveling and preaching over this large circuit between the Pee Dee River and the Cape Fear River.[34]

Reverend Norman was a welcome guest at many homes and often led group singing in the evenings. He would sometimes stay at one home several days and from there travel to several preaching places. When he had leisure time, he went hunting game in the woods; it is not certain whether he provided his own gun or borrowed from his hosts to satisfy his "great propensity to gunnery."

Jesse Lee visited and preached February 13, 1800, while Norman was at Lockwood's Folly. The following week on February 22 occurred the first commemoration of Washington's birthday. In the late president's honor and remembrance, Norman eulogized and preached a sermon in a Saturday service at the Court House.[35]

Asbury in Brunswick in 1801

Bishop Asbury visited Brunswick County in March of 1801 after a six-hundred-mile trip in "barrens, swamps, savannahs, rivers, and creeks in South Carolina." He wrote of his restful stay at Gause's

Manor and of his visit to the "sea beach" where he thought of his people across the ocean, wondering if he would ever see them again. On this visit to the area he preached first at Gause's and at Charlotte meeting house (Shallotte). At Lockwood's Folly he stayed in comfort with the Bellune family, preached to the "public congregation," and visited the "class meeting."[36] (For sermon outline see Chapter 16, quote from Asbury's *Journal*, 1801.)

After preaching at Town Creek, Asbury stopped and dined with General Benjamin Smith at Belvedere Plantation where he was cordially received. Afterwards the preachers proceeded across the Cape Fear River to Wilmington where Jeremiah Norman preached in the crowded "tabernacle." This building was also called "the chapel" and was considered "excellent" by Bishop Asbury who recorded its size as 66' x 36'. This chapel had been turned over to the Methodists by William Meredith who requested administration and support which he knew was available only in the Methodist Episcopal Church led by Asbury.[37]

Although Jeremiah Norman had at first been discouraged by conditions on the Bladen Circuit, he was able to see improvements. He was assisted by John Campbell the first year and by Hanover Donnan the second year. He had made friends in Brunswick, including the families of Gause, Bellune, Rourk, Wingate and Smith. He found help and encouragement in the visits of Bishop Asbury, Jesse Lee, Nicholas Snethen and Richard Whatcoat.[38]

Annual Conference of 1802

The 1802 Annual Conference held at Camden was the first of the South Carolina conferences in which a major reorganization was effected. From the organization conference in 1787 through 1801, preachers were appointed for circuits and stations in the South Carolina District. By action of the Conference of 1802, the South Carolina District became three distinct districts of the South Carolina Conference: The Camden District included the northeastern section of South Carolina and the southeastern counties of North Carolina; Saluda District included western South Carolina and part of western North Carolina; Georgia became the third district. Presiding elders chosen for these districts were James Jenkins for the Camden District, George Daugherty for the Saluda District, and Stith Mead for the Georgia District.

This conference heard preaching at noon and at night. Finances were low, but preachers were paid eighty dollars each. There was not enough money left to pay an extra stipend for their children.

Asbury Returns to
the Bladen Circuit

From the conference, Bishop Asbury and Nicholas Snethen traveled to the Bladen Circuit by way of Georgetown, Kingston, and Little River. Upon arrival at William Gause's home, they found that William, Senior, had died; but the Bishop and Snethen were welcomed.

The next stop was at "Charlotteville meeting house" where Snethen spoke on "Faith, Hope, and Charity."[40] Asbury followed with his sermon on "Let Us Come therefore Boldly to the Throne of Grace." The congregations of the last three meetings were "not many more than a hundred souls" in all.

John Gause, a local minister, provided lodging for Bishop Asbury and Mr. Snethen. At Lockwood's Folly, Nicholas Snethen spoke on a portion of Psalm CXIV; Asbury spoke from the Epistle General of John III, 1,2.

Continuing on their way, they "dined in the woods" and spent the night with Charles Gause at upper Bell Swamp. After preaching at New Hope, they went to "Rolks" [Rourk's] and lodged for the night; the next morning both preached again and then went on to Wilmington.[41]

The next year, the Bishop crossed the northern portion of Bladen Circuit through Robeson County, to Fayetteville, Purdy's, Union Chapel and Lake Waccamaw. After two rain storms, he and his companion preacher arrived at a ferry by Wilmington and there had an unpleasant crossing over the Cape Fear River in wind and rain. They found in the Wilmington fellowship 878 Africans and a few whites. They preached Saturday afternoon, Sunday morning, noon, 3:30 p.m. and again at night. Consideration was given to the possibility of establishing a school in that town.[42]

Annual Conference of 1804

The eighteenth South Carolina Annual Conference was held in Augusta, Georgia, the first week in January of 1804. There was preaching every night by the bishops and others. Bladen Circuit was scheduled to receive Benjamin Jones, a native of South Carolina who had been admitted to the conference in 1801. He was about thirty years old when he was given this appointment. He did not complete

70

his first trip around the circuit; near Lake Waccamaw he was drowned in Brown Marsh, supposedly because of his apoplexy. Bishop Asbury was saddened by the loss of this pious, good young man; others remembered the deceased as being "deeply serious with a gentle Christian spirit."[43]

Hugh Porter was left to continue traveling and preaching over the large Bladen Circuit. This young man, a native of South Carolina, was admitted to the conference in 1802. He became an elder in 1805 and located in 1807.[44]

After the January Conference, Bishop Asbury visited part of the Bladen Circuit in February of 1804. Arriving at Waccamaw River, he was uncertain about the prospect of crossing in a "broken flat." His uncertainty was accentuated when the flat upset and all passengers had to wade out. Luckily they were not in the deepest part of the river. The Bishop recalled "by making three trips of the horses, men and baggage, our crazy skiff put us safe over." For the next thirty miles they had no food and traveled in the rain. After arriving in Smithsville, the horses broke away and were returned only after some time and trouble. Asbury and Alexander McCaine spoke at Smithville.

From there they made a visit to Brunswick, the old colonial town with only four houses remaining. In his *Journal* Asbury mentioned "the noble walls of a brick church"; these walls were, and still are, the remains of St. Philip's Anglican Chapel that was burned during the Revolution.[45] The Bishop preached at Mrs. Grimshaw's.

By the time the preachers reached Town Creek the Bishop felt "pressed down by weather and hard labor of riding and preaching." They learned here of a recent camp meeting which had brought a revival of religion among whites and blacks. After both preached at Rourk's, they traveled toward Wilmingotn, arrived there "faint and feeble," but preached to nearly a thousand souls.[46]

The Year of 1805

The nineteenth South Carolina Annual Conference in 1805 sent three preachers to the Bladen Circuit. One was Lewis Myers who had been ordained deacon by Asbury in 1801 and was commended by the Bishop for outstanding work in various positions. (See Chapter XVI for more on Lewis Myers.) Assisting him on the Bladen Circuit were James Russel and John Porter.

After the conference of 1805, the Bishop and Richard Whatcoat traveled across South Carolina to Robeson County, North Carolina.

71

They visited Lumberton, then a town of about twenty families, and continued on another cold ride to Fayetteville. There the Bishop was invited to speak at the State House[47] but declined so as to meet the Methodist congregation in their plain chapel.

After a stormy morning on January eighteenth, the preachers rode through swamps and spring tides. At one place where the bridge was missing, an overseer identified by Asbury as "one of our sheep" brought a ladder for them to walk upon and placed planks so that the horses could pass over. The next morning they crossed the Northeast Cape Fear River before sunrise and arrived in Wilmington for breakfast, and morning preaching by Whatcoat. Both preached Sunday at "our enlarged house" which was filled with both colors in spite of the severe weather.[48]

In the year of 1805, two conferences were held, the second beginning December 30. Twenty-six sermons were preached; Bishop Asbury heard progress reports and news of revivals; Whatcoat ordained the deacons.

From this conference at Camden, South Carolina, the Bishop traveled to Rockingham and Fayetteville, North Carolina; then ninety-one more miles in two days to Wilmington. It was estimated that one-fourth of this city's inhabitants were in attendance at the preaching service in the chapel. The Bishop on this trip did not preach in Brunswick County, but from Wilmington went northward.[49]

1806 Appointments

For this *one year* (1806) appointments were made for the "Bladen and Brunswick" Circuit with three preachers dividing responsibilities.

After this year Bladen and Brunswick became two separate circuits, both remaining in the Camden District. Two preachers served the Brunswick Circuit which included Brunswick County and the South Carolina county of Horry. In December of 1807 the reported membership was 1,092.[50]

Circuit Riders of Bladen Circuit, 1787-1806

Name	Received on Trial	Full Connection	Ordained Deacon	Ordained Elder	Located or Transferred
Daniel Combs	1787				Tr. 1789
Thomas Hardy	1789	1790	1790		Tr. 1790
Thomas Humphries	1783	1785			1798
Lemuel Moore	1789				Tr. 1790
Jonathan Bird	1789	1791	1791	1794	1799
John Ahair	1791	1793	1794		1794 d.
William Bellamy	1791	1793	1793	1795	1799
Joshua Cannon	1790	1791	1791	1793	1797
Samuel Edney	1791	1793	1793		1794
Sihon Smith	1786		1789	1793	1794
Benjamin Denton	1793	1795	1796		1797
Robert Cox	1794	1795	1795	1797	1797
Rufus Wiley	1790	1792	1792	1795	1801
John Shepperd	1795	1797	1797		1797
Anthony Sale	1793	1795	1796	1797	1799
Christopher Mooring	1789	1791	1791	1795	1799
Moses Black	1796	1798	1798	1800	1806
James Jenkins	1792	1794	1794	1797	1812
Moses Wilson	1795	1798	1798		
Thomas Milligan	1798	1800	1800		
John Simmons	1786	1788	1791	1795	
Jeremiah Norman	1792	1794	1797		
John Campbell	1789	1790	1791	1798	
Hanover Donnan	1798	1800	1800		
Moses Matthews	1799	1801	1801	1803	1809
Samuel Mills	1802	1806	1806	1808	1811 d.
William Jones	1801	1803	1804		1805
William Avant	1799	1801	1803		1805
Benjamin Jones	1801	1803	1804		1804 d.
Hugh Porter	1802	1804	1804	1805	1807
Lewis Myers	1799	1801	1801	1804	Tr. 1830
George Dougharty	1798	1800	1800	1804	1807 s.
Wiley Warwick	1804	1806	1806	1808	Tr. 1830
Robert Porter	1806	1808	1808	1810	1816
Samuel Dunwoody	1806	1808	1808	1810	1854 d.

Hymns

O for a thousand tongues to sing My great Redeemer's praise,
The glories of my God and King, The triumphs of His grace !
My gracious Master and my God, Assist me to proclaim,
To spread through all the earth abroad The honors of Thy Name.
Jesus the Name that charms our fears, That bids our sorrows cease,
'Tis music in the sinner's ears, "Tis life, and health, and peace.

* * * * *

Rejoice the Lord is King: your Lord and King adore!
Rejoice, give thanks and sing, And triumph evermore:
Lift up your heart, lift up your voice! Rejoice, again I say, Rejoice!
Jesus, the Saviour, reigns, The God of truth and love;
When he had purged our stains, He took his seat above:
Lift up your heart, lift up your voice! Rejoice, again I say, Rejoice!

* * * * *

A charge to keep I have, A God to Glorify,
A never-dying soul to save, And fit it for the sky.
To serve the present age, My calling to fulfill;
O may it all my powers engage To do my Master's will!
Arm me with jealous care, As in Thy sight to live,
And O, Thy servant, Lord, prepare A strict account to give!
Help me to watch and pray, And on Thyself·rely,
Assured, if I my trust betray, I shall forever die.

* * * * *

Gentle Jesus, meek and mild, Look upon a little child;
Pity my simplicity, Suffer me to come to Thee.
Lamb of God, I look to Thee; Thous shalt my example be;
Thou art gentle, meek and mild; Thou wast once a little child.
Fain I would be as Thou art; Give me Thine obedient heart;
Thou art pitiful and kind; let me have Thy loving mind.
Loving Jesus, gentle Lamb, In Thy gracious hands I am;
Make me, Saviour, what Thou art, Live Thyself within my heart.

— Charles Wesley

74

Chapter VII

South Carolina Conference, Camden District Brunswick Circuit Societies, 1806-1816

On December 29, 1806, the South Carolina Conference convened in Sparta, Georgia, with Bishop Francis Asbury presiding. Fifty traveling preachers were present and their combined membership reports showed an increase of a thousand.

After leaving Georgia, the Bishop traveled northward through snow, hailstorms, and dangerous river crossings.[1] The Brunswick Circuit, after its separation from Bladen, was still a large circuit extending from Wilmington to Georgetown, South Carolina, and from the seashore to the Waccamaw River. In this

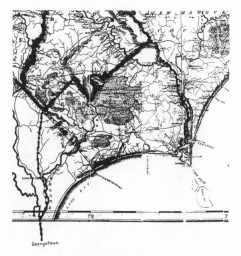

The Brunswick Circuit of 1808 included Brunswick County and part of Horry County to Georgetown, South Carolina.
Price - Strother Map 1808, Department of Cultural Resources, Division of Archives and History.

75

area were Methodist societies at Wilmington, Town Creek, Smithville, Lockwood's Folly, Shallotte, Conwayboro, and Georgetown. Additional preaching places were scattered among other communities.

Young Joseph Travis
and John Collinsworth

To the new Brunswick Circuit, the Conference sent two young preachers, Joseph Travis and John Collinsworth. As described by Chreitzberg, "The two preachers were of the same class, both young and inexperienced, the first-named mild and loving, the second rather ascetic; but both were zealous and faithful. They had no presiding elder, Kendrick having died; and Jonathan Jackson, appointed in his palce, did not reach the circuit until the close of the year."[2]

After many years of preaching, Mr. Travis in his *Autobiography* related some incidents from his trip toward the Brunswick Circuit. He recalled that he began traveling and stopped to eat with a lady acquaintance. She showed great surprise at his intended preaching plans and said "Joe, it will be a poor preach that you will make." These words seemed to come to his ears as he stood up for his first preaching efforts and were not forgotten during his many years as a successful preacher and presiding elder.

The Reverend Joseph Travis

One of his friends by the name of Riddick Pierce, on his way to Montgomery Circuit in North Carolina, traveled part of the way with Travis and Collinsworth and had the misfortune of being thrown off his horse. He concluded that this was his judgment for traveling on the Sabbath.

After reaching the Brunswick Circuit, the young preachers were welcomed at the home of Julius Gause, a local preacher of note, who later shared some of his wisdom with the young inexperienced men when in eagerness to be effective, Travis became vociferous. "More faith and less noise would be better than yelling like a Camanche Indian," said Brother Gause.

Travis and Collinsworth found little advice on the management of the singular "jerks" and "dancing exercises" that appeared a few times in the public congregations. Travis concluded that religious people might have the jerks but there was "no religion in the jerks."[3]

Mr. Travis recalled that his assigned territory was a five-week circuit with appointments in both North Carolina and South Carolina. He had long trips between preaching places and experienced difficulties and privations. He adopted a rule to spend in close meditation and prayer one hour each day while riding. In this practice he was "peculiarly blessed" and encouraged.

Early in this large and laborious circuit, Travis began to doubt whether God ever designed him for such a work, and concluded that if no soul became converted under his preaching within six months after his coming to the circuit, he should take it as a signal that he was not in his proper place and would travel homeward. Before the six months passed, young Travis was reassured by the dramatic conversion of a young man. This convert became "an acceptable and useful itinerant preacher in our Church."[4]

This incident and other encouragement helped Mr. Travis live and work above significant personal misfortunes that had occurred in his childhood. When he was three days old, he was barely rescued from a burning house. At age three an injured knee and ensuing complications brought on him a stooped posture for life. In good humor he told of his first appearance in Wilmington, arriving late:

> Ultimately I hopped in, when behold the congregation was about rising en masse, supposing I was bowing to them, and believing me to be the most polite preacher they had ever seen, believed it was but right to bow in return. They soon found, however, that my act of politeness was from necessity, not of choice.[5]

Local Preachers of Brunswick County

In the Travis *Autobiography*, the Asbury *Journal*, and the Chreitsburg *Early Methodism in the Carolinas* there are records of several local preachers in the early Brunswick Circuit.

The first one, Stephen Daniel of Town Creek, was mentioned in 1785 by Asbury. Later Travis stated, "He was in truth a lovely man, of most amiable temper, humble, holy, and affectionate in his universal deportment. Saint and sinner admired Stephen Daniel. His house was my home and I always left it with reluctance."

Another was Julius Gause who was mentioned by Travis as a "local preacher of note," and Chreitzberg stated that Gause was "of high standing in church and state."

Others included Edward Sullivan who was remembered as a humble fervent Christian; John King, "of great pulpit eloquence"; Dennis Hankins, "a sincere, devout, and humble good preacher"; Richard Green "a good preacher and much beloved." Also, Peter William Gautier, educated for the bar, was mentioned by Travis as "a preacher of considerable standing." Benjamin Sellers was remembered as "a local preacher and faithful servant of God"; Father Lyell, a seventy-year-old "good man and acceptable preacher." In later years Travis wrote that Sellers and Lyell were "truly coadjutors to our fathers in the itineracy in planting Methodism in that section of the country" (eastern Carolinas).[6]

Bishop Asbury did not visit Mr. Travis in Brunswick County, but the two met in Camden, South Carolina, at the end of the year. Mr. Travis was on his way to see his dying mother; the Bishop, on his way to Charleston for the Annual Conference. Asbury requested that the young preacher go to Charleston, but Travis went to his mother's bedside. The latter preacher was given an appointment anyway.[7]

Brunswick Circuit Membership
and Early Appointments

The Brunswick Circuit remained in the Camden District of the South Carolina Conference. The circuit membership in December of 1807 was 1092 (752 white, 340 black).

Appointments for Brunswick Circuit:

December, 1807, James Hunter and Charles Fisher
December, 1808, John Henning and Lewis Hobbs
December, 1809, Alberton Jones and John Rye
December, 1810, Thomas Griffin and Aaron Mattox
November, 1811, John Gamewell and Benjamin Scott[8]

78

During these years, the number of blacks in membership was growing. The total of Methodist memberships in America included 34,724 blacks.[9]

Daniel Asbury

One of the memorable ministers of this period was Daniel Asbury, not a relative of the Bishop. In early life he had been captured by Indians in Kentucky and had suffered many hardships with them when he was taken to Canada and there imprisoned by the British. After his escape in 1783, he returned to his father in Virginia. There he opposed Methodist preachers in the area, but was converted, became a minister, and was admitted to the Methodist itineracy in 1786. He was a presiding elder for fourteen years. His life's greatest experiences took place on the Sabbath. On a Sabbath he was born; on a Sabbath he was captured by Indians. On later Sabbaths he returned to his father; he was converted; and finally, he went to his eternal rest.[10]

Pee Dee District, Brunswick Circuit

In 1812 the Pee Dee District was formed from the eastern section of the Camden District, and Daniel Asbury was transferred to become presiding elder of the new Pee Dee District, which included Brunswick County, North Carolina. Ministers were sent from the last South Carolina conferences that were attended by Bishop Asbury.

The Conference convening December 19, 1812, had Asbury and Bishop William McKendree presiding. Appointed to the Brunswick Circuit were John Gamewell, John Boswell, and West Harris.

The Conference beginning at Fayetteville January 12, 1814, had Asbury and McKendree again presiding. They appointed to Brunswick Circuit Jacob Hill and William Collinsworth.

Later that year the Conference convening at Milledgeville, Georgia, December 21, 1814, with Asbury and McKendree presiding, appointed to Brunswick Circuit James Norton and John Murrow.

The Conference that convened in Charleston December 23, 1815, had Bishop William McKendree presiding. Bishop Asbury was ill and unable to complete his attempted trip. John McClendon was appointed for Brunswick Circuit. He was the first Methodist preacher on this circuit who could not look forward to visits by Bishop Asbury.[11]

Last Visit of Bishop Asbury

Bishop Asbury's last visit to Brunswick County was on his return from the Conference at Milledgeville, Georgia. James Norton and John Murrow were on the circuit when the Bishop made his ninth and last visit. On this final trip here Bishop Asbury visited Frink's and Gause's by the sea; then Shallotte, Lockwood's Folly and Town Creek.

While in the Brunswick area, the Bishop was troubled by his expectorating blood and was hindered by a rainstorm before reaching Wilmington.[12] He suffered along another long trip through Ohio, Kentucky, Tennessee, and the Carolinas. After this difficult traveling, he attempted to attend the next South Carolina Conference, but his strength failed before he could arrive in Charleston. As his friends helped him begin his return trip northward, they went by Marion, South Carolina, and passed on the west side of Brunswick County; the Bishop was unable to attend the Virginia Conference then being held in Raleigh. He reached Richmond, unable to stand, and there preached his last sermon while he was supported on a table. In this weak condition he still had in mind the missionary collection and the General Conference in Baltimore; but in the home of one friend and with his head on the hand of another friend, he breathed his last breath. The message that Bishop McKendree received was: "Our dear father has left us and has gone to the church triumphant. He died as he had lived — full of confidence, full of hope — at four o'clock this afternoon, Sunday, March 31, 1816."[13]

Chapter VIII

Bishop Asbury's Efforts
on the Crescent

The message concerning the departure of "Our Dear Father" did not arrive promptly on the Crescent, but in the slow mode by which traveled the post and the preachers in 1816. Slower still was the comprehension and measurement of the Methodists' loss in the passing of the pastor of our earliest preachers, and of the whole country's loss in the closing of the Asbury era.

Now after two hundred years and countless hours of study by scholars, more information is available and more people can find reason to appreciate Asbury's selfless service to America. He began as an evangelist-missionary. With his magnetism and management he was able to organize societies, appoint "local preachers", supervise the traveling preachers, provide Methodist books, start schools, and collect offerings for the needy.

The resident bishop in America traveled in the conferences and districts; he presided over 224 annual conferences. A good portion of his time was used in southern work. The Coastal Crescent was under his watchcare thirty years. After his first visit here in 1785, he sent and supervised circuit riders as long as he lived.[1]

The preservation of the Bishop's records and the studies by Asbury scholars have made available a storehouse of knowledge and inspiration for all people, both in and outside his beloved Methodist Church, which he believed and declared to be the *purest* and organized the *nearest to God's plan.*

Francis Asbury's aims and aspirations were examined by himself many times. Before landing in America, he passed his own self-examination while ocean waves tossed the ship. He was going to the New World "to live for God and to bring others to do so."[2]

Bishop Asbury found at Brunswick Town the walls of St. Philip's Anglican Chapel and graves of some Anglican ministers and colonial leaders. Photograph from collection at Brunswick Town State Historic Site.

Three years later he recorded one of his prayers: "Lord, keep me from all superfluity of dress and from preaching empty stuff to please the ear, instead of changing the heart."

This young preacher arrived in America at a time when there was widespread suspicion of all English people. As the Revolutionary War approached, the English Methodist missionaries were returning to their old country. With one who was preparing to leave, Asbury fasted and prayed. Later he found himself to be the only one of the eight preachers who chose to remain in America. His decision is recorded in the entry of August 7, 1775, of his *Journal*: "I can by no means agree to leave such a field for gathering souls to Christ, as we have here in America. It would be an eternal dishonor to the Methodists that we should all leave 3000 souls who desire to commit themselves to our care; neither is it the part of a good shepherd to leave his flock in time of danger; therefore, I am determined by the Grace of God not to leave them, let the consequence be what it may."[3]

He would find an American way to disseminate the Word: start with the heart, and strengthen the mind. He would win souls, support and encourage preachers as he had been supported and encouraged. He dedicated himself to the young Methodist Church in America to serve by travel, teaching, testimony and travail.

Of Asbury's fifty-five years as missionary and bishop, forty-five were spent in the American states and frontier. During thirty of these years, he made annual visits to South Carolina and Georgia; in so doing he traveled southward and northward through North Carolina. Fortunately for the southeastern North Carolina area, the Bishop visited along the way and recorded nine trips to Brunswick County. Not recorded was another passing through without time to visit or preach. The rigors of seashore travels through swamps and savannahs were different from but probably as difficult as his hazardous travels on mountain trails.

Potential misfortunes and problems were unpredictable. On his way southward to hold the first South Carolina Conference in 1787 he encountered difficulties, one of which he described as follows: "At night we were poorly provided against the weather; the house was unfinished; and, to make the matters worse, a horse kicked the door open and I took a cold and had the tootheache with a high fever."[4]

The following year near the same area he wrote that he "had to break the ice in two swamps." In another trip toward southeastern North Carolina, he wrote, "We set out by sunrise and had to work our way through the swamps, where I feared being plunged in head foremost."[5]

Leaving Charleston in January of 1800, he faced cold weather and bad roads. His Journal for that time reads: "In the evening my carriage got set fast; the second draught, the hook upon my swingletree gave way, and I had to take to the mud to fix the traces."

There were many references to "hail and wind," "boggy places," "swimming the horse" over rivers; also "no food for thirty miles," which meant fasting most of the day.

It took only a few years of hazardous travel and uncomfortable accommodations to bring on health impairments which escalated with time. Extreme cold or extreme heat, damp clothing in rainstorms, irregular or scanty meals — all did their damage. When frequent illness came, he longed for more spirituality and determined to "spend the remnant of my days and strength altogether for God."[6]

During the Revolutionary War it was sometimes necessary to hide in the swamps to protect himself. At those times when he was not allowed to preach, he deplored the "dumb, silent Sabbaths."

In spite of recurring weakness, he tried to keep on a schedule: "Unwell as I was, I stood up and spoke." At a later time he could not speak because he nearly lost his breath while walking to the house; still he and his companion went on in the rain and were compelled to ferry themselves "over the Cape Fear River after being detained nearly half an hour in the rain."

On a trip to Canada in 1811, one of his feet became swollen and inflamed; he had such pain that his "whole body was disordered."

In 1813 the high fevers and great pain continued. In 1814 he was unable to walk at times and elected to speak from his carriage; but he recorded November 20 "God is with me in all my feebleness."[7]

In his last long trip of 1815-16 he passed through Massachusetts, New York, New Jersey, Pennsylvania, West Virginia, Ohio, Kentucky, Tennessee and North Carolina. In South Carolina he made his last journal entry December 7, 1815: "We met a storm and stopped at William Baker's, Granby."

In January of 1816 in Sumter County, South Carolina, a preacher requested the Bishop to return him to a circuit. Asbury answered, "I am a dying man or I would give you one. I will never see another conference in South Carolina."[8]

Slowly the Bishop traveled toward Charleston, but he was unable to arrive at the Conference. Friends helped him begin the return trip northward, but he was unable to go by Raleigh where the Virginia Conference was being held. He continued, hoping to arrive in Baltimore for the General Conference, but no! No more conferences.

Before leaving South Carolina, the Bishop conversed with a minister friend in Camden concerning whether one is saved by his own righteousness. John Wesley Bond saved notes on Asbury's review of his own efforts:

> I am now in the forty-fifth year of my mission in this country, during which time I have laboured extensively. Sixty times I have crossed the wide range of the Alleghaney [sic] mountains in going and returning to and from the western country; and often before there was even a bridle path to point the way, or a house to shelter us; and when Indian depredation was committed before and behind and on either side of me. Twenty-nine visits I have made to North and South Carolina, and various parts of Georgia; and frequently when their rude pole bridges would be floating by the waters that at times inundate the lowland of that country, so that sometimes I had to wade and lead my horse along the best way I could. And there it was that I caught such colds as have fastened like a vulture on my lungs ever since. And by frequent exposure to bad weather and having to sleep in pole-cabins, where there was nothing between the logs to keep out the wind, I have had such attacks of the rheumatism that my feet and legs have been so swollen that I was unable to walk, and would have to be carried and sit on my horse; where, not being able to keep my feet in the stirrups, I had to let them hang. And in painful condition I have traveled hundreds of miles preaching the gospel. And from these repeated swellings, and the severe pains accompanying them, the use of my limbs [was so taken] from me that I have not been able to stand to preach a sermon for seven years, but have had to rest myself against a table or stool. Besides all my labors and sufferings in other parts of this newly settled country. But what of all this? True it is not forgotten before God. Yet, I can trust in nothing I have ever done or suffered. I stand alone in the righteousness of Christ. I stand in the justifying and in the sanctifying righteousness of Jesus Christ. And, Glory to God! I feel as great a verity in the doctrine I have preached as ever I did in my life. It is the doctrine of the Scriptures; it is the doctrine of God.[9]

The shepherd of many flocks and pastor of many preachers did not, because of his declining health, relinquish his concern for either group. In his own endeavor to live for God and bring others to do so, he hoped to implant the same desire in his preachers. To warm hearts and to enlighten minds, he set high goals and gave his unlimited efforts to help the preachers become effective.

Knowing that their pay was insufficient, he offered to the most needy occasional contributions from the "mite fund", the Book

Concern, and from his own personal funds. At conference he once stated "Our poor preachers keep Lent a great part of the year," and "we ought not to let them starve for clothing". He was able to persuade the General Conference to raise their pay from $64.00 a year to $80.00; also $80.00 for the wife, $16.00 for each child under seven and $24.00 for each child seven to fourteen.[10]

Concerned with the need for preachers to improve their preparation and presentations, he arranged for books to be available at conferences. He was also concerned with continuous searches for prospective preachers. These efforts were successful, apparently, since he ordained four thousand of his prospects. Of the Methodist growth in America he wrote: "In 45 years the poor little daughter mission church in America has overgrown her mother in Europe of nearly 70 years' standing. We have no Doctors of Law and Divinity, no commentators."[11] He lived to see the 1773 statistics (10 preachers, 1160 members) grow to 678 preachers and 214,367 members in 1813.

Not only did Bishop Asbury encourage the preachers to read widely and speak well; he also wanted all people to have educational opportunities. In North Carolina he raised the first money ever given for Methodist education in America. Here also he began the first periodical of American Methodism, the *Arminian Magazine.*[12]

The Bishop felt some uneasiness when he thought the New England Congregationalists were "cooling off" his Methodists; in addition, he feared the consequences of a potentially threatening schism among the South's Methodists. He felt a loss each time he thought a preacher's family drew from ever important preaching time. Perhaps this feeling prompted his writing, "Jonathan Jackson is married: O thou pattern of celibacy, thou art caught."[13]

Asbury's concerns extended even to include his "poor lame mare," his "Little Jane," "Little Fox," "Spark," "Tipple," "Old Glory," "Relief" and other cherished and faithful helpers on the road. Appreciation and sympathy led him to have included in the first *Discipline*, "Be merciful to your beast; not only ride moderately, but see with your eyes that your horse be rubbed and fed."[14]

James McGraw, author of *Great Evangelistic Preachers*, stated that Asbury feared formalism more than fanaticism. He noted the Bishop's belief that only the preaching which molds the lives of people is great. He judged Asbury's preaching as being "out of the heart of God to the hearts of hearers."[15]

Asbury's favorite text was I Timothy 1, 15-16: "How true it is, and how I long that everyone should know it, that Christ Jesus came into the world to save sinners—and I was the greatest of them all. But God had mercy on me so that Christ Jesus could use me as an example to show how patient he is with even the worst sinners so that others will realize that they, too, can have everlasting life.''[16]

His frequent choice of this text is in itself testimony of his devotion to God. The Last Will and Testament of Francis Asbury is final evidence of his incredible adherence to Christian principles.

Francis Asbury's
Last Will and Testament
in the name of Almighty God, Amen

June 6, 1813

I, Francis Asbury, native of Great Britain, born at Great Barr, Handworth Parish, Staffordshire County, Superintendent and Bishop of the Methodist Episcopal Church in America, in common health of body and firm exercise of mind, having deliberated upon the shortness of life and the certainty of death. I make my last will and testament revoking all others. *Item*, I give my body to the dust, from which it was originally taken, in hopes of a glorious ressurection to everlasting life! I commit my Spirit to the Father of all Spirits, in the justifying, sanctifying, preserving, and Glorifying Grace of the Son of God and only Savior of the world. *Item*, I give and bequeath all my wearing apparel to the traveling and local preachers of the Methodist Episcopal Church that shall be present at my death. *Item*, I give and bequeath my horses, or horse and carriages, together with all my Books and Manuscripts, to William McKendree, the first American Bishop of the Methodist Episcopal Church. *Item*, I give and bequeath in Special Trust and Confidence to William McKendree, David Hitt, and Henry Boehm, the sum of two thousand Dollars now deposited in the Book Concern, be the same more or less, to be applied in printing Bibles and Testaments, with other pious Books and Tracts and Pamphlets upon experimental and practical Godliness; and upon the decease of said Trustees, then in that case I devise the trust and confidence shall be founded upon the Bishops elected by the General Conference in succession on the one part, the Baltimore Annual Conference on the other part, shall elect two elders of their Body in joint Trust and especial confidence to insure the deposit in the Book Concern as long as the General union of Order and interest shall be maintained, and an equal dividend is made to all the Conferences in Union and within the United States. Should the present order of things be changed, then and in that case, I wish the money to be funded, and the Interest by the Special Trust and Confidence to be equally and annually divided among the Ten Conferences as now appointed by order of the General Conference, or if the number shall hereafter be increased, there shall be an equal dividend to the whole number. Be it known that I have not laid up treasure upon Earth; more than the sum I have bequeathed, in the principal and interest, has been left to me in legacies by persons that died childless, some thinking possibly I might live to advanced age, and to need an Independent Support; these legacies were left me chiefly by persons of the first Generation of Methodists. I have appropriated the interest and some of the principal, and as a faithful steward return it to the Church; should Elizabeth Dickens survive me and continue in her widowhood, it is my will she should be paid, during her natural life, Eighty Dollars annually; as to all my nominal children, male and female, whose parents have thought proper to put any part of my name upon them, I wish the Book Concern to give these each a Bible, as one of my nominal children. *Lastly*, I appoint my three before-mentioned friends, viz: William McKendree, Daniel Hitt and Henry Boehm as sole executors of this my Last Will and Testament, revoking all former wills by me made; my Burial decent and solitary, a gravestone or not, but plain; my funeral expenses paid by money in my pocket, or from the Interest of the deposit in the Concern. Given under my hand and seal this Seventh day of June, in the year of our Lord one thousand eight hundred and thirteen.

Francis Asbury (seal)

Signed, sealed, published and declared by the above Francis Asbury, to be his last Will and Testament, in the presence of us, who have hereunto subscribed our names as witnesses in the presence of the testator: Baltimore County, to wit:

> Michael Coate
> Isabel Coate
> John W. Bond[17]

Tributes

In memory of his friend, Jesse Lee published this "Sketch of Bishop Asbury."

He was of a slender constitution and yet never spared himself, but ventured through the greatest difficulties and dangers, in order to preach to the people and to attend to the preachers. He was an excellent preacher; and his gift in prayer was exceedingly great. He was deeply pious, remarkably fervent and constant in prayer. His peculiar talent was for governing the preachers, and taking care of the Church of Christ. He generally rose early in the morning, traveled many miles a day, preached often and slept but little. He was generally known throughout the United States, much esteemed and greatly beloved. His presence was generally courted, his advice requested, and his directions attended to. It pleased God to spare him for many years; and, at last, to give him safe and happy passage out of this world.

And his numerous friends have no room to doubt but that their loss is his infinite gain. He has not left behind many, if any, to equal him in the Church to which he belonged. And notwithstanding, his loss is, and will be greatly lamented. We have full confidence in the Lord and He will take care of and provide for his Church.[18]

At the unveiling of the Asbury Statue in Washington, D.C. President Calvin Coolidge said:

> His outposts marched with the pioneers, his missionaries visited the hovels of the poor, that all might be brought to a knowledge of the truth • • • one of the builders of our nation.[19]

Elmer T. Clark, an outstanding Asbury scholar and author of many books on Methodism, wrote of the Bishop:

> This was the preacher who was known as the man who rambles America: and of whom it was said that he was "the most familiar figure on every road". Across the years American Methodism has had many great leaders, but in administration and executive ability, in self-abnegation and evangelistic zeal, none has quite attained the stature of Francis Asbury.[20]

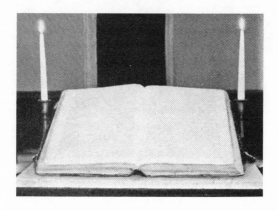

Asbury's Bible, at Old St. George's

89

Photograph by Nancy Brenholtz

The Prophet of the Long Road
Bishop Francis Asbury
(1745-1816)
Washington, D.C.
Erected by American Methodists
Dedicated by President Coolidge 1924
Augustus Lukeman, Sculptor

90

Chapter IX

The Years After Bishop Asbury

As Elmer T. Clark wrote, no one has attained the stature of Bishop Asbury; but devoted followers tried to carry on his work. Among these were the next three bishops: William McKendree, Enoch George, and Robert R. Roberts.

William McKendree was born in Virginia, served with George Washington in the Revolution, and was present at the surrender of Cornwallis at Yorktown.

McKendree was converted in 1787 and entered the itineracy in 1788. He was made presiding elder in 1796 and spent the next twelve years extending Methodism in the frontiers of Tennessee, Kentucky, and north of the Ohio River. After becoming the first American-born bishop in 1808, he served twenty-seven years reaching the entire church. He was recognized particularly for his strict adherence to established rules, and his ability to expedite business. Many churches have been named "McKendree" in memory of this great Bishop of the Church.

Enoch George also was born in Virginia. He entered the itineracy in 1790 and served several years in South Carolina. As bishop he returned to South Carolina five times for Annual Conferences. He was remembered as a "powerful preacher, much loved among the preachers and the people."

Robert R. Roberts was born in Maryland but was reared in Pennsylvania. He was converted at fifteen years of age and was admitted on trial in the Baltimore Conference in 1802. In 1816 he was chosen bishop, the first married man to be elected a Methodist bishop.

After serving several years in the eastern states, he moved to Indiana and, four years later, died there.

Bishop T. A. Morris wrote of his venerable colleague: "He possessed by nature the elements of an orator — an imposing person, a clear and logical mind, a ready utterance, a full-toned melodious voice. He was always patient and pleasant; above all, unpretending."[1]

James O. Andrew   *Robert R. Roberts*

Joseph Travis, Presiding Elder

Joseph Travis, who had his first appointment on the Brunswick Circuit and served there the year of 1807, became presiding elder of the Pee Dee District in 1818. He recorded this list of appointments for his first year there:

South Carolina Conference, Pee Dee District —
Lynch's Creek Circuit, Elija Bird
Black River Circuit, James Parsons, William Hankins
Little Pee Dee Circuit, John W. Norton, Josiah Evans
Deep River Circuit, John Bosewell
Georgetown Station, John McVean
Bladen Circuit, John Dix
Fayetteville Station, Whitman C. Hill
Wilmington Station, James O. Andrew
Brunswick Circuit, Samuel Harrison, A. Hamil

Mr. Travis considered his appointment very pleasant since he would be seeing friends he had made while he was serving the Brunswick Circuit, Georgetown, Wilmington and Fayetteville. Also, his family would be better situated. He had married Elizabeth Forster, daughter of Colonel A. M. Forster of Brunswick County, and had one daughter.[2]

Records from 1818 to 1824

The Brunswick Circuit of the Pee Dee District received the following appointments. The dates indicate the beginning of each conference.

January 27, 1818, Samuel Harrison, Andrew Hamil
December 24, 1818, Elijah Bird, Samuel Jenkins
January 13, 1820, David Hilliard, Anthony Simmons, Aquila Norman
January 11, 1821, Daniel F. Christenberry, Benjamin L. Hopkins
February 21, 1822, William Hankins, David Riley
February 20, 1823, Elisha Calloway, Joel Townsend
February 19, 1824, John Boswell, John L. Greaves.[3]

Local preachers continued to have an important part in the growth of Methodism in the Lower Cape Fear area. An early list by Chreitzberg and by Travis has already been noted. *The North Carolina Directory 1822-23* lists the following as local Methodist ministers of the Brunswick Circuit:

Edward Sullivan	Edward Fizgerald	Joshua Newell
Hezekiah Hewitt	Moses McKeithan	John Butler
John J. Gause	Josiah Lewis	Samuel Hankins
William Gause	Samuel Sarvis	Benjamin Lisle
Nicholas Prince	Levi Dunn	Wilson Longley

Deacons: Rev. A. M. Forster, Rev. Thomas Durant, Rev. Thomas King
Elders: Rev. James L. Berlin, Rev. J. W. Norton.[4]

Methodist society memberships in the Brunswick Circuit increased during the twelve years as part of the Pee Dee District. In 1812 the membership was 500 whites, 249 blacks. In 1824 there were in memberhsip 664 whites, 420 blacks. The Pee Dee District membership increased by 1783 whites and 841 blacks. Five traveling preachers were added the last year.[5]

Reports at the 1824 South Carolina conference showed the following membership record.

Georgetown	92w	1232c
Black River	352w	748c
Lynch Creek	535w	152c
Little Pee Dee	1165w	332c
Deep River	254w	51c
Brunswick	664w	420c
Bladen	271w	351c
Fayetteville	113w	287c
Wilmington	118w	817c
	3546w	4380c [6]

93

At this conference the usual listing of "superannuated or worn out preachers" was made. All the active preachers had their characters examined by the calling of their names before the conference members.[7]

South Carolina Conference of 1818

Three states were represented at the Conference of 1818. The following is taken from James O. Andrew's notes:

> Arriving from Wilmington, N.C., I found my friends all well [in Charleston], and after a few days I left for Conference which was held in Augusta, Georgia . . . Let it be borne in mind that a trip to Augusta was a much more serious affair in those days than now. We had then no puffing, snorting express which could land us there in four or five hours. It was then a four-day job, with the delightful variety of swamps, mud-holes, and pine roods. During the three days of our journey which brought us to Tinker's Creek, our company was excellently pleasant. Bishop McKendree was very communicative and interesting, and what with his intelligent conversation, his general good humor, and the keenness of his wit, he kept us all the while interested and amused, but when we reached Tinker's Creek, the scene changed. The Bishop as unwell and we began to fear that in consequence of the unusually heavy floods of rain, Bishop Roberts would not arrive in Augusta. ... but toward the last of the week he did arrive. He had been prevented from arriving earlier by high waters. ...
> The first number of the *Methodist Magazine* was displayed by Bishop McKendree and a committee was appointed to gather original matter for monthly issues. The Conference closed and I was ordered back to Wilmington.[8]

Fayetteville District, Brunswick Circuit

When the Pee Dee District was divided by the South Carolina Conference in 1825, the Brunswick Circuit was included in the newly-formed Fayetteville District, which extended over the coastal area from Cape Fear to Georgetown, South Carolina.

At the end of the first year in the Fayetteville District, the Brunswick Circuit societies had 402 white members and 427 black members. During the ten years in the Fayetteville District, the membership of the circuit increased by 1085. For this ten-year period the following preachers served:

94

1825 — John Boswell, Reuben Mason; William Kennedy, P.E.
1826 — Archibald Peurifoy; Bond English, P.E.
1827 — Benjamin Haskins, Ebenezer Leggett; Charles Betts, P.E.
1828 — Simeon Stevens: Charles Betts, P.E.
1829 — Angus McPherson, James Hitchener; Charles Betts, P.E.
1830 — Henry Ledbetter, John G. Humbert; Charles Betts, P.E.
1831 — Ebenezer Leggett, William Whitby; Nicholas Talley, P.E.
1832 — Ebenezer Leggett, Charles Wilson; Nicholas Talley, P.E.
1833 — Kenneth Murchison, William Smith; Nicholas Talley, P.E.
1834 — Leonard Rush, Campbell Smith; Nicholas Talley, P.E.[9]

Notes from Minutes of the South Carolina Conference beginning February 16, 1825, at Wilmington:

Located this year:

Elijah Sinclair	James B. Turner	Reuben Tucker
John Covington	John Howard	Travis Owen
Anderson Ray	John Murrow	Jeremiah Freeman
Joseph Travis	Matthew Raeford	Jesse Sinclair

"Superannuated and worn out preachers":

Andrew Hamill	John Greaves
William Kennedy	Jesse Richardson
Daniel Asbury	John Gamewell

Pee Dee District membership: 3,518 white; 4,181 black.

Appointments for southern part of Fayetteville district:

Wilmington —	Thomas L. Winn
Brunswick Circuit —	John Boswell
	Reuben Mason
Waccamaw Circuit —	Archibald Peurifoy[10]

Brunswick Circuit Progress
in the Fayetteville District

In 1830 the South Carolina Conference reports showed the largest membership to that time. The Brunswick Circuit membership had increased to 1042. Five years later it was 1195. In 1833 the mission to the slaves of the Cape Fear area was still active and a Temperance Society wsas organized at Lockwood's Folly.

Some Notable Presiding Elders

Among the early Methodist preachers who contributed to the growth of Methodism were presiding elders, a few of whom are noted as follows:

Nicholas Tally was one of three brothers who preached; he did more service in this area than the other two. He was born in Virginia, converted in Georgia, and received into the South Carolina Conference in 1811. He became an itinerant minister in 1812 and in December, 1849, was appointed Presiding Elder of the Wilmington District. Afterwards, working in missions, he completed fifty-five years and retired. in 1873 at the age of 82 he died.

William McGhee Kennedy was born in North Carolina and joined the South Carolina Conference in 1805. Among his many appointments was Wilmington; later he was presiding elder of the Pee Dee District (1826-1827). He was secretary of the South Carolina Conference for fourteen years and was elected eight times to the General Conference while he served forty-six years.

Bond English was a native of South Carolina admitted to the Conference in 1797. He was Presiding Elder of the Fayetteville District in 1826 and of the Wilmington District in 1839 and 1840. He gave forty-six years of his life in the advancement of Methodist churches.[11]

Chapter X

Wilmington District Formed

When the Fayetteville District was divided in 1835, its coastal area became the Wilmington District of the South Carolina Conference.

The Brunswick Circuit and the Cape Fear Mission were placed in the new Wilmington District. Also in this district were the two Wilmington station churches; the Bladen Circuit; the Waccamaw Circuit; Georgetown; the Black River and Pee Dee circuits in South Carolina. In 1836 the Wilmington District had five charges and one mission in North Carolina; five charges and three missions in South Carolina.

Charles Betts served as presiding elder during the first four years of the Wilmington District (1835-1839). The Brunswick Circuit was served in 1835 by Morgan C. Turrentine and John N. Davis; the next year by Edward J. Fitzgerald and Sampson D. Laney.

In 1837 the South Carolina Annual Conference was held in Wilmington, North Carolina. The Brunswick Circuit reported society memberships of 487 whites, 664 blacks and three Sunday Schools. Appointed to serve these were William M. D. Moore and Andrew J. Green. The following year Archibald McGilvray and James H. Chandler were appointed.

The North Carolina Conference was formed in 1838, but the South Carolina Conference continued to send preachers to Brunswick County Methodist societies and other societies in the Wilmington District. The Brunswick Circuit in 1839 was served by William Harrison and Martin Myers; they reported at the end of the year 992 members with four licensed preachers and two Sunday Schools.

The preachers for 1840 were Simpson Jones and Joseph Kerton, assisted by four local preachers. For 1841 Claudius Pritchard and

Hugh A. C. Walker were appointed. By that time the Brunswick Circuit membership had again exceeded a thousand, but no appointments were made for Brunswick Circuit by the next conference. The circuit name was changed to "Smithville"; no explanation of the name change was recorded in the Annual Conference Minutes for that year (1842).[1]

The Smithville Circuit, formerly Brunswick Circuit, remained in the Wilmington District of the South Carolina Conference for 1842 and the next eight years. The circuit appointments for this period were:

Theophilus Huggins	Simpson Jones
Charles S. Walker	John R. Pickett
William H. Fleming	David Seale and Stephen Miller
John R. Pickett and William Lee	George Moore and Israel
William Crook	Hughes

The Wilmington District until 1850 extended to Georgetown, South Carolina. The presiding elders for 1842 through 1849 were:

Hugh A. C. Walker, 3 years
Whiteford Smith, 1 year
Charles Betts, 4 years
Nicholas Talley, 1 year[2]

More Volunteer Servants

It has earlier been noted that the South Carolina Conference in 1787 began sending to Brunswick County the first itinerant preachers who organized there the earliest Methodist societies. This County was only a part of the large Bladen Circuit that covered territory which later formed six counties. With such a large territory, a preacher could not visit more than once a month at any location. To assist these traveling preachers, plans were made for some local men to become prepared to fill in at meetings between the regular appointments.

Stephen Daniel was the first "local preacher" in Brunswick County. He was the son of John Daniel who had earlier lived in Charleston, South Carolina, and had been a generous supporter of the St. Thomas Anglican Church there. To each of his five sons, John Daniel bequeathed a plantation in Brunswick County. Stephen Daniel's plantation was near Town Creek and was first visited by Superintendent Asbury in 1785. At that time Asbury was on his first Episcopal tour and en route to Green Hill's home at Louisburg.[3]

It is possible, and even probable, that the present name of *Green Hill Plantation* may have had its origin in Asbury's first visit here at Town Creek in 1785.

Edward Sullivan was another local preacher at Town Creek. He welcomed Bishop Asbury's visits and preaching in 1801 and afterwards.

About the same time, Dennis Hankins and John Julius Gause were local preachers in the southern part of the county. James King was active in societies west of them.[4]

The Exhorters

Other volunteer servants were the exhorters; they were licensed but had less responsibility than the local preachers. They were not expected to take a text and deliver a formal sermon, but they were expected to urge the congregation to practice Christian teaching and to give evidence and testimony of Christian living. With fervent spirit they attempted to "draw the net" and to encourage exercise of faith, communion in society and individual responsibility in Methodist classes.[5]

Some of these volunteer servants were mentioned in the early records of the old Bladen Circuit; more were licensed and listed officially in later records of Methodist classes in the Cape Fear area.

During the first four years of the Wilmington District, the Brunswick County Methodist Societies grew in number and became better organized. Reverend Charles Betts was the presiding elder. For each group, he provided the rules for Methodist societies and opened each quarterly meeting with "Dear Brethren, live in love and peace and the God of love will be with you all. Remember your fast days, the Friday before each quarterly meeting, and pray for us your preachers."[6]

An early Methodist class membership list for Zion (1847) included eighteen names:

Daniel Evans	Jacob A. Evans
Miles Potter	Henry Evans
Samuel Potter	Nathan Register
Richard Sullivan	George Hays
Whitefield Potter	William Henry Potter
John Mercer	G. W. Rabon
Thomas A. Durant	Hugh Mc[illegible]
Josiah Smith	George Smith
William T. Potter	Junius Evans

This is the earliest Methodist class roll available at this writing.[7]

The sixty-fourth session of the South Carolina Conference of the Methodist Episcopal Church, South, was held at Camden beginning December 19, 1849. This was the last session of this Conference in which appointments were made for Brunswick County Methodists of the Wilmington District. These and others of the Wilmington District follow:

Presiding Elder, Nicholas Talley

Cape Fear Mission (around Smithville) — J. T. Munds
Smithville Circuit, N.C. — G. W. Moore, Israel P. Hughes
Wilmington, N.C. — H. A. C. Walker, J. T. Munds
Bladen, N.C. — D. J. Simmons, R. Washburn
Waccamaw Neck, S. C. — John A. Minnick, A. L. Smith
Marion, S.C. — A. McCuorquodale, O. A. Chreitzberg
Conwayboro, S.C. — James H. Chandler
Black River, S.C. — J. M. Bradley, J. Parker
Black River Mission, S.C. — M. Eaddy, A. P. Martin
Santee Mission, S.C. — W. Carson, A. Ervin
Sampit Mission, S.C. — L. M. Little[8]

1849 Statistics for Wilmington District

Cape Fear Mission — 5 whites, 433 blacks

Smithville Circuit — 589 whites, 657 blacks, 2 local elders, 1 licentiate

Wilmington — 283 whites, 749 blacks, 1 local elder, 1 local deacon

Bladen — 686 white, 854 black, 2 local deacons, 2 licentiates

Waccamaw Neck — 25 white, 487 black

Georgetown — 148 white, 1015 black, 1 local elder, 1 local deacon

Marion — 1000 white, 704 black, 4 local elders, 6 local deacons, 8 licentiates

Conwayboro — 763 white, 293 black, 1 local elder, 4 licentiates

Black River — 694 white, 1161 black, 1 local elder, 3 local deacons, 2 licentiates

Pee Dee Mission — 63 white, 1182 black

Sampit Mission — 226 black[8]

Cape Fear Mission and Plantations

The Cape Fear Mission (1812-1861) served the black people on the plantations in southeastern Brunswick County below the forks of Cape Fear River, including some of the oldest plantations. Among these were Orton, York, Kendall, Howe, Lilliput, Pleasant Oaks, Charles Town, Clarendon, The Forks, Buchoi and Belville.

Farther up the river were Belvidere, Woodburn, Gabriel Bluff, Cobham, Shawfield, Prospect, Mulberry, Dallison, Auburn, Magnolia, McFadden, Point Repose and Rowan.

The plantations along Town Creek were: Dalrymple, Hullfield, Watters, Dobbs, Spring Garden, Bel Grange, Bigford, Nathaniel Rice, J. Davis, Russell, Gause, Green Hill, Stanaland, Whitlock House, Walker.

By Lockwood's Folly River and by the seashore were: Swain, Wingate, Evans, Bell, Galloway, Goose Marsh, Myrtle Grove, Russ, Hewett, Holden, Leonard, Robinson, Boone, Simmons, Gause.

The western area of the county included the families of Babson, Formyduval, Smith, Carlisle, Mintz, Thomas Gore, Frink, Grissett.

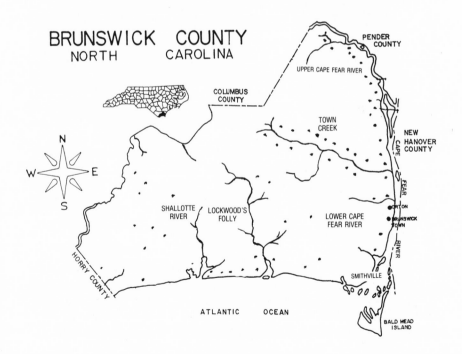

101

CONTENTS.

HYMNS.

PART I.

FOR PUBLIC WORSHIP.

SECTION I.

Being and Perfections of God.

1   C. M.   C. Wesley.
          The Trinity.
A THOUSAND oracles divine
     Their common beams unite,
That sinners may with angels join
     To worship God aright!

2 To praise a Trinity adored
By all the hosts above;
And one thrice holy God and Lord
Through endless ages love.

3 Triumphant host! they never cease
To laud and magnify
The Triune God of holiness,
Whose glory fills the sky :

4 Whose glory to this earth extends,
When God himself imparts,
And the whole Trinity descends
Into our faithful hearts.

5 By faith the upper choir we meet,
And challenge them to sing
Jehovah, on his shining seat,
Our Maker and our King.

6 But God made flesh is wholly ours,
And asks our nobler strain;
The Father of celestial powers,
The Friend of earth-born man.

7 Ye seraphs, nearest to the throne,
With rapturous amaze

On us, poor ransom'd worms, look down,
     For heaven's superior praise !

8 The King, whose glorious face ye see,
     For us his crown resign'd ;
That fulness of the Deity,
He died for all mankind !

2   7s.   C. Wesley.
          The Trinity.
HOLY, holy, holy Lord,
     God the Father, and the Word,
God the Comforter, receive
Blessings more than we can give.

2 Mix'd with those beyond the sky,
Chanters to the Lord most high,
We our hearts and voices raise,
Echoing thy eternal praise.

3 One, inexplicably three,
One, in simplest unity :
God, incline thy gracious ear,
Us thy lisping creatures hear.

4 Thee, while man, the earth-born, sings,
Angels shrink within their wings ;
Prostrate seraphim adore
Breathe unutterable love.

5 Happy they who never rest,
With thy heavenly presence blest !
They the heights of glory see,
Sound the depths of Deity !
7

This early Hymn Book of the Methodist Episcopal Church was indexed by subject, by texts, and by all lines. The Preface was signed by Joshua Soule, James O. Andrew, William Capers, and Robert Paine. The hymns had to be learned, since there were no instruments in early churches. The preacher learned the tunes and tried to teach the congregations.

Chapter XI

The Transfer Debate and Decision

A major event occurred when the General Conference of the Methodist Episcopal Church, South, met in St. Louis in May of 1850. Bishop J. O. Andrew opened the Conference with the reading of the sixth chapter of Corinthians; the assemblage sang "And Are We Yet Alive?"

Delegates from North Carolina were Charles F. Deems, Peter Doub and D. B. Nicholson. South Carolina was represented by William M. Wightman, Hugh A. C. Walker, J. Stacy, W. A. Gamewell, Charles Betts and Nicholas Talley.

The North Carolina delegates to the General Conference presented their plea for Annual Conferences to adhere to state lines, emphasizing their claim to the authority to make appointments for all Methodist churches in North Carolina.

Delegates from South Carolina offered amendments and requested further discussions, so that the decision was not made the first day.

The second day's session brought the vote which set conference boundaries at the state line. Because of the opposition of South Carolina ministers, another effort was made by Charles Betts and A. M. Shipp:

> Resolved, that the privilege is hereby granted to the preachers who may at the time of the next sessions of the conferences concerned, be found in the territory aforesaid, to adhere, at pleasure either to the South or North Carolina Conference; and that the same privilege be granted to the societies in the same territory.

Another resolution was presented, but tabled:

> The undersigned, learning that the boundary line as now ordered between the North Carolina and the South Carolina Conferences,

will sever the several circuits along the border; and fearing that the results will be sadly injurious to that section of the Church — with the distinct understanding, that the vote for reconsideration and final adjustment will be taken without debate do now respectfully move a reconsideration of the vote by which the boundary line in questions was ordered to be changed.

Signed

W. Hicks and

W. H. Rogers

The requested reconsideration of the vote was not granted, but approval was given for entering into the minutes the following protest of the South Carolina delegates:

We, the delegates of the South Carolina Conference of the Methodist Episcopal Church, South, in behalf of the entire ministry and membership whose interest we officially protested against any change in the boundary between the North Carolina and the South Carolina Conferences, do most earnestly and solemnly remonstrate against the action of the General Conference depriving us of a large portion of our territory by the violent removal of a landmark established by our fathers and left unchanged for the last half-century.

We regard the action aforesaid as an unjust usurpation of power over the rights and privileges appertaining to Annual Conferences — violative of the customs and usages of our Church toward old and well-established conferences — revolutionary in its principles and tendency, and frought with disastrous consequences of the Church of God, whose interests are paramount to all considerations earthly and temporal.

Signed,

W. M. Wightman	C. Betts
H. A. C. Walker	N. Talley
A. M. Shipp	S. W. Capers
J. Stacy	R. J. Boyd[1]
W. A. Gamewell	

After the General Conference debated at length and decided to change the conference boundaries to coincide with the state lines, the South Carolina Annual Conference met in Wadesboro, North Carolina, December 18, 1850. The South Carolina delegates to the General Conference reviewed their efforts to keep in the South Carolina Conference the North Carolina territories and preachers and expressed their regrets in not prevailing; but their report continued with "We hold the peace of the Church in the ceded territory, and the unwavering attachments of the multitudes of the

104

membership of the South Casrolina Conference demand the temporary sacrifice at our hands. The integrity of our Church Union is sufficiently important to warrant another effort to secure it by bringing back the General Conference to original principles."[2]

The South Carolina Conference had lost the territory between the South Carolina line and Fayetteville and from Rockingham to the coast in North Carolina. The transfer included the North Carolina territory of the Wilmingotn District and its presiding elder; Bladen Circuit with its ministers John H. Robinson and D. D. Byars; Fayetteville Station with J. H. Wheeler; Fayetteville Circuit with Abner Ervin and C. H. Phillips; Rockingham with L. W. Pegues; Montgomery with A. M. Rush; Cape Fear Mission with J. T. Munds. Transferred also was Smithville Circuit, which included all the twelve Methodist societies and one African mission in Brunswick County. For these, appointments would hereafter be made by the North Carolina Methodist Conference.[3]

Cokesbury School in North Carolina was the first Methodist Conference school in America. Funding for this school was started in 1780. The site, now in Davie County, has a North Carolina Historical Marker.

Cokesbury College, the first Methodist college in America, opened in 1789 at Abington, Marylnad, It was named in honor of Bishops Coke and Asbury.

Chapter XII

Recapitulatory Records
and Dual Chronology

In recognition and appreciation of the contributions from the South Carolina Conference to Southeastern North Carolina, the following addenda are included with information on the General Conference representatives; the circuits and appointed preachers; the sessions of the South Carolina Conference; summarized statistics of the circuits; and one Pastoral Letter from one great bishop. Also, supplementary information is given in a chronology of church history and related historical events.

South Carolina General Conference Delegations
From the General Conference of 1804 to 1850

Members who attended the General Conference of 1804: Josias Randle, George Dougherty, Honover Donning, Moses Mathews, James Jenkins.

Members who attended the General Conference of 1808: Josias Randle, Britton Capel, Joseph Tarpley, James H. Mellard, William Phoebus, John Gamewell, Wiley Warwick, Lewis Myers, Epps Tucker, Daniel Asbury, Samuel Mills.

After that time they were elected, as follows:

1812. Lewis Myers, Daniel Asbury, Lovick Pierce, Joseph Tarpley, William M. Kennedy, James Russell, James E. Glenn, Joseph Travis, Hilliard Judge, Samuel Dunwody. No reserves.

1816. Lewis Myers, Daniel Asbury, Joseph Tarpley, William M. Kennedy, Thomas Mason, Hilliard Judge, Samuel Dunwody,

Anthony Senter, John B. Glenn, Sol. Bryan, James Norton, Henry Bass, Reuben Tucker, Alexander Talley. No reserves.

1820. Joseph Tarpley, Joseph Travis, William Capers, James Norton, Lewis Myers, Daniel Asbury, S. K. Hodges, Samuel Dunwody, William M. Kennedy. Reserve: J. O. Andrew.

1824. James O. Andrew, Lewis Myers, William M. Kennedy, S. K. Hodges, Lovick Pierce, Nicholas Talley, Joseph Travis, James Norton, Henry Bass, William Capers, Samuel Dunwody. Reserve: Andrew Hamill.

1828. J. O. Andrew, William Capers, William M. Kennedy, Lovick Pierce, Henry Bass, Samuel Dunwody, S. K. Hodges, George Hill, William Arnold, Andrew Hamill, M. McPherson, Robert Adams, Elijah Sinclair. No reserves.

1832. William Capers, Malcom McPherson, William M. Kennedy, Henry Bass, Samuel Dunwody, N. Talley, Hartwell Spain, Charles Betts, Bond English. Reserves: Robert Adams, Daniel G. McDaniel, Joseph Holmes.

1836. William Capers, Samuel Dunwody, William N. Kennedy, N. Talley, M. McPherson, C. Betts. Reserves: H. Bass, William M. Wightman, H. Spain.

1840. William Capers, C. Betts, William M. Wightman, William M. Kennedy, Bond English. Reserves: H. Spain, H. A. C. Walker, N. Talley.

1844. William Capers, William M. Wightman, Charles Betts, Samuel Dunwody, H. A. C. Walker. Reserves: Whitefoord Smith, Bond English.

Delegates to Convention 1845: William Capers, William M. Wightman, Charles Betts, H. A. C. Walker, Samuel Dunwody, Bond English, Whitefoord Smith, Samuel W. Capers, Robert J. Boyd.

1846. William Capers, William M. Wightman, H. A. C. Walker, Charles Betts, N. Talley, B. English. Reserves: W. Smith, S. Dunwody, S. W. Capers.

1850. William M. Wightman, Whitefoord Smith, H. A. C. Walker, C. Betts, A. M. Shipp, James Stacy, W. A. Gamewell, N. Talley, S. W. Capers. Reserves: R. J. Boyd, H. Spain.[1]

South Carolina District — Bladen Circuit

Date of Conference	Appointments for Bladen Circuit	Members in Society W	C
3-22-1787	Daniel Combs James O'Kelly, Elder		
3-17-1788	James Hardy John Tunnell, Elder	35	
3-17-1789	Thomas Humphries, Lemuel Moore Reuben Ellis, P. Elder; Ira Ellis, Elder	34	
2-15-1790	Jonathan Bird Thomas Ware, Elder	167	61
2-22-1791	John Ahair, William Bellamy Thomas Bowen, Elder	232	57
2-14-1792	Joshua Cannon, Samuel Edney Thomas Bowen, Elder	403	64
12-24-1792	Sihon Smith, Benjamin Denton Thomas Bowen, Elder	480	72
1-1-1794	William Bellamy, Robert Cox Thomas Bowen, Robert Cox, Elders	480	55
1-1-1795	Rufus Wiley, John Shepperd John Fore, Elder; Thomas Bowen, Book Steward	375	22
1-1-1796	Anthony Sale James Meacham, Elder	386	42
1-5-1797	Christopher Mooring, Moses Black; Thomas Humphries, P. Elder	436	104
1-1-1798	James Jenkins, Moses Wilson, T. Milligan; Jonathan Jackson, P. Elder	462	143
1-1-1799	John Simmons, Moses Wilson Benjamin Blanton, P. Elder	450	200
1-1-1800	Jeremiah Norman, John Campbell Benjamin Blanton, P. Elder	730	114
1-1-1801	Jeremiah Norman, Hanover Donnan James Jenkins, P. Elder	653	130

South Carolina Conference — Camden District

Date of Conference	Appointments for Bladen Circuit	Members in Society W C
1-1-1802	Moses Matthews, Samuel Mills James Jenkins, P. Elder, Camden District	543 217
1-1-1803	William Jones, William Avant James Jenkins, P. Elder, Camden District	633 418
1-2-1804	Benjamin Jones, Hugh Porter James Jenkins, P. E. Camden District	722 511
1-1-1805	Lewis Myers, James Russell, J. Porter, George Dougharty, P. E. Camden District	1031 22
12-30-1805	For Bladen and Brunswick: Wiley Warwick, Robert Porter, Samuel Dunwoody, George Dougharty, P.E. Camden District	1301 430

Appointments for
Brunswick Circuit

Date of Conference	Appointments for Brunswick Circuit	Members in Society W C
12-29-1806	Joseph Travis, John Collinsworth Bennett Kendrick, P.E. Camden District	No numbers given
12-28-1807	James Hunter, Charles Fisher Moses Matthews, P.E. Camden Dist.	752 340
12-26-1808	John Henning, Lewis Hobbs Jonathan Jackson, P.E. Camden Dist.	697 313
12-23-1809	Alberton Jones, John Rye Daniel Asbury, P.E. Camden District	757 408
12-22-1810	Thomas Griffin, Aaron Mattox Daniel Asbury, P.E. Camden District	677 399
11-30-1811	John Gamewell, Benjamin Scott Daniel Asbury, P.E. Camden District	682 380

South Carolina Conference — Pee Dee District

Date of Conference	Appointments for Brunswick Circuit	Members in Society	
		W	C
12-19-1812	John Gamewell, John Boswell, West Harris; Daniel Asbury, P.E.	500	249
1-12-1814	Jacob Hill, William Collinsworth William M. Kennedy, P.E.	703	404
12-21-1814	James Norton, John Murrow; William M. Kennedy, P.E.	682	339
12-23-1815	John McLendon; William M. Kennedy, P.E. Pee Dee District	557	248
12-25-1816	Allen Turner, Thomas Roseman William M. Kennedy, P.E.	525	368
1-27-1818	Samuel Harrison, Andrew Hamill Joseph Travis, P.E.	765	280
12-24-1818	Elijah Bird, Samuel Jenkins Joseph Travis, P.E. Pee Dee Dist.	647	311
1-13-1820	David Hilliard, Anthony Simmons Aquila Norman; Joseph Travis, P.E.	773	484
1-11-1821	Daniel F. Christenberry, Benjamin Haskins; Joseph Travis, P.E.	661	357
2-21-1822	William Hankins, David Riley William M. Kennedy, P.E.	687	374
2-20-1823	Elisha Calloway, Joel W. Townsend William M. Kennedy, P.E.	633	402
2-19-1824	John Boswell, John L. Greaves William M. Kennedy, P.E.	664	420

South Carolina Conference — Fayetteville District

	Appointments for Brunswick Circuit		
2-16-1825	John Boswell, Reuben Mason William M. Kennedy, P.E.	712	438
1-12-1826	Archibald Peurifoy; Bond English, P.E. Fayetteville District	402	427

111

South Carolina Conference — Fayetteville District

Date of Conference	Appointments for Brunswick Circuit	Members in Society W	C
3-11-1827	Benjamin L. Hoskins, Ebenezer Leggett; Charles Betts, P.E.	314	385
2-6-1828	Simeon L. Stevens Charles Betts, P.E.	350	389
1-28-1829	Angus McPherson, James Hitchener Charles Betts, P.E.	433	553
1-27-1830	Henry W. Ledbetter, John G. Humbert; Charles Betts, P.E.	495	547
1-26-1831	Ebenezer Leggett, William Whitby Nicholas Talley, P.E.	485	528
1-26-1832	Ebenezer Leggett, Charles Wilson Nicholas Talley, P.E.	502	525
1-30-1833	Kenneth Murchison, William R. Smith; Nicholas Talley, P.E.	615	547
1-5-1834	Lenoard Rush, Campbell Smith Nicholas Talley, P.E.	640	555

South Carolina Conference — Wilmington District

Brunswick Circuit Appointments

Date	Appointments	W	C
2-11-1835	Morgan C. Turrentine, John N. Davis; Charles Betts, P.E.	637	448
2-10-1836	Edward J. Fitzgerald, Sampson D. Laney; Charles Betts, P.E.	562	514
1-4-1837	William M. D. Moore, Andrew J. Green; Charles Betts, P.E.	487	664
1-10-1838	Archibald McGilvray, James H. Chandler; Charles Betts, P.E.	455	566
1-9-1839	William T. Harrison, Martin P. Myers; Bond English, P.E.	493	480
1-8-1840	Simpson Jones, Joseph P. Kerton Bond English, P.E.	377	615
2-10-1841	David W. Seal, Cladius H. Pritchard Hugh A. C. Walker, P.E.	477	526

2-26-1842 Brunswick County became Smithville Circuit

Smithville Circuit Appointments

Date of Conference	Appointments for Smithville Circuit	Members in Society	
		W	C
1-26-1842	Theophilus Huggins Hugh A. C. Walker, P.E., Wilmington District	not recorded	
2-8-1843	Charles S. Walker Hugh A. C. Walker, P.E. Wilmington District	702	620
2-7-1844	William H. Fleming Hugh A. C. Walker, P.E. Wilmington District	508	682
12-25-1844	David W. Seale, Stephen H. Miller Whiteford Smith, P.E. Wilmington District	166	142
2-10-1845	William Crook Charles Betts, P.E. Wilmington District	515	590
1-13-1847	Simpson Jones Charles Betts, P.E. Wilmington District	500	580
1-12-1848	John R. Pickett Charles Betts, P.E. Wilmington District	486	547
12-20-1848	John R. Pickett, William M. Lee Charles Betts, P.E. Wilmington District	596	569
12-19-1849	George W. Moore, Israel P. Hughes Nicholas Talley, P.E. Wilmington District	589	567
12-18-1850	Smithville Circuit transferred to North Carolina Conference[2]		

Sessions of the South Carolina Conference

No.	Place	Date	President	Membership	
1.	Charleston, S.C.	Mar. 22, 1787	Coke and Asbury	2,075W	141C
2.	Charleston, S.C.	Mar. 12, 1788	Francis Asbury	2,246W	224C
3.	Charleston, S.C.	Mar. 17, 1789	Coke and Asbury	3,087W	290C
4.	Charleston, S.C.	Feb. 15, 1790	Francis Asbury	2,962W	496C
5.	Charleston, S.C.	Feb. 22, 1791	Coke and Asbury	3,830W	699C
6.	Charleston, S.C.	Feb. 14, 1792	Francis Asbury	3,655W	742C
7.	Charleston, S.C.	Dec. 24, 1792	Francis Asbury	3,371W	826C
8.	Finch's	Jan. 1, 1794	Francis Asbury	5,192W	1,220C
9.	Charleston, S.C.	Jan. 1, 1795	Francis Asbury	4,428W	1,116C
10.	Charleston, S.C.	Jan. 1, 1796	Francis Asbury	3,862W	971C
11.	Charleston, S.C.	Jan. 1, 1797	Coke and Asbury	3,715W	1,038C
12.	Charleston, S.C.	Jan. 1, 1798	Jonathan Jackson	4,457W	1,381C
13.	Charleston, S.C.	Jan. 1, 1799	Francis Asbury	4,806W	1,385C
14.	Charleston, S.C.	Jan. 1, 1800	Francis Asbury	4802W	1,535C
15.	Camden, S.C.	Jan. 1, 1801	Asbury, Whatcoat	4,745W	1,562C
16.	Camden, S.C.	Jan. 1, 1802	Francis Asbury	5,663W	1,780C
17.	Camden, S.C.	Jan. 1, 1803	Francis Asbury	9,256W	2,815C
18.	Augusta, Ga.	Jan. 2, 1804	Coke and Asbury	11,064W	3,456C
19.	Charleston, S.C.	Jan. 1, 1805	Asbury, Whatcoat	12,258W	3,831C
20.	Camden, S.C.	Dec. 30, 1805	Asbury, Whatcoat	12,665W	4,387C
21.	Sparta, Ga.	Dec. 29, 1806	Francis Asbury	12,484W	4,432C
22.	Charleston, S.C.	Dec. 28, 1807	Francis Asbury	14,417W	5,111C
23.	Liberty Chapel, Ga.	Dec. 26, 1808	Asbury, McKendree	16,344W	6,284C
24.	Charleston, S.C.	Dec. 23, 1809	Asbury, McKendree	17,788W	8,202C
25.	Columbia, S.C.	Dec. 22, 1810	Asbury, McKendree	19,404W	9,129C
26.	Camden, S.C.	Dec. 21, 1811	Asbury, McKendree	20,863W	11,063C
27.	Charleston, S.C.	Dec. 19, 1812	Asbury, McKendree	23,966W	13,771C
28.	Fayetteville, N.C.	Jan. 14, 1814	Asbury, McKendree	23,711W	14,348C
29.	Milledgeville, Ga.	Dec. 21, 1814	Asbury, McKendree	23,240W	14,527C
30.	Charleston, S.C.	Dec. 23, 1815	William McKendree	25,065W	16,429C
31.	Columbia, S.C.	Dec. 25, 1816	McKendree, George	22,383W	16,789C
32.	Augusta, Ga.	Jan. 27, 1818	William McKendree	20,965W	11,714C
33.	Camden, S.C.	Dec. 24, 1818	R. R. Roberts	21,059W	11,587C
34.	Charleston, S.C.	Jan. 20, 1820	Enoch George	21,221W	11,748C
35.	Columbia, S.C.	Jan. 11, 1821	Enoch George	22,105W	12,485C
36.	Augusta, Ga.	Feb. 21, 1822	McKendree, George	21,290W	12,906C

Sessions of the South Carolina Conference

No.	Place	Date	President	Membership	
37.	Savannah, Ga.	Feb. 20, 1823	R. R. Roberts	23,121W	13,895C
38.	Charleston, S.C.	Feb. 19, 1824	Enoch George	24,909W	14,766C
39.	Wilmington, N.C.	Feb. 16, 1825	R. R. Roberts	27,756W	15,293C
40.	Milledgeville, Ga.	Jan. 12, 1826	Joshua Soule	28,405W	15,708C
41.	Augusta, Ga.	Jan. 11, 1827	McKendree, Roberts, Soule	29,419W	16,552C
42.	Camden, S.C.	Feb. 6, 1828	Joshua Soule	35,173W	18,475C
43.	Charleston, S.C.	Jan. 28, 1829	William McKendree	38,708W	21,300C
44.	*Columbia, S.C.	Jan. 27, 1830	John Howard	40,335W	24,554C
45.	Fayetteville, N.C.	Jan. 26, 1831	W. M. Kennedy	20,513W	19,144C
46.	Darlington, S.C.	Jan. 26, 1832	Elijah Hedding	21,731W	20,197C
47.	Lincolnton, N.C.	Jan. 30, 1833	J. O. Andrew	24,773W	22,336C
48.	Charleston, S.C.	Feb. 5, 1834	Emory and Andrew	25,186W	22,788C
49.	Columbia, S.C.	Feb. 11, 1835	J. O. Andrew	23,789W	22,737C
50.	Charleston, S.C.	Feb. 10, 1836	J. O. Andrew	24,110W	23,643C
51.	Wilmington, N.C.	Jan. 4, 1837	Malcolm McPherson	23,615W	23,166C
52.	Columbia, S.C.	Jan. 10, 1838	Thomas A. Morris	24,016W	23,498C
53.	Cheraw, S.C.	Jan. 9, 1839	J. O. Andrew	24,756W	24,822C
54.	Charleston, S.C.	Jan. 8, 1840	Thomas A. Morris	26,974W	27,630C
55.	Camden, S.C.	Feb. 10, 1841	J. O. Andrew	26,945W	30,481C
56.	Charlotte, N.C.	Jan. 26, 1842	B. Waugh	27,475W	30,860C
57.	Cokesbury, S.C.	Feb. 8, 1843	J. O. Andrew	30,540W	33,375C
58.	Georgetown, S.C.	Feb. 7, 1844	Joshua Soule	31,568W	37,952C
59.	Columbia, S.C.	Dec. 25, 1844	Joshua Soule	32,306W	39,495C
60.	Fayetteville, N.C.	Dec. 10, 1845	J. O. Andrew	33,387W	41,074C
61.	Charlotte, N.C.	Jan. 13, 1847	William Capers	32,371W	40,475C
62.	Wilmington, N.C.	Jan. 12, 1848	J. O. Andrew	32,753W	40,988C
63.	Spartanburg, S.C.	Dec. 26, 1848	William Capers	33,313W	41,888C
64.	Camden, S.C.	Dec. 19, 1849	J. O. Andrew	33,788W	41,617C
65.	‡Wadesboro, N.C.	Dec. 18, 1850	R. Paine	30,906W	37,860C[3]

* Georgia Conference set off

‡ South Carolina Conference lost jurisdiction over Southeastern North Carolina

Circuit Ministers and Memberships

Bladen Circuit (Brunswick County and five other counties)

1788	1 minister, 1 elder	35 white members
1798	3 ministers, 1 presiding elder	462 white, 143 colored
1801	2 ministers, 1 presiding elder	653 white, 130 colored
1805	2 ministers, 1 presiding elder	1301 white, 430 colored

Brunswick Circuit (Brunswick County, N.C. and Horry County, S.C.)

1808	2 ministers, 1 presiding elder	697 white, 313 colored
1811	2 ministers, 1 presiding elder	682 white, 380 colored
1814	2 ministers, 1 presiding elder	682 white, 339 colored
1818	2 ministers, 1 presiding elder	647 white, 311 colored
1820	3 ministers, 1 presiding elder	773 white, 484 colored
1824	2 ministers, 1 presiding elder	664 white, 420 colored
1826	1 minister, 1 presiding elder	402 white, 427 colored
1829	2 ministers, 1 presiding elder	433 white, 553 colored
1834	2 ministers, 1 presiding elder	640 white, 555 colored
1838	3 ministers, 1 presiding elder	455 white, 566 colored
1841	2 ministers, 1 presiding elder	447 white, 526 colored

Smithville Circuit (all of Brunswick County, also eastern Horry County)

1844	1 minister, 1 presiding elder, 5 Sunday Schools	508 white, 682 colored
1849	2 ministers, 1 presiding elder 3 Sunday Schools	589 white, 657 colored
1850	12 Methodist societies in Brunswick County; 1 mission	

The Wilmington District began the year of 1850 with memberships of 4254 whites and 8438 blacks. After several societies were lost to the North Carolina Conference in May, the Wilmington District of the South Carolina Conference reported at the end of the year 2855 white members and 5704 black; 15 Sunday Schools; 61 teachers, 629 volumes in libraries; 439 children; 51 Bibles given.[4]

Pastoral Letter of the South Carolina Conference, to the Churches within its Bounds

Dearly Beloved Brethren,—Having been again permitted in the providence of God, to meet in another Annual Conference, we have thought it well to address you a pastoral letter, affectionately urging upon your attention such considerations as seem to us important to your spiritual welfare, exhorting you to perserverance and patience in the work of the Lord. There are many things concerning which we might speak, brethren, but as time will not allow us to say all that might be said, we beg your patient and prayerful hearing of a few things.

1. *Family Religion.*—We cannot too strongly renew the advices we have given you in reference to family religion. We are deeply impressed with the conviction that whatever labours we may minister for the salvation of the rising race, little can be effected without the hearty and untiring co-operation of Christian parents. The religion we preach and which you profess, must receive its practical illustration in your domestic life and family conversation. It is not enough that your children hear that you are professors of religion; they must see in your daily deportment, the proof that your hearts are properly affected by the spirit of religion. None but a father can possess a father's influence; none but a mother can know a mother's love. We entreat you let not the morning or the evening sacrifice of thanksgiving and prayer and praise be forgotten or neglected; but with every opening and closing day, commend your assembled household to the providence of that God whom you have taken for your portion and your all. And let not your servants be forgotten. If you reap the fruits of their carnal labours, let them receive the influence of your spiritual instructions. Remember, we beseech you, your responsibility to God on their behalf. Give no credit to the supposition that you cannot do them good. Spare no effort for their religious instruction. They are members of your household; oh, let them be members with you of the household of faith. We recommend that your hours for family worship be carefully selected with reference to the convenience of all your family.

2. *Class Meetings.*—The class meetings of our church have always been considered of great importance as means of spiritual improvement. They have been one of the peculiar features of our economy from the beginning, and are happily adapted to the encouragement of the young, the timid, and the tempted. We entreat you, forsake not the assembling of yourselves together, as the manner of some is; but encourage one another, and so much the more, as ye see the day approaching. Some have feared that we were becoming forgetful of this blessed institution. Let it not be said of you, brethren, that you have lost your first love; but remembering the comfort of the class-meeting to you in your early religious experience, mind the same thing, walk by the same rule.

3. *The Sabbath.*—The institution of the Sabbath is of ancient date.— It has its sanction as well in the reasonableness of the appointment, as in the authority which has fixed it. Too much regard cannot be had for the day which has been hallowed by God himself. Let no common cares or worldly business intrude upon the sanctity of the Lord's day. Remember it is not our day, but God's. And the thoughts and conversation, and anxieties of common life should all be laid aside, as well as its ordinary pursuits and employments, and the entire day be consecrated to a sacred communion with heaven. Nor should we permit those in our employ

117

to profane that precious rest, nor allow circumstances of seemingly pressing importance to induce a violation of the fourth commandment. Let a discreet forecast be used in anticipation of the Sabbath, that no travelling or other labour be done in that day. *Remember the Sabbath day to keep it holy.*

4. *Sunday Schools.*—We are apprised that in some places our Sunday Schools are in a flourishing condition and doing well, while in others, the difficulties of forming and conducting them are very great. Where the greatest attention has been given to this interest, it has been generally found that the Sunday School is a nursery for the church. God has signally owned this institution, and crowned it with His special approbation and blessing. Many who were scholars have become teachers, and have been made partakers of the divine grace, and members of the mystical body as well as of the visible church of Jesus Christ. Cultivate then, dear breathren, your Sunday Schools, and God will give the increase to your labours.

5. *The Times.*—Great complaints are heard on all hands concerning the hardness of the times. It is true that a great pressure seems to rest upon our country in this regard; but the hardness of the times, and the scarcity of money are not so much to be deplored as the unfortunate wreck of moral character which in some instances they have involved. Let us advise you one and all to keep in view that excellent requirement of our discipline, which teaches us to borrow no money, and incur no debt without a probability of paying. Whatever losses you may meet—through whatever misfortunes you may be called to pass, let there be no stain upon your moral characters, but maintain at the sacrifice of your dearest earthly interests your Christian integrity. And let all these embarrassments remind you of the uncertainty of worldly good, and warn you to lay up for yourselves treasure in heaven; where neither moth nor rust doth corrup, and where theives cannot break through nor steal.

6. *Missions.*—On the subject of missions, beloved brethren, we desire to speak freely, out of the fulness of our hearts. We have fallen short, grievously short of our duty as a church in this most Christian interest.—We feel it, we humble ourselves under the conviction of it, and with sincere desires to fetch up what is lacking "to the help of the Lord, to the help of the Lord against the might," we would commune with you in the spirit of our Christian brotherhood, if peradventure we may quicken one another to greater diligence.

When our fathers began the work of their calling, "to spread Scripture holiness over these lands," some seventy years ago, the way was plain before them. From the places of their first beginnings in New York and Maryland they spread abroad, raising societies, and forming circuits on every hand, till circuits grew into conferences, and the land was pervaded with their labours. It was one continuous work, extending itself among the same people, of the same language, religion, temper, and habits, and requiring only that the surplus of support in the older circuits should be carried to the new. The preachers, indeed, were frequently deficient of their quarterage, (as they still are,) but there needed no separate system of support for a particular class; they were one body of ministers interchangeably serving the same people, now in one circuit, and then in another, in the same general work. After a time we reached the borders of the Indian tribes and with them our missions, as distinct from the itinerancy of the circuits, were commenced. We might have begun before that time, in some of those fields which are now cultivating among the negroes in parts of the Southern States, where the white population did not, (as it still does not,) admit of an extension of the work on the circuit plan; but Dr. Coke's most unfortunates persuasion of its being his duty to array the church against a civil institution, and his influence in the General conference, prevailing for a time over the meek, but wiser counsels of Bishop Asbury, so as to induce acts of that body, giving great, and we must think, just umbrage to the Southern people, hindered and prevented us.

With the Indians, then, we began; and at our first beginning it was apparent that some system of support, separate from the circuit plan of surplasage and conference collections, was indispensably necessary to carry on the work. The work itself was peculiar, requiring peculiar expenditures, and done among an uncivilized people who could not be expected to support it, or, hardly, to contribute a fraction of the amount which it imperatively called for. For the service of such a people, there must be afforded not only a preacher, whose time should be taken up with preaching the Gospel, but there must also be afforded instruciton in letters, that they might be able to read the holy Scriptures; and, at least, some insight into the plainer arts of civilized life. To furnish them a preacher without the necessary helps , should seem like crying to the poor, "be ye warmed and filled," whilst we should withhold from them the things needful for the body. To supply this lack of service, our Missionary Society was instituted. Its object was expressed to be, that "of enabling the several annual conferences more effectually to extend their missionary labours throughout the United States, and elsewhere; and also to assist in the support and promotion of missionary schools, and missions in our own and foreign countries." And such only is its object still. The plan was simple, and contemplated the support of missions and mission schools, by means of auxiliary and branch societies: the annual Conferences being expected to form themselves into auxiliaries, having for branches as many similar societies as should be formed in their several Conference districts.

As in the work of planting churches by circuit preaching, so also in the missionary field among the Indians, the work begat its increase; and we went on from tribe to tribe, till we had establisehd missions in most of the tribes skirting our western and north-western frontiers. Meanwhile the mission to the western coast of Africa was undertaken; the door was opened for preaching and catechetical instruction to the most needy portions of the slave population in our own States; a mission was commenced in South-America at Rio Janeiro, Buenos Ayres, and Monte Video; and lastly, and with wonderful encouragement, to the Indians beyond the Rocky Mountains. All this time we had experienced no reverses. The system of supporting missions by means of missionary societies had indeed but partially been put in practice; but means were always furnished as our wants arose, partly by the operations of the societies, and partly by spontaneous contributions by numerous wealthy friends. The increase of labour also in this department of the work, was furnished with no less facility than the means of support:—a facility evidently resulting in every instance from the clearest conviction on the part of those called, that they were following in the way of God's especial providence. Thus it was with us till the late reverses in the monetary affairs of the country suddenly surprised us with the painful fact that our means were exhuasted, our treasury in debt, and the very existence threatened of some of our missions. Appeals for relief, loud and repeated, were made to the church by the Treasurer at New York, and others, with a hope and expectation that a fact so painfully mortifying to Christian piety needed only to be known in order to its being corrected. But until this time the evil continues without abatement; our debt for the missions is even increasing; and time only serves to show that the country, embarrassed as it is, and our system of supplies for our missions by missionary societies neglected as it is, there is no hope of supporting the work so happily commenced, and hitherto, successfully carried on. The wealthy friends, on whom alas, we too much relied, and the sufficiency of whose liberality we vainly trusted, instead of engaging the whole church to unite as one man to bear on and on the Gospel banner, have been impoverished with the times, and can only sigh for their inability to assist us.

But it is right; and God, in all this, rebukes our negligence, and forces on us a conviction of our duty. We have been egregiously in fault in all this matter. We ought to have learned wisdom from the example of the Saviour noticing the contributors to the treasury of the Temple.—"He saw the rich men casting their gifts into the treasury; and he saw also a certain poor widow casting in thither two mites." The service of God, consist in what it may, is intended for all, and shall be shared by all. And thus it is with respect to the support of missions. Those do well who of their *"abundance"* cast in *"much;"* and those still better who of their *"penury"* cast in *"mites.* All are alike bound to the duty, that all may alike be partakers of the benefit. "For if there be first a willing mind, it is accepted according to that a man hath, and not according to that he hath not." "And God is able to make all grace abound towards you, that ye always having all sufficiency in all things may abound to every good work." We have wronged you brethren, especially the poor, by not having been diligent to carry out into every class in all the circuits and stations where we labour, such a system of collections for the support of missions as would engage you all, rich and poor, men, women and children, as contributors to this blessed cause. A system which is fully carried out, taking but little from any, yet a little from every one, would furnish by "mites," week after week, and year after year, an unfailing supply for the wants of the work till the last of the heathen shall be converted to God. Most earnestly do we as a Conference, recommend this plan to you and while we do so, we have engaged together to exert ourselves individually as we go among you, to promote its adoption in every place, by every member of the church.

The monthly meeting of prayer for the missions, we would also strongly recommend. Let every society be zealous to maintain it, and every member constant to attend it. We beg of our brethren, the local preachers, the exhorters, the class-leaders, to engage heartily in it as a work precious to the Lord. O, what a time is this! The missions to South-America given up, and the Misisonaries called home, for want of means to support them! Africa literally crying to us in God's name for the Gospel, and we unable to impart it to her. Oregon shouting with her thousand converts her salvation come, threatened with the unnatural danger of the night coming back upon her risen sun—her risen sun sinking back into the dusk of night, not like the sun of Joshua for a longer day of triumph to the Lord, but because our Israel have not done their duty, and our Joshua will not triumph without them. Truly, brethren, it is a time for prayer—nay, more, for humiliation and repentance.

But we will not weary you with regrets for the past, but would rather encourage you to the performance of present duty. And indeed we cannot but feel, brethren, amidst the gloom which has been cast about us by the disatrous failure of our means for the support of missions, a hope, a cheering hope that even this calamity shall be over-ruled for good. Shall it not rouse the whole church, ministers and members, to take part, if individually but a small part, according to their ability, in the blessed work of rolling off this stone of stumbling and offence, and helping on the triumphs of the Gospel steadily and continually till the whole world shall rejoice in the name of Jesus. Who might withhold so small a mite as one cent a week, or fifty cents a year, for this great cause?—Surely none. No, not one.

Finally, brethren, we exhort you by the love of God and Jesus Christ our Lord, that ye abound more and more in faith and love, and the fruits of righteousness, according to the hope of the Gospel that your labour shall not be in vain. Hold fast the form of sound doctrine which you have been taught. Live as knowing that the time is short. Beware of covetousness and a worldly mind. Remember the Sabbath day to keep it holy. Abide in prayer—in the unity of the Spirit—in the fellowship of saints—in the comfort of the Holy Ghost—in the joyful expectation of eternal life. And may the peace and grace of God the Father and our Lord Jesus Christ, by the power of the Holy Ghost, be Multiplied unto you, and abound in you and among you always. Amen.

BEVERLY WAUGH,*President, 1843*

J. H. WHEELER, *Secretary.*[5]

The Reverend Doctor Beverly Waugh was born in Fairfax County, Virginia, in 1789. He was converted at age fifteen and joined the Baltimore Conference in 1809. He was in charge of the South Carolina Conference in 1842.

Selected Chronology

Church History		World History
	1501	Amerigo Vespucci reported on New World
Martin Luther launched Protestant Reformation	1517	
	1520	America's eastern shore attracted Spanish adventurers
	1523	Spanish Royal patent for colonizing Chicora
	1524	Ian Verrazano visited Carolina Crescent
First Christian service on Carolina shores	1526	Lucas Vasquez de Ayllón brought large colony
Church of England separated from Rome	1534	
Society of Jesus formed	1540	
	1558	Queen Elizabeth ascended throne of England
Thirty-nine articles of Church of England	1563	
Massacre of Huguenots in France	1572	
Irish Catholic movements against queen	1579	
	1584	Roanoke Island explored
	1585	Dangerous shoals named "Cape of Fear"
Clergy of Roanoke baptized first child	1587	Virginia Dare born
Huguenots of France received rights	1598	
	1603	Queen Elizabeth died; James I ascended
King James version of the Bible	1611	
	1618	Sir Walter Raleigh beheaded
	1620	Plymouth Colony founded
Puritans and Roaylists struggled	1625	Death of James I
	1629	Charles I granted Carolina to R. Heath
The First Bishop's War	1639	
The Second Bishop's War	1640	
The Ulster Rebellion	1641	
	1662	William Hilton visited Charles River
		Nicholas Shapley mapped Lower Cape Fear

122

The Proprietors promised "freedom and Liberty of Contience in all religious or Spirrituall things"	1663	Charles II granted Carolina to Lords Proprietors A New England group settles on Charles River William Drummond first governor of Carolina William Hilton named river "Cape Fear"
	1664	John Vassal started Charles Town settlement
	1667	Charles Town abandoned
Carolina visited by founder of Quakers	1672	
First Episcopal church in Charleston, S.C.	1681	
French Hugeunots lost rights and fled	1685	
Quakers' opposition to Church of England	1700	Carolina's first public library (from SPG)
Vestry Act, first church law in N.C.	1701	
SPG Charter granted by William III First SPG missionary to America John Wesley born in England	1703	
	1704	Tar first made in North Carolina
First church in Carolina at Bath	1705	First school teacher in N.C.
	1706	Bath became first incorporated town of N.C.
	1707	Union of Scotland and Ireland
	1711	Massacre of Whites began Tuscarora War
	1712	Colonel James Moore moved toward Neuse River Divided Carolina became N.C. and S.C.
	1713	Cape Island granted to Thomas Smith
	1714	Thomas James was granted land west of Cape Fear
Church of England established nine parishes for Carolina	1715	Small white settlement destroyed Money allocated for road from Neuse to Cape Fear
	1718	Year of the pirates — Stede Bonnet surrendered at Cape Fear
Thirteen Anglican parishes in South Carolina		

124

Left	Year	Right
	1748	Spanish attacked Brunswick Town
Brown Marsh Presbyterian Church established	1750	
Moravians began Wachovia settlement	1753	Arthur Dobbs occupied Russelboro
St. Philip's Church under construction	1754	Dobbs made governor
Legislation to establish Anglican church	1755	
	1756	Increase of settlers on Lockwood's Folly
Lockwood's Folly Baptists sought preachers	1757	
John McDowell to St. Philip's	1758	
Francis Asbury converted at age 13 Lottery to support Anglican Church building Methodist colonists arrived in America Second lottery for Anglican Church Roof of St. Philip's struck down by lightning	1759 1760	George III began his reign An academy opened in Wilmington
	1761	George III proclaimed king in ceremony at Brunswick
Lockwood's Folly Separate Baptists organized St. Philip's communicants, 15, 2 black St. Philip's Parish heads of families listed	1762 1763	Thomas Godfrey wrote first play in America "The Prince of Parthia"
Independent preachers organized Methodists in Maryland Whitefield called for Wesley's preachers to work in America George Whitefield preached in Wilmington Governor Tryon requested one clergyman for each parish Beginning of Wesleyan movement in America (Old John Street Church New York City) Lockwood's Folly Baptists offered meeting house for Anglican use	1764 1765 1766	Brunswick County created Boundary House built on state line William Dry agreed to build first causeway over Eagles Island Governor Dobbs died at Brunswick Town Parliament passed Stamp Act Armed defiance of British Stamp Act March on Brunswick Town to stop Stamps Governor Tryon recommended North Carolina—South Carolina line Legislation for erecting governor's residence at New Bern
Saint Philip's Church consecrated	1768	Drawbridge built across Cape Fear River near Wilmington

	1768	Collet map published by Parliament
John Wesley's first missionaries arrived in America	1769	Official Royal Post began between Wilmington and Charleston
		Hurricane destroyed Court House and many homes in Brunswick Town
St. James Church in Wilmington completed	1770	Tryon Palace completed in New Bern
Francis Asbury preached his first sermon in America (Philadelphia)	1771	Governor Tryon led militia against Regulators
Joseph Pilmore preached in Wilmington; at Brunswick Town and Lockwood's Folly January and February, 1773	1772	Wilmington constables ordered to prevent disturbance of worship services
First Methodist conference in Philadelphia	1773	Elizabethtown established
Nicholas Christian at St. Philip's Church	1774	First assembly of North Carolina people independent of the crown
St. Philip's and Brunswick Town abandoned	1775	American Revolution began
		Committee of Safety formed in Wilmington
Asbury planned to visit North Carolina		Fort Johnston burned
Anglican Church disestablished in North Carolina	1776	Continental Congress approved Declaration of Independence July 4
St. Philip's Church burned by British		Moore's Creek Battle February 27
Carolina Circuit of Virginia Conference		Plantations near Wilmington plundered
Ashbury chose to stay in America		
Reverend John Wills resigned from St. James	1777	Inauguration of first governor of independent state, R. Caswell
	1778	Legislation for Court House near Lockwood's Folly Bridge
Over 90% of Methodists were in the South	1779	
Lockwood's Folly Baptist Church constituted		
Asbury's first visit in Western North Carolina	1780	Wilmington surrounded by British
		Cornelius Harnett captured, abused, dead
	1781	Cornwallis surrendered at Yorktown
		"Lighthorse Harry" Lee reports in Wilmington
Asbury approved as "general assistant" to Methodists in America	1782	
	1783	Official end of Revolution
		Assembly authorized lighthouse on Baldhead

126

American Methodist Episcopal Church organized December 27 Asbury consecrated bishop Asbury's first visit in Brunswick County First regional conference of American Methodists in Louisburg, North Carolina	1784	Walkersburg incorporated Court held at Robert Bell's
	1785	
	1786	June 26 first use of new courthouse at Lockwood's Folly
First Methodist Conference in Charleston, South Carolina Bladen Circuit formed, included Brunswick County	1787	Constitution drafted
Charles Wesley died in England Asbury presented Methodist Resolution to president Washington Methodist Publishing House was begun "Sunday School" in some Methodist records	1788	South Carolina entered the Union May 23 Thalian Association founded
	1789	U.S. Constitution ratified at Fayetteville University of North Carolina chartered
President Washington visited Reverend William Gause John Wesley died March 2, London, age 88 First General Conference of American Methodists	1791	Washington toured Brunswick County
	1792	Legislation to establish Fort Johnston Raleigh chosen for State Capital
	1794	First legislation in new State House
Asbury crossed Brunswick County to Norman's Cokesbury College lost by fire	1795	Crusoe Island settled Hinton James became first enrolled at Chapel Hill First N.C. lighthouse lighted— Baldhead
Asbury from Wilmington to Lockwood's Folly, Shallotte, Gause's Lockwood's Folly Baptists reconstituted as Mount Pisgah Church First Methodist Class of white people in Wilmington	1796	January court adjourned to Bellune Tavern
	1797	
	1798	Lotteries planned to finance an academy in Smithville

127

Asbury visited Gause, Shallotte, Lockwood's Folly and Town Creek	1799 President Washington died December 14
Methodist "districts" became "conferences"	
Lockwood's Folly Methodists had first commemoration of Washington's Birthday, February 22	
Wilmington became Station Church, Nathan Jarret preacher	1800 White House completed in June
United Brethren in Christ organized	
Jeremiah Norman preached in Methodist Societies	1801 Thomas Jefferson began two-term presidency
Asbury visited several societies in Brunswick	Smithville had July 4 celebration
"The House" dedicated for Methodists in Smithville	
Asbury and Snethen visit Gause, Charlotteville, Lockwood's Folly, Town Creek	1802 James Turner became North Carolina governor
South Carolina Conference divided into districts: Camden, Saluda, Georgia	1803
First camp meeting in Brunswick County	1804 Cornelius Galloway house and whaleboat for sale
Asbury visits Smithville, Brunswick, Town Creek	Daniel Bellune Tavern for sale
Brunswick Circuit included this county and Horry to Georgetown	1805 Yellow fever epidemic
	1806 Storm washed many boats ashore
Hymn book for American Methodists	1807 Benjamin Smith introduced bill to sell Court House at Lockwood's Folly
Delegated General Conference for Methodists	1808 County seat moved to Smithville
First American-born Methodist Bishop	
	1810 Riots among Smithville pilots and foreign boat pilots
Methodists in Smithville proposed to build chapel like Wilmington's (30' x 50')	1812 Yellow fever epidemic
Asbury's Last Will and Testament	1813
South Carolina Methodist Conference at Fayetteville	1814 School for girls at Smithville
Bishop Coke died at sea	British captured Washington, burned White House and Capitol
	Dolly Madison saved original copy of the Constitution

128

Asbury's last visit to Brunswick County	1815	
Virginia Methodist Conference at Raleigh January 24	1816	
Bishop Asbury died March 31		
Methodists had 700 preachers, 214,000 members		
Episcopal Church organized Diocese of North Carolina	1817	First steamboat arrived in Wilmington
Methodist camp meeting at Town Creek	1818	Packet boat service Wilmington to Smithville
A.M.E. Zion Church founded	1821	Mexico wins independence from Spain
South Carolina Conference at Wilmington	1825	Appropriation to construct Fort Caswell
	1826	General Smith died in Smithville
	1827	Improved access to port of Wilmington
Reformers exit to form Associated Methodist Church	1828	
	1829	Andrew Johnson became president
Methodist Protestant Church formed	1830	Storm refugees in fort at Smithville
Baptist State Convention organized		
	1831	Mail route established Wilmington to Smithville
		Stage line to Georgetown
Temperance Society at Lockwood's Folly	1833	
	1834	Wilmington and Raleigh Railroad chartered
		Passenger packet Norfolk to Charleston
South Carolina Methodist Conference formed Wilmington District	1835	Ice covered Cape Fear River
Reverend William Hankins drowned in boat accident		
Original of *Asbury Journal* destroyed by fire in New York City Publishing House	1836	Edward Dudley, First governor elected by direct vote of the people
South Carolina Conference at Wilmington	1837	Lockwood's Folly Post Office established in February; later named Shallotte
		Depression; severe storms
At Greensboro, North Carolina Methodist Conference was organized, separated from Virginia	1838	"S.S. Pulaski" blew up off Brunswick coast; 140 killed

129

Greensboro Female College established—first in state with authority to grant degrees to women	1838	
First regional Methodist Historical Society	1839	North Carolina's first public school law
	1840	Disastrous fire in Wilmington —150 houses lost New State Capitol finished Wilmington and Weldon Railroad
South Carolina Conference sent to Brunswick Circuit David Seal and Claudius Pritchard	1841	
South Carolina Conference of January 26 changed "Brunswick Circuit" to "Smithville Circuit"	1842	
	1843	Great fire in Wilmington
Separation of M.E. Church, North and South	1844	First telegraph message transmitted
South Carolina Methodist Conference in Fayetteville	1845	State school for deaf in Raleigh
South Carolina Methodist Conference in Charlotte	1847	Daniel Webster, guest of Governor Dudley, Wilmington
South Carolina Methodist Conference in Wilmington	1848	Congress appropriated funds for Cape Fear River light
	1849	Oak Island lights illuminated
South Carolina Methodist Conference at Wadesboro Southeastern North Carolina transferred to North Carolina Conference	1850	John Bell, first keeper of the lights
	1856	Supply Post Office established
Brunswick County had 12 Methodist classes, 1 mission	1858	Thalian Hall established
	1861	North Carolina seceded
Full clergy rights for black preachers Two chaplains from Wilmington District; 16 from North Carolina Conference	1864	
	1865	Wilmington surrounded by Union Forces
First woman with Methodist Local Preachers License	1866	
North Carolina divided; Western North Carolina Conference formed	1889	

130

Methodist Societies, Classes, Missions, Camp Meetings Wilmington District 1805-1900

The North Carolina Conference in 1850 began its administration of the Wilmington District, most of which had been transferred from the South Carolina Conference. This district included Wilmington with two societies; Fayetteville Station; Fayettev ille Circuit; Sampson; Bladen; Rockingham; Topsail; Topsail Academy; Smithville Circuit, including twelve societies; and Cape Fear African Mission for the plantations around Smithville. This list indicates that the Wilmington District of the North Carolina Conference in 1851 included the areas that presently make up the counties of New Hanover, Pender, Brunswick, Bladen, Columbus, Cumberland, Robeson, Sampson, Duplin, Richmond and Scotland.

1851 Wilmington District
Charges and Membership

Wilmington	295 white	815 black
Topsail	168 white	253 black
Sampson	682 white	454 black
Fayetteville Station	186 white	333 black
Fayetteville Circuit	432 white	338 black
Bladen	576 white	572 black
Rockingham	637 white	294 black
Cape Fear Mission	5 white	433 black
Smithville Circuit	673 white	473 black
Total	3,654 white	3,965 black[1]

Smithville Circuit

The Smithville Circuit included all the twelve Methodist Societies in Brunswick County: Bethel, Governor's Creek, Hewett's, Hood's Creek, Horeb, Myrtle Branch, Rehoboth, Shallotte, Smithville, Wayman, Zion, and Zoar. The total membership reported at Conference in November, 1850, was 696 white and 622 black.

The trustees for Smithville Circuit in 1851 were Daniel B. Evans,

Francis W. Potter, Thomas G. Drew, Christopher C. Mercer, William H. Walker, John J. Drew, and Ezekiel Skipper.[2]

The Census of 1850 lists five families of Methodist ministers in Brunswick County. These included the three preachers appointed that year, and two others who were probably retired or "local preachers."[3]

The North Carolina Conference appointed the following preachers who served in Brunswick County before the War Between the States.

Conference	Smithville Circuit	Cape Fear Mission
November 1850	William J. Langdon	J. T. Munds
	J. M. Fulton	
November 1851	William J. Langdon	J. L. Fisher
	J. H. Brent	
November 1852	James H. Brent	William Walsh
November 1853	Paul J. Carraway	Jere Johnson
November 1854	John Andrews	George Farrabee
November 1855	J. A. Cunningham	George Farrabee
November 1856	J. A. Cunningham	(to be supplied)
December 1857	William F. Clegg	Marble N. Taylor
December 1858	Alexander D. Betts	Marble N. Taylor
December 1859	Jeffrey H. Robbins	William M. D. Moore
December 1860	Alexander D. Betts	William M. D. Moore[4]

The first eight years in the North Carolina Conference brought improvements in organization and in participation. The preachers had local assistants; most of the Methodist classes had local leaders, and some had licensed exhorters. Their activities are summarized in these circuit records of 1858:

> Zoar Class— $65.00 apportionment, 55 members, 3 class leaders
> Shallotte Camp Class— $60.00 apportionment, 47 members, 1 class leader
> Zion Class—$20.00 apportionment, 45 members, 3 class leaders, 1 exhorter, 1 steward
> Rehoboth Class—$20.00 apportionment, 38 members, 2 class leaders
> Shallotte Village—$25.00 apportionment, 24 members, 2 class leaders
> Sharon Class—$20.00 apportionment, 20 members, 1 leader, 1 exhorter
> Governor's Creek—$35.00 apportionment, 14 members, 1 class leader
> Hewett's Class—$15.00 apportionment, 13 members, 1 class leader
> Smithville Class—$90.00 apportionment, 70 ,members, no class leader
> Macedonia—$15.00 apportionment, 6 members, no class leader
> Union (later "Patmos")—$10.00 apportionment, $5.00 paid[5]

Methodist Classes and Class Leaders

Methodist classes were made up of society members who assumed responsibility for support and leadership. The class leader was chosen for his evident piety and devotion, to lead a specific class. He kept a loving watchcare over his group, conducted class meetings, encouraged testimony, and collected gifts for the society. Thus he led the active members, the "workers of the hive."

Smithville Circuit class leaders in 1859:

Thomas Drew, Rev. C. C. Mercer, Duncan Harvel at Zoar;
Washington Holden, John Liles at Shallotte Camp;
Daniel B. Evans, Ezekiel Skipper, John Drew at Zion;
John B. Stanaland, James Potter at Rehoboth;
William McKenzie, Nathan Register at Shallotte Village;
George Kirby, John Davis at Sharon;
William Drew at Governor's Creek.[6]

The progress of Methodist classes in Brunswick County was made possible principally by the dedication, organizational ability, and the preaching of Reverend Alexander D. Betts. His years in this county produced immeasurable results, but as the secession movement grew in the South, serious setbacks were experienced by the churches.

Chaplains and Churches 1861-65

Reverend Betts was asked in 1861 by the Conference to become a chaplain in the Confederate Army. He was assigned to the 30th Regiment of General Robert E. Lee's troops. He traveled with the troops, visited and prayed in their prisons, and was the soldiers' spiritual father. Remembering his horseback ride to Richmond he said, "When I knelt at sunset in the woods and prayed for the chaplains, the soldiers, my country and my family, my soul was so happy."

The North Carolina Conference had the following ministers serving as chaplains:

A. D. Betts	W. B. Richardson
O. J. Brent	J. J. Hines
John D. Buie	A. B. Alford
Jeffrey H. Robbins	William H. Moore
Franklin H. Wood	E. A. Wilson
Richard S. Webb	C. M. Pepper
C. C. Dodson	J. S. Long
Calvin Plyles	Benjamin F. Guthrie[7]

133

With some ministers and many other men in military service, the Methodist classes suffered and showed little progress. Sunday Schools were at a low ebb, and most of them closed during the winter months.

Some quotations from Thomas Gattis's report to the Conference give brief descriptions of problems existing at that time:

> November 1862: "I have failed to reach some of my appointments on account of family afflictions and the yellow fever which has been raging in some parts of the circuit."

> November 1864: "Brethren, we have much cause to be thankful, that in the midst of the terrible excitement of war, and the actual presence of an army in some parts of the circuit, so few have grown cold, and so many are clinging to the church, trying to glorify God and secure their salvation."

Appointments during the War of 1861-1865

N. C. Conference	Smithville Circuit	Cape Fear Mission
December 1861	Thomas J. Gattis	William M. D. Moore
December 1862	James B. Bailey	William M. D. Moore)
December 1863	Thomas J. Gattis	(to be supplied)
December 1864	Thomas W. Guthrie	(to be supplied)
December 1865	J. M. Smoot and Thomas Gattis	local pastor to supply[8]

After Wilmington surrendered in January 1865, the Quarterly Conference could not be held because of the occupancy of the surrounding territory by Federal troops.[9]

Postwar Hopes and Efforts

Minutes of postwar Methodist conferences show that efforts were being made to establish priorities and to concentrate on improvements. In September, 1866, the Wilmington District Conference had representatives from Smithville Circuit, Wilmington's two station churches, Bladen Circuit, Whiteville Circuit, Robeson Circuit, Sampson Circuit, Duplin Circuit and Topsail Circuit. On the third day this resolution was passed:

> That the preachers in each station and circuit in the Wilmington District be urged to take the personal oversight of all the baptized children in his charge, and if possible, all the children, and that he be required to catechize them—teaching them personally so much of our catechism as is incorporated in the *Discipline* of our Church—that he require them to learn the Articles of Religion, and that he instruct them thoroughly in the doctrine and discipline of the church.[10]

134

Smithville and Brunswick

Soon after the war ended, the Smithville Society moved to become a station church. The circuit preacher already residing in Smithville was assigned to this station church and the other societies became the Brunswick Circuit churches waiting for supply preachers to visit them in all parts of the county.

Appointments for the next two years were:

North Carolina Conference	Smithville Station	Brunswick Circuit	Cape Fear Mission
November 1866	J. F. Smoot	W. M. D. Moore	no appointment
November 1867	W. M. D. Moore	V. W. Pugh to supply	no appointment[11]

In 1868 reports to the Wilmington District conference stated that class meetings were "badly attended," some stewards were "delinquent," and Smithville appeared to be in "deplorable condition." War casualties and the separation of black Methodists left only 39% of the previous membership to begin the postwar period.

After two years and little progress, the scattered classes of Brunswick Circuit were joined again with Smithville and the all-county circuit became "Smithville Circuit"; but there was *no preacher available* to serve the *eleven societies* in this large county, which then was larger than the present area of 854 square miles.[12]

It was possible to fill the Smithville Circuit appointment for the next eight years, and to supply Waccamaw Mission, beginning in 1875 and continuing through 1883. Then the mission became Waccamaw Circuit and continued over twenty years.

N.C. Conference	Smithville Circuit	Waccamaw Mission
December, 1868	to be supplied	
November, 1869	John E. Thompson	
November, 1870	H. F. Wiley and W. R. Ferguson	
November, 1871	J. L. Keen	
December, 1872	W. R. Ferguson	
December, 1873	I. W. Avent	
December 1874	T. P. England	
December, 1875	J. W. Randle	to be supplied
November, 1876	J. W. Randle	T. J. Browning to supply
November, 1877	D. Culbreth	T. J. Browning
November, 1878	H. F. Wiley to March 1879 followed by J. H. Tart[13]	T. J. Browning

Wilmington District in the 1870's

The Wilmington District in 1872 had twelve charges, one local mission and one northern mission. For these, the following appointments were made:

Wilmington
  Front Street—R. S. Moran
  Fifth Street—to be supplied
Topsail—John Jones
Kenansville—C. M. Anderson
Magnolia—R. F. Bumpass
Clinton—James Mahoney
Onslow— R. B. Bibb
Cokesbury—J. B. Bailey,
    J. D. Buie

Bladen—J. T. Bagwell
Elizabethtown—J. T. Gibbs
Whiteville—M. H. Hoyle
Smithville—W. R. Ferguson
Sneeds Ferry Mission—
  to supply
Church of the Strangers,
  N.Y. City—
  Charles F. Deems

In 1872 the church property values in the Wilmington District were reported as follows:

Smithville Circuit	$3,600.	Onslow, Richlands	$8,000.
Cokesbury	3,700.	Abbotsburg	1,500.
Bladen	6,000	Elizabethtown	8,000.
Wilmington Fifth	4,500.	Whiteville	6,400.
Wilmington Front	50,000.	Magnolia	3,800.
Topsail	1,500.	District Parsonage	3,000.
Kenansville	3,000.	Total	103,000.[14]

One of the concerns of the Wilmington District Conference in 1876 brought the passage of this resolution:

> Whereas class meetings have in former days been great utility in bringing many of our people to a higher state of spiritual enjoyment and enlarged Christian experience and, Whereas these meetings scarcely exist now among us; and Whereas all the enterprises of the church with regard to its temporal and spiritual prosperity are mainly dependent on the vigilance and care of our pastors; therefore, Resolved that the pastors are requested to urge upon the people of their respective charges the importance of attending to the use of this most excellent prudential means of Grace and that they call the members of the churches together as often as practicable *after preaching* and *lead the class in person.*[15]

At the District Conference in September of 1876, the Smithville Circuit pastor reported seven churches, 443 members, 30 received, 1 expelled, 15 children baptized. The pastor's salary was $500; $230.73 had been paid. The Conference approved continuing

Waccamaw Mission. The Smithville Circuit Quarterly Conference had raised $47.25 toward building a new church at Lockwood's Folly; the original Methodist congregation at Lockwood's Folly had at first used the Old Brunswick County Courthouse, which later was dismantled and used elsewhere to build a dwelling.

At the conference in July, 1878, the Smithville Circuit pastor, H. F. Wiley, reported 11 appointments (places with regular preaching schedules); 400 members; 9 Sunday Schools, 275 members.

Reverend Wiley served the Smithville Circuit until March 1879. At that time he limited his service to Smithville where a station church and parsonage were planned. J. H. Tart served the other eleven Brunswick churches until the end of that year.[16]

Late Nineteenth-Century Methodism

The last twenty-year period in the nineteenth century was a time of organization and growth of Methodist churches in Southeastern North Carolina. In Brunswick County the rate of growth had been matched only by the Asbury years, 1785-1815, when the Bishop visited and encouraged preachers of the Bladen Circuit until 1805 and of the Brunswick Circuit until his last visit in 1815.

J. M. Ormand, in his *The Country Church of North Carolina*, stated that in 1872 there was in Brunswick County one church for each 635 in population.[17] Baptists had by that time increased their memberships and had built as many church buildings as had the Methodists.

The Brunswick Circuit in 1879 had eleven regular appointments: Bethel, Concord, Leland, Macedonia, New Hope, Piney Grove, Shallotte Camp, Shallotte Village, Shiloh, Summerville, Zion. Most of the classes had by that time been organized as churches. Southport was made a station church that year, and Waccamaw Mission was being served by N. A. Hooker. Most of these early-organized churches remained active and increased in membership, but the *number* of Methodist churches in Brunswick County did not grow beyond the eleven of 1879 until 1908; then the number was fifteen.

Reverend T. J. Browning reported for Brunswick Circuit in 1881 an increase in attendance at eight churches; a few class meetings; nine Sunday schools (two in winter); 526 members; four regular drinkers; no dancing.[18]

137

A summary of the 1890 report shows:

	Church Members	S. Schools	S. Schools Members	Property Value
Southport	240	1	156	$4,100.00
Brunswick Circuit	558	10	394	3,500.00
Waccamaw Circuit	348	7	240	1,700.00
Brunswick Mission	205	6	275	925.00[19]

In 1891 five Methodist Conference preachers were living and working in Brunswick county. Waccamaw Circuit had 2 preachers, 396 members. Brunswick Circuit had 1 preacher, 590 members. Brunswick Mission had 1 preacher, 228 members, Southport Station had 1 preacher, 355 members.[20]

Circuit *churches* were not listed individually with their statistics; only the *circuit* statistics and *station church* statistics were listed. In 1926 the churches were listed, but not in 1927. In 1928 and each year afterwards, *every church* and its statistics were recorded in the Annual Conference *Minutes* and published in the *Journal* of each year's conference proceedings.

The earliest Epworth League organized in Brunswick County was at Southport in 1901. Zion organized one in 1906.[21]

Methodist Appointments for Brunswick 1879-1898

Conference	Smithville Station	Brunswick Circuit	Waccamaw Mission	Brunswick Mission
December				
1879	Hugh F. Wiley	J. H. Tart	N. A. Hooker	
1880	T. L. Hoyle	T. J. Browning	Jeremiah Johnson	
1881	W. B. North	J. T. Kendall	J. T. Kendall	
1882	W. B. North	D. A. Watkins	D. A. Watkins	
1883	Daniel H. Tuttle	T. J. Daily	J. H. Tart	
			Waccamaw Circuit	
1884	C. M. Gentry	Z. T. Harrison	J. H. Tart	
1885	M. M. McFarland	Thomas C. Lovin	C. W. Godwin	
1886	J. M. Ashby	Hilliard Eure	T. J. Browning	
1887	J. M. Ashby	Hilliard Eure	D. A. Futrell	J. M. Marlow
November				
1888	J. M. Ashby	R. L. Warlick	J. Milliken (supply)	J. M. Marlow

138

Conference	Smithville Station	Brunswick Circuit	Waccamaw Circuit	Brunswick Mission
November				
1889	J. M. Ashby	J. B. Thompson	N. A. Perkins	J. M. Marlow
December				
1890	C. P. Jerome	J. B. Thompson	T. J. Browning	J. M. Marlow
November				
1891	C. P. Jerome	J. B. Thompson	J. M. Marlow	T. J. Browning
December				
1892	Oliver Ryder	Daniel Reid	T. J. Browning	
1893	Oliver Ryder	Daniel Reid	T. J. Browning	
1894	Oliver Ryder	R. F. Taylor	J. M. Marlow	
1895	H. B. Anderson	R. F. Taylor	J. M. Marlow	
1896	H. B. Anderson	J. A. Rouse	J. M. Marlow	
1897	H. B. Anderson	J. J. Porter	J. M. Marlow	
November				
1898	R. W. Bailey	J. J. Porter	B. F. Deloach (to supply)	

Reported for 1898:   Waccamaw Circuit, 7 Sunday Schools, 280 members
Brunswick Circuit, 8 Sunday Schools, 225 members
Southport Station, 1 Sunday School, 178 members[22]

The General Assembly on March 4, 1887, amended the charter of the town of Smithville, changing the name to *Southport.*[23]

Two Methodist Conferences in North Carolina

In 1889 the western part of North Carolina became a separate conference and was given the name "Western North Carolina Conference." The eastern part of the state retained the name "North Carolina Conference." That same year Methodist youth movements consolidated into the Epworth League. The year of 1895 was the year of the advent of the official Methodist magazine entitled *North Carolina Christian Advocate.*

In 1899 the North Carolina Conference had:

109 local preachers in the membership of 65,255
38 Epworth Leagues with membership of 1,437
618 Sunday Schools with membership of 39,520
671 Methodist Societies
643½ houses of worship

The Annual Conferences from 1850 to 1900 were held in November or December, and appointments were made for the *calendar* years.

1898 Wilmington District Charges and Membership

Wilmington

Grace	845	Clinton Circuit	742
Fifth Street	513	Bladen Circuit	669
Market	112	Elizabeth Circuit	595
Scott's Hill Circuit	206	Whiteville Circuit	184
Onslow Circuit	723	Carvers Creek (new)	
Jacksonville and		Waccamaw Circuit	574
Richlands	274	Brunswick Circuit	635
Magnolia Circuit	500	Southport Station	352
Kenansville	599	Total	7,964[24]
Burgaw Circuit	429		

New Circuits: Atlantic, Zion

In 1899 a new organization was set up for Brunswick County Methodist churches. Southport remained as the only station church in the county. The other Methodist churches made up three circuits: Zion Circuit, in the northern part of the county, Atlantic Circuit in the southern section, and Waccamaw Circuit in the western area.

The December Annual Conferences made the 1899 and 1900 appointments as follows:

	Southport	Zion Circuit	Atlantic Circuit	Waccamaw Circuit
1899	R. W. Bailey	T. J. Browning	J. M. Marlow	B. F. Deloach
1900	R. W. Bailey	T. J. Browning	J. M. Marlow	B. F. Deloach

Reports to the Annual Conference included the following:

	Local Preachers	Members	Number Societies	Church Buildings
Waccamaw Circuit				
1900	3	500	--	8
1901	1	421	6	6
Atlantic Circuit				
1900	1	385	6	6
1901	1	429	7	7
Zion Circuit				
1900	--	255	5	4
1901	--	287	7	6
Southport				
1900	--	287	1	1
1901	--	282	1	1

140

The 1901 total collections and average per member:

Waccamaw Circuit	$112.84	.25 per member
Atlantic Circuit	845.32	1.97 per member
Zion Circuit	196.14	.68 per member
Southport	900.23	3.19 per member 25

Wilmington District Conference Official Rolls For Brunswick County Charges 1899-1902

1899

Southport
Rev. R. W. Bailey
M. C. Guthrie
B. F. Green
J. R. Newton
M. T. Craig

Brunswick Circuit
Rev. J. J. Porter
Jas. H. Swain
E. W. Taylor
G. W. Kirby
R. N. Swain
E. M. Parker

Waccamaw Circuit
Rev. B. F. DeLoach
Rev. E. Milliken
Rev. J. Q. Long
Rev. J. M. Marlowe
S. H. Ward
J. M. Long
J. A. Carrol

1900

Southport
Rev. R. W. Bailey
J. A. Drew
J. A. Newton
Richard Dozier
M. T. Craig

Atlantic Circuit
Rev. J. M. Marlowe
Rev. J. H. Swain
J. F. Tripp
David Ward
J. W. Worthington
E. M. Parker

Zion Circuit
Rev. T. J. Browning
E. W. Taylor
J. D. Danford
G. H. Cannon
A. V. Goodman

Waccamaw Circuit
Rev. B. F. DeLoach
Rev. J. L. Long
Rev. E. Milliken
D. M. Cox
John Russ
S. M. Long

1901

Southport
Rev. R. W. Bailey, P.C.
J. B. Ruark
J. A. Drew
S. P. Swain
Richard [not given]

Atlantic Circuit
Rev. J. M. Marlowe, P.C.
J. H. Swain, L.P.
Guilford Sellers
John Russ
Walter Leonard
A. M. Moore

Zion Circuit
Rev. T. J. Browning, P.C.
O. A. DuRant
J. D. Robbins
C. N. Harvell
A. V. Goodman

Waccamaw Circuit
Rev. E. Milliken, P.C.
J. K. Long, L.P.
L. L. Holmes
B. A. Marlowe
H. P. Long
J. M. V. Reaves

1902

Southport
A. R. Goodchild, P.C.
William St. George
W. J. Newton
J. A. Drew
M. C. Guthrie

Shallotte Circuit
J. M. Marlowe, P.C.
J. H. Swain, L.P.
C. N. Lenoard
Samuel Bell
A. M. Moore
E. M. Parker

Zion Circuit
G. H. Cannon
D. R. Walker
J. W. Gay
Alvin Mercer

Waccamaw Circuit
C. W. Ray, P.C.
G. L. Holmes
B. A. Marlowe
J. B. Cox
J. M. V. Reaves

Note: Pastor in charge is designated by ''P.C.''; licensed preacher, ''L.P.'' This chart shows how the Brunswick Circuit of 1899 was divided to form Atlantic Circuit and Zion Circuit, for two years only. In 1902, Atlantic Circuit became Shallotte Circuit.

Methodist Missions in Brunswick County
Cape Fear Mission

In addition to the preachers appointed to regular preaching places, some were sent as missionaries to the more populous plantations that had slaves.

At the South Carolina Annual Conference in December of 1812, Hugh McPhail was appointed to serve in a mission to the black people of the Cape Fear Area, which was at that time within the Pee Dee District of the South Carolina Conference. The next year, Benjamin Scott was appointed for six months and was followed by Griffin Christopher.

No other appointments for the Cape Fear Mission were made until 1833 when Ebenezer Legett was sent. His work reached out to the black people of twenty plantations on the Cape Fear River. His report to the South Carolina conference of 1834 shows a membership of 304 blacks.

The eastern section of the Fayetteville District became the Wilmington District in 1835 and included the Cape Fear Mission. Leonard Rush served the Mission that year. No more preachers were appointed until 1841 when James H. Chandler was sent. At the end of that year he reported 225 black members.

Morgan C. Turrentine was appointed to this mission in 1842 and served through 1849 when the membership had increased to 5 white and 433 black members. Hugh F. Porter was appointed by the South Carolina Conference for the Cape Fear Mission.

As the number of missions increased in South Carolina, there was a need for money to be raised locally for the Cape Fear Mission. Besides the special offerings in the Brunswick Circuit, there were public collections and individual solicitations for funds. The 1843 donor list included: Dr. D. F. Hill; "a lady"; S. L. Hall, Esquire; T. G. Drew, Esquire; J. H. Watters, Esquire; J. G. Hill, Esquire; T. Green, Esquire; Captain S. Potter, Esquire; Dr. A. J. DeRosset; Dr. J. D. Bellamy; D. Godwin, Esquire; public collection.[26]

When the Smithville Circuit, all of Brunswick County, was transferred to the North Carolina Conference in 1850, the Cape Fear Mission was also transferred. Thereafter, the mission appointments were made by the North Carolina Conference. These appointments included the following: J. T. Munds, William Walsh, Jere Johnson, George W. Farrabee, Marble Taylor; William M. D. Moore served four years, 1860-1864.

142

Membership at the Mission in 1861 was 350 blacks. No Cape Fear Mission reports of membership were made after that year.[27]

Waccamaw Mission

A mission was planned for the areas near the Waccamaw River. There most of the inhabitants were white. J. W. Abernathy was serving there in 1874, but he was released, and a supply preacher was sought in 1875. In 1876 the North Carolina Conference sent T. J. Browning, who served four years. After him, came N. A. Hooker, J. L. Keen, J. Johnston and J. H. Tart, in that order.

In 1884 Waccamaw Mission became Waccamaw Circuit with regular preaching schedules at several places. Appointments for 1885 to 1907 are listed with other appointments to charges in Brunswick County. While J. M. Marlowe was serving this circuit, New Home Church was organized and a new building erected on New Brittain Road.[28]

Brunswick Mission

The southern part of Brunswick County was served as Brunswick Mission from 1887 to 1894. In 1891 the membership was 228.

C. W. Godwin served this mission in 1888. Appointed after him were J. M. Marlowe and T. J. Browning, both of whom increased the membership and organized some churches. New Hope was organized in 1890 near the present location of Seaside. Some churches that were in the Brunswick Mission were later in the Atlantic Circuit (1898 and 1899), and afterwards in the Shallotte Circuit.

In 1892 T. J. Browning served the last year of the Brunswick Mission and continued working in the circuit of the same area. As new churches were organized, some were later assisted by funds available from the Duke Endowment.[29]

A Northern Mission

Mission offerings were collected in Brunswick County Methodist churches for the Church of the Strangers, an independent church founded by Charles Force Deems in New York. That mission church grew rapidly and in 1885 had capacity congregations of 1250 people.

When Cornelius Vanderbilt and his second wife became parishioners and benefactors, the New York church no longer needed the meager offerings from Methodist churches in Brunswick County.[30]

Camp Meetings

In the early years of Methodist circuit riders it was not possible for the Bishop and elders to visit all remote areas. Isolated families found it necessary to travel and to meet wherever possible in order to participate in sacramental and baptismal services. In some cases where no chapel had been built and no home was suitable, they met in the woods and improvised means of camping for the "sacramental meeting." There was a program of preaching, praying, singing, testimonies, and fellowship. These meetings proved successful in reaching more people and effecting more conversions.[31]

Camp meetings were never legislated into the Methodist *Discipline*, but their effectiveness was recognized and soon after 1800, the bishops urged each district to provide them on a regular basis. The Wilmington District provided a camp ground at Town Creek in Brunswick County. The District Camp Ground Committee was dismissed in 1875.

Bishop Asbury participated in numerous camp meetings, and in conversation and letters he expressed his views: "We hear of blessed work in James River District, camp meetings the instrument." Near Georgetown, South Carolina, he observed: "Is not this man a brand plucked from the burning? Camp meetings have done this—they do great good, and prosper in the sandhills." When nearing the South Carolina Conference in 1812, he noted, "I am happy to inform you camp meetings prevail with general use in great success. In the Allegheny Mountains late, in storm and rain, hail and snow with frost."[32]

In the earliest camp meetings about 1800, there was cooperation among Methodists, Baptists, and Presbyterians; together they were able to have great community revivals.

The Methodist camp meetings grew naturally from the "Quarterly-meeting Conference" where ministers met with class leaders and officials. As the meetings grew to include others and visiting preachers, the time was extended from two-day meetings to a week or more, and more preachers participated. None of the small Methodist chapels would hold the crowds; thus, it was necessary for each family to come prepared to camp.[33]

James Jenkins, Presiding Elder of Camden District 1801 through 1804, gave encouragement to camp meetings and is credited with establishing camp grounds in that District. He mentioned in a letter of October 18, 1804, a camp meeting at Beauty Spot with "ten preachers, and numbers of people" attending; also, at Brother Gautier's with ten preachers and 1600 people participating. Reverend Jenkins said of the latter, "This exceeded all I ever saw. The work broke out the first day, and increased rapidly until we left the ground. The Lord rode forth conquering and to conquer. The devil's kingdom fell like lightning."

At Town Creek in Brunswick County June 22, 1804, a camp meeting began. Of this one Jenkins wrote, "The power of God was present to wound and to heal. The cries of the distressed, and the shouts of joy from those that were healed, were truly awful, and pleasing. The work broke out the first day, and increased until Sunday evening and Monday morning; when God seemed to bow the heavens and came like the rushing of am mighty wind. The slain of the Lord were many; every mouth was stopped and confessed that it was the power of God. On Monday morning we had three persecutors struck with the power of God; two fell, and never rose until God spoke peace to their souls. We supposed that there were seventy souls who found peace with God through our Lord Jesus Christ."[34]

Joseph Travis, presiding elder of the Pee Dee District in 1818 and until 1822, told in his *Autobiography* how he conducted an early camp meeting at Town Creek in Brunswick County:

> I had a camp meeting on Town Creek, Brunswick Circuit. The encampment was pretty large—the congregation good; the preachers were gifted and sufficient in number. The meeting commenced on Thursday. Day after day I continued appointing the greatest men to preach. Saturday night came—nothing effected; not a groan or a tear, that I heard or saw. I feared a perfect "water haul," as a result of our meeting. However, on Sabbath morning, I concluded to reverse the order of the day, and selected the weakest preachers on the ground—one to preach, and the other to exhort after him. The one preached a good short sermon: the other rose to exhort, and in short time he commenced weeping and in his simple or plain manner he related his experience of conversion by the aid of his pious mother, then in glory. The hallowed fire caught in the congregation. A general weeping took place, and finally loud bursts of shouting. From that hour the work went on; and many were happily converted before Monday morning—plainly evincing that "the race is not to the swift, nor the battle to the strong."[35]

Concord
United Methodist Church
Supply, North Carolina

146

Chapter XIV

Brunswick County's
Methodist Leaders
1901-1950

Large Circuits, Slow Growth

For the fifty years of 1901 to 1951, the Brunswick County Methodists had three ministers each year to serve the two charges and one station church. Smithville, later named Southport, was the first station church. The two other charges in 1908 included fourteen churches. Town Creek Charge in the northern part of the county included Zion, Leland, Summerville, Shiloh, Piney Grove, Bethel, and Macedonia. Shallotte Charge included Shallotte Camp, Shallotte Village, Union, Andrews, New Hope, Sharon and Concord.[1]

Southport had a parsonage in that town. Town Creek Charge parsonage was located by Zion Church. In 1897 Albert S. Kirby provided a lot at Supply for the building of a parsonage, but the Shallotte Charge parsonage was later (1901) built on Mulberry Street in Shallotte.[2]

By 1901 in Brunswick County the Methodist classes had been reorganized as churches. By 1914 all the churches had Sunday Schools. The following list shows superintendents of each Sunday School and their addresses:

Shallotte Circuit

Andrews	McD. McLamb	Wampee, S.C.
Concord	Guilford Sellers	Supply, N.C.
New Hope	W. F. Price	Shallotte, N.C.
Shallotte Camp	James Holmes	Shallotte, N.C.
Shallotte Village	R. M. Sellers	Shallotte, N.C.
Sharon	G. A. Robinson	Supply, N.C.
Union	W. S. Canaday	Mill Branch (Ash), N.C.

Town Creek Circuit

Bethel	C. N. Leonard	Bolivia, N.C.
Leland	J. T. West	Leland, N.C.
Macedonia	F. H. Willard	Suburb, N.C.
Piney Grove	R. W. Simmons	Town Creek, N.C.
Zion	R. S. McKeithan	Town Creek, N.C.

Southport

Trinity	E. H. Cranmer	Southport, N.C.[3]

1910 Membership

Shallotte Circuit, 128; Town Creek Circuit, 309; Southport Station, 297

1920 Membership

Shallotte Circuit, 434; Town Creek Circuit, 280; Southport, 313

1930 Membership

Shallotte Circuit, 421; Town Creek Circuit, 294; Southport, 344[4]

Reports of Pastors in Brunswick to the District Conference August 7, 1901

Zion Circuit:

Spiritual conditions are not very good at this time. Attendance on "ordinance" not very good. There is mission territory and an appropriation for that charge, but with the present arrangement, it will not be likely to develop. We think that an appropriation, as it now stands, is about thrown away.

Seven Sunday Schools not doing as well as they should. Conducted mainly according to our usual plan.

Nothing done as yet for the Bible Society.

Finances are low. We have some system but this nearly all. Church buildings are in right good condition, except one which we are now trying to rebuild. One new church we are trying to pay for, and we intend to build a new church at another point, not as yet begun.

Records of Quarterly conference present.

(pastor not present)[5]

Trinity at Southport:

The spiritual condition of our church is only fairly good. The attendance upon the services is usually very good.

We have a Women's Home Missionary Society that is doing some work.

148

We usually have a very good Sunday School, but we find it very difficult to keep it up this summer on account of the summer excursions that come down from Wilmington and demoralize our young people. And, too, our superintendent has been kept away for several months on account of sickness in his family.

We have not taken the collection for the American Bible Society, but will.

We use the voluntary assessment plan in raising the salary. Our people are not very liberal in the support of the church. We have a nice church and a very good parsonage: the parsonage is now being painted and we hope to paint the church in the near future.

The Quarterly conference record is here for inspection.

Our League still has vivacity. We have some money in the Savings Bank towards building a League Hall, and hope to build in a few years.

Respectuflly submitted,
Robert W. Bailey, P.C.[6]

Atlantic Circuit:

The spiritual state of our charge is not as good as we desire. Our people, some of them, are not as loyal to the church as they should be. Yet, there are others that are true and faithful, ready to do every good word and work. Our people attend very well upon the ordinances and social meetings of the church. There is some fine missionary territory in the bounds of the charge.

Our Sunday Schools are in excellent condition, well organized and doing good work. We use our literature and conduct schools in the usual way. We have an excellent high school at Shallotte Camp conducted by Professor Leonard, continues ten months in the year.

There has been no work done by the American Bible Society and no collections taken as yet.

We use the assessment plan at some of the churches, at others we do not. We use different methods in securing the collections ordered by the Annual Conference.

Our houses of worship are in fair condition. We are completing a very neat church at Shallotte Camp. We began work on our parsonage the 1st of April; it is now about completed.

J. M. Marlowe, P.C.[7]

Waccamaw Circuit:

The spiritual state and the attendance upon the ordinances and social meetings of the church are good. There is a good per cent of the members that appear to enjoy the grace of God. There is a right good percent that pray in public and in their families. There is a remnant that is not as loyal to the church as they should be. I am trying

149

to build them up again. I have not held any protracted meetings yet on account of poor health, but expect to begin soon if health will permit.

There are two very good points of mission territory in the bounds of the circuit.

Womens F.M.S., none; Home Missionary Society, none.

There are 6 Sunday Schools, all of which are conducted in the opening, followed by religious services. Some use Bible lessons, others the quarterlies. We have very good singing in most of our schools. Number of pupils, 343; officials and teachers 26, total 369.

Collection for Bible Society has not been taken yet. The financial system is not very good. They do not use the assessment plan as much as should be done. I think the stewards leave it to the members as to what they shall pay. Houses of worship very common. This work needs a parsonage.

Cheerfully submitted,
Erwin Milliken[8]

Methodist "Local Preachers"

In 1740 John Wesley began selecting a few local laymen to become his "assistants" in their own societies. Bishop Asbury began the same practice in America and was always alert in selecting "local preachers" with some potential for the itineracy.

For over a century after Asbury's time, local preachers continued to have important responsibilities in Methodist societies and churches. These preachers were of two classes. Some were former members of the Annual Conference but had located voluntarily because of health or family. These retained their credentials but did not travel; they served as opportunity came.

Other local preachers were duly licensed laymen who, after certain studies, might possibly be ordained. These were not members of the Conference, but they found opportunities to preach, sometimes supplying a small charge when Conference members were not available. They reached remote communities that were not provided with Conference ministers.

Available records are insufficient for a complete listing of the local preachers that assisted the Methodist growth in the Cape Fear area, but there is evidence of their contribution to the cause.

In 1859 Zoar, near Bolivia, was being served by C. C. Mercer, and William Gause helped in the general area.

In 1871 the Wilmington District had ten local preachers. In 1881 Smithville had one local preacher, Brunswick Circuit had two, and

Waccamaw Circuit had one. In 1890 G. B. Andrews was licensed at Shallotte, Benjamin Williams at Supply, and W. R. Ferguson at Southport. Wilmington District in 1918 had sixteen local preachers. In 1920 local preachers in Brunswick County were: J. K. Worthington at Shallotte, W. R. Ferguson at Southport and J. M. Carrol at Bolton.

Wilmington District reported in 1944 the following local preachers:

W. B. Ward, Clarendon
Dennis Kinlaw, Asbury College
L. B. Jacobs, Maxton
Paul Edwards, Duke Divinity
  School
R. A. Mercer, Louisburg College
O. F. McBride, High Point
  College
Guy Jones, U. S. Army
Clyde McCarver, on trial

Z. V. Cowan, Council
W. J. Freeman, White Oak
J. D. Maides, High Point College
Kenneth Johnson, U. S. Army
Robert C. Elkins, U. S. Army
J. M. Carrol, Scotts Hill
Richard Evans, Louisburg
  College
J. W. Smith, Pembroke[9]

Wilmington District Local Preachers in 1954

Nathan Byrd, Earl Crow
Charles Howell
Ed Lewis
Nash Locklear
Samuel McMillan
Emerson Thompson
Leo Thompson, Hubert Hodgin
Maurice Waddell
W. B. Ward
G. B. Webster
Thomas White
Ernest Williamson

Wilmington
Bolton
Sneeds Ferry
Pembroke
Wilmington
Burgaw
Wilmington
Fair Bluff
Clarendon
Wilmington
Lumberton
Chadbourn

Wilmington District Local Preachers in 1962

Carl D. Andrews
J. P. Bullard
Kenneth Crutchfield
Oscar Cummings
Bruce Dowless
Mark Hawthorne

Rebecca Moddlemog
James Oliver
John Ross
Donald Sellers
T. L. White

1965 Virginia Franks, T. N. Railey, R. T. Taylor

1970 W. D. Ward, (Retired) Clarendon, N.C.

1973 B. Ward and Horton Clayton[10]

The Laity

Methodism in its beginning was a movement by concerned laymen in the Anglican Church. Lay workers continued to serve in important roles as American Methodism grew. Licensed exhorters, local preachers, and class leaders gave significant service, especially where appointed preachers had large circuits.

As churches became organized, these volunteer servants were replaced by "lay speakers" and "lay pastors." Gradually the title "exhorter", "class leader", and "local preacher" disappeared from use, but active laymen continued their contribution as "lay leaders", "lay speakers", and "local pastors".

The Laymen's Movement has grown in both of the North Carolina Conferences. Students are listed and observed as they progress at Duke Divinity School, and other colleges, so that they may serve as student local pastors wherever they are needed.

Local Methodist churches are now more adequately represented with multiple numbers of lay delegates to the Annual Conference.

The church youth no longer see themselves as just a part of the local youth organization; they are now a part of the total ongoing life of the Church with opportunities to make their contribution.

The Conference Board of Laity through planning and encouragement of conference, district, and local church activities, continues to emphasize lay participation in program events and outreach.

North Carolina Conference 1920
Report of the Sunday School Board

The following report is submitted by your Sunday School Board:

We wish again to emphasize the importance of the work of the Sunday School and to ask your co-operation in carrying it on. It must be very manifest to all who are informed as to church work that upon the work of the Sunday school depends much of the success of the church in promulgating the principles and promoting the program of Jesus Christ. The Sunday school is the only institution that can reach all of the people. It is especially important in that it gets hold of the children in their most impressionable years. Ideas instilled in the days of youth are not easily forgotten. It is peculiarly fitting that we should redouble our efforts now at a time when religious education is receiving so much emphasis. We shall hardly be able to rebuild the shattered ideals of our people except through systematic work such as may be done in the Sunday School.

We offer the following recommendations:

1. That standard training schools be held in as many districts as possible and that such appropriation be made for this as may seem necessary.

2. That other schools be set up in towns and country communities wherever desirable and practicable and that a sum not exceeding $500.00 be appropriated for this purpose.

3. That the Executive Committee shall be empowered to employ workers in every district wherever practicable, such workers to be selected after consultation with the presiding elders and Field Secretary.

4. That an appropriation of $200.00 be made for the Wesley Bible Class Federation.

5. That we co-operate with the Managers of the Trinity College Summer School for Preachers in providing for training courses for Sunday school workers.

6. That we co-operate with the Epworth League Board in providing a credit course for young people at the Epworth League Institute.

7. That the Executive Committee be instructed to continue their efforts to secure an elementary worker provided a suitable person can be found who is available.

8. That we urge our people to attend the Lake Junaluska Training School.

We respectfully urge our pastors and laymen to assist us in putting over the program which we have planned for the year and we pledge our greatest efforts to assist them in promoting the cause of Christ.

Respectfully submitted,

H. E. SPENCE, *Chairman.*

R. C. CRAVEN, *Secretary.*

Report of the Board of Temperance
and Social Service - 1920

ABNORMAL TIMES

Your Board believes that in these abnormal times the influence of the Church ought to be felt along all practical lines and that only as the principles of Christianity shall permeate the actions of men in the changes that are now taking place will our nation be saved from strikes, lock-outs, anarchy, and other forms of lawlessness. The various "isms" and organizaitons spreading evil abroad in the land give the clarion call to the Church to apply the doctrines of Christ to all the details of human society.

A LEAGUE OF NATIONS.

We believe that all difficulties, differences and misunderstandings arising between nations should be settled by some organization of nations. We deplore the fact that the "League of Nations" has not yet been ratified by this country and we still hope that a way will be found whereby this nation may become a member of the League. We do not believe in the spirit of militarism, nor in the increase of the armies and the navies. Our faith is in the God of nations and our protection is under His wing.

THE NEGRO PROBLEM AND LYNCHING.

When Christians learn to do unto others as they would have others do unto them, the negro problem will be in the process of solution and profiteering and lynching will become a thing of the past.

THE CIGARETTE.

We repeat our statement of one year ago that "the cigarette is an evil and its use is injurious. The law of the State forbids its use or gift to any one under sixteen. Our conviction is that this law is not properly enforced. We give it our endorsement and call on citizens and officers to see to its enforcement."

MOVING PICTURE SHOWS.

In view of the many indecent and immoral pictures that are exhibited in the moving picture theaters all over this country, threatening the morals and Christian ideals of our people and poisoning the minds and hearts of our children, we believe that this Conference should memorialize our State Legislature to provide for a State Board of Censors who shall pass upon all films sent into the State for public exhibition.

SUNDAY BASEBALL, GOLF AND LIKE GAMES.

We deplore the practice of games such as golf, baseball, etc., on the Sabbath, and hereby memorialize our State Legislature to enact a State-wide law prohibiting the same.

STREET CARNIVALS.

We believe that the Street Carnivals exhibited in many of our towns and cities do no good and much harm, and we urge the authorities of the municipalities to use all present law to prohibit them. We name J. J. Boone, Dr. M. Bolton and Luther Hamilton as a committee to cooperate with like committees from other organizations to investigate the matter of legislation concerning the exhibiting of such carnivals and to secure further legislation, if need be. This committee is also authorized to act with other committees to secure any other State legislation asked for in this report.

NATIONAL LAW FOR SABBATH OBSERVANCE.

We urge Congress to enact a law for Sabbath Observance in the District of Columbia and a law for the nation to stop all Sunday mails, postoffices, railroad trains and newspapers. To this end, we endorse the law proposed by the Tennessee Conference as it now appears on page 3377 of the Congressional Record of February 20, 1920 (a copy of which is hereto attached). We name W. W. Peele, W. B. Cooper and R. L. Davis as a committee to co-operate with the committee of three appointed by the Tennessee Conference and other like committees for the purpose of securing such legislation.

WORLD PROHIBITION.

The Board is glad to note the progress that has been made for world prohibition. The International Congress of the World League Against Alcoholism, which met in Washington in September, had representatives from more than twenty-five nations, in which nations there are temperance organizations that are engaged in the work of exterminating the beverage liquor traffic. We endorse the action of the Anti-Saloon League in aiding the world movement.

THE ANTI-SALOON LEAGUE.

Your Board is gratified at the report that comes through the Superintendent of the North Carolina Anti-Saloon League concerning the work of that organization. In the States of Massachusetts, New York, New Jersey, Ohio and Wisconsin, where the wet forces were

155

trying to nullify the Eighteenth Amendment and the law-enforcement code, the drys had signal victories at the polls on election day, and the next Congress will have more friends and supporters of prohibition in it than the last Congress. New Jersey and New York have elected Legislatures that, in all probability, will pass law-enforcement legislation rather than nullification legislation, as their Legislatures did a year ago.

The Board of Trustees of the North Carolina Anti-Saloon League has memorialized the next General Assembly to pass legislation that will harmonize our State laws with the Volstead prohibition code and has asked the leaders of prohibition everywhere to make 1921 a law-enforcement year. The Board endorses the action of the Anti-Saloon League Trustees and urges our General Assembly to enact such legislation. We endorse the work of the Anti-Saloon League and suggest that our pastors avail themselves of every opportunity to use her speakers for the purpose of building up sentiment against the lawless liquor traffic in every community.

We recommend that the Conference request the Bishop to appoint R. L. Davis, Superintendent of the Anti-Saloon League of North Carolina, for another year, he having been re-elected to that position by the Board of Trustees of the Anti-Saloon League.

J. J. BOONE, *Chairman, Pro Tem.*
R. L. DAVIS, *Secretary..*

BE IT ENACTED BY THE SENATE AND HOUSE OF REPRESENTATIVES OF THE UNITED STATES IN CONGRESS ASSEMBLED:

1. Hereafter it shall be unlawful for any person in the employment of the United States to work or carry on his ordinary vocation on Sunday;

2. It shall be unlawful for any person or corporation to operate on Sunday any freight or passenger train, or mail train or any other train, or part of a train on Sunday in the carrying on of Interstate Commerce, trade or traffic of any kind;

3. It shall be unlawful for any postoffice to be open on Sunday or to deliver mail on Sunday; it shall be unlawful for any mail to be carried or delivered on Sunday by any employee of the United States, whether in city or country;

4. It shall be unlawful for any newspaper or other paper or publication published or purporting to be published on Sunday to be received, carried, or delivered as mail by any agency of the United

States, in any postoffice, or over any route under the jurisdiction of the United States.

5. It shall be unlawful for any person or corporation engaged in Interstate Commerce or carrying on any business or vocation under the laws of or with the permission or license from the United States, or any of its agencies, to do or carry on any ordinary vocation or business on Sunday; the purpose of this act being to express our national determination to honor the Sabbath day and keep it holy, as God commands; thereby securing for all that opportunity for spiritual and bodily refreshment decreed by our Lord for the happiness of all men and the safety of all nations.

Brunswick County Methodist Churches
1940

Shallotte Circuit	Church Members	Sunday School
Andrews	98	55
Camp	74	65
Concord	39	32
Dixon	21	38
New Hope	26	--
Sharon	122	81
Union	53	--
Village	97	86
Town Creek Circuit		
Bethel	140	67
Piney Grove	67	46
Shiloh	30	31
Zion	98	60
Delco	30 (removed)	
Southport Station	313	195

Appointments for Brunswick County 1901-1917

Conference Date	Southport Station	Town Creek Charge	Shallotte Charge	Waccamaw Circuit
December 1901	A. R. Goodchild	R. T. Wyche	J. M. Marlowe	to be supplied
December 1902	Euclid McWhorter	W. R. Royal to supply	N. H. Guyton	T. J. Browning
November 1903	Euclid McWhorter	W. R. Royal to supply	N. H. Guyton	T. J. Browning
November 1904	W. D. Sasser	T. F. Sawyer to supply	to be supplied	T. J. Browning
November 1905	W. D. Sasser	A. D. Betts	J. M. Wright	L. E. Sawyer
December 1906	G. D. Langston	A. D. Betts	D. A. Watkins	L. E. Sawyer
December 1907	G. D. Langston	C. T. Rogers	A. D. Betts	L. E. Sawyer
December 1908	G. D. Langston	T. H. Bain to supply	T. C. Ellers	
November 1909	W. V. McRae	T. H. Bain	T. C. Ellers	
November 1910	L. T. Singleton	C. P. Snow to supply	J. M. Marlowe to supply	
November 1911	C. M. Lance	F. A. Lupton to supply	J. M. Marlowe to supply	
November 1912	C. M. Lance	F. A. Lupton to supply	J. M. Marlowe to supply	
December 1913	C. M. Lance	R. L. Carraway	J. M. Marlowe to supply	
November 1914	C. M. Lance	R. L. Carraway	R. L. Beasley to supply	
December 1915	T. G. Vickers	R. R. Jones	R. M. Fitts	
December 1916	T. G. Vickers	E. W. Glass	R. M. Fitts	
December 1917	C. B. Culbreth	A. H. Andrews	J. F. Usry	

Brunswick County Appointments 1918-1934

Conference Date	Southport Station	Town Creek Circuit	Shallotte Circuit
December 1918	C. B. Culbreth	D. A. Watkins	J. F. Usry
November 1919	M. D. Hix	D. A. Watkins	W. J. Underwood to supply
November 1920	M. D. Hix	Samuel Johnson to supply	W. J. Underwood to supply
November 1921	D. E. Earnhardt	B. F. Watson	J. W. Dimmette
November 1922	J. C. Whedbee	Shanklin Salyer	J. W. Dimmette
November 1923	J. R. Edwards	W. J. Freeman	J. C. Harmon
November 1924	J. R. Edwards	C. D. McLamb	W. J. Freeman
November 1925	J. R. Edwards	C. D. McLamb	W. J. Freeman
November 1926	J. H. Miller	E. C. Sell	W. J. Freeman
November 1927	J. H. Miller	E. C. Sell	W. J. Freeman
October 1928	J.H. Miller	E. C. Sell	W. J. Dubois to supply
October 1929	R. H. Broom	Z. A. Faison, Jr. to supply	W. J. Dubois
November 1930	R. H. Broom	E. H. Measemer	O. C. Melton
November 1931	R. H. Broom	E. H. Measemer	O. C. Melton
November 1932	R. H. Broom	D. D. Traynham	O. C. Melton
November 1933	C. A. Jones	D. D. Traynham	R. N. Fitts
November 1934	C. A. Jones	D. D. Traynham	R. N. Fitts

158

Brunswick County Appointments 1935-1950

Conference Date	Southport Station	Town Creek Circuit	Shallotte Circuit
November 1935	E. M. Hall	J. C. Harmon	W. R. Hardesty
November 1936	E. M. Hall	J. C. Harmon	F. M. Spence
November 1937	E. M. Hall	J. C. Harmon	C. N. Phillips
November 1938	E. M. Hall	W. J. Freeman to supply	C. N. Phillips
November 1939	R. S. Harrison	W. J. Freeman to supply	C. N. Phillips
November 1940	R. S. Harrison	Walter Pavy	J. C. Whedbee
November 1941	R. S. Harrison	Walter Pavy	W. G. Lowe
November 1942	R. S. Harrison	Walter Pavy	W. G. Lowe
November 1943	R. S. Harrison	J. C. Harmon	W. G. Lowe
November 1944	O. I. Hinson	J. C. Harmon	W. G. Lowe
November 1945	O. I. Hinson	J. C. Harmon	W. G. Lowe
November 1946	P. H. Fields	W. B. Gregory	to be supplied
November 1947	L. D. Hayman	R. H. Caudill	Richard Braunstein
November 1948	L. D. Hayman	R. H. Caudill	Richard Braunstein
November 1949	L. D. Hayman	R. H. Caudill	J. M. Carroll
November 1950	N. L. Jones	R. H. Caudill	J. M. Carroll[11]

In October 1947 at Concord Methodist Church, Tracie Varnum was granted a license to preach and began part time work in Brunswick County. Since that year he has served continuously in Southeastern North Carolina churches, and this year of 1988-1989 he is serving at Concord where he was licensed in 1947.[12]

Reverend Tracie Varnum and wife Clementine

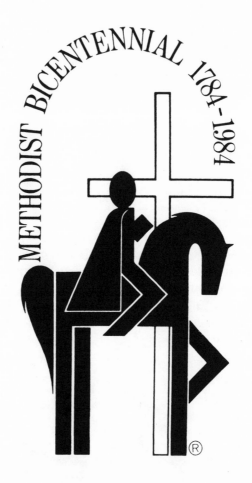

Methodism in America (1784-1984) was celebrated in FESTIVAL 200 in which the theme was "Claim the Past, Celebrate the Present, Challenge the Future."

Chapter XV

Methodist Churches and Ministers After 1950

For the fifty years of 1901 to 1951, preachers were appointed to one station church (Southport) and two circuits in Brunswick County. Then the Shallotte Camp congregation wanted station status. At the North Carolina Conference in Wilmington, October-November, the request was granted and L. J. Bridges was appointed to serve this newly-made station church.

For the next seven years, the Brunswick County Methodist churches included two station churches and two combination charges with appoitments as follows:

	Southport	Town Creek Charge	Shallotte Camp	Shallotte Charge
November 1951	N. L. Jones	C. L. Warren	L. J. Bridges	J. T. Fisher
October 1952	N. L. Jones	C. L. Warren	L. J. Bridges	J. T. Fisher
October 1953	R. H. Jordan	C. L. Warren	L. J. Bridges	J. T. Fisher
October 1954	R. H. Jordan	C. L. Warren	L. J. Bridges	J. T. Fisher
June 1955	R. H. Jordan	C. L. Warren	R. D. Ricks	Travis Owen
June 1956	R. H. Jordan	John Pfister	L. C. Ledford	Travis Owen
June 1957	L. J. Bridges	Richard Blake	W. B. Starnes	W. R. King

After 1955 The North Carolina Annual Conference met each year in the month of June. By 1958 the number of station churches in Brunswick County had exceeded the number of combination charges. Appointments for Brunswick's Methodist churches:

1958

Southport: Trinity—L. J. Bridges
Shallotte Camp—W. B. Starnes
Ocean View—L. D. Hayman
Bethel (Feb.)—Alden Hemingway

Shallotte Charge (Village, Andrews, Sharon, Concord)—W. R. King
Town Creek (Zion, Shiloh, Piney Grove)—Charles F. Eakin

161

1959

Southport—L. J. Bridges
Camp—H. A. Phillips
Ocean View—L. D. Hayman
Bethel—Jack Fulgum

Concord-Evergreen—Gerald Vaiden
Shallotte Charge—W. R. King
Town Creek—Charles F. Eakin

1960

Southport—L. J. Bridges
Camp—H. A. Phillips
Ocean View—L. D. Hayman
Bethel—Kermit Norris

Concord-Evergreen—Gerald Vaiden
Shallotte Charge—H. T. Pickett
Town Creek—Charles F. Eakin

1961

Southport—C. H. Lancaster
Camp—H. A. Phillips
Ocean View—L. D. Hayman

Bethel-Concord—H. K. Jeannerett
Shallotte Charge—H. T. Pickett
Town Creek—C. F. Eakin

1962

Southport—C. H. Lancaster
Camp—H. A. Phillips
Ocean View—B. H. Lamb

Bethel-Concord—H. K. Jeannerett
Shallotte Charge—H. T. Pickett
Town Creek—H. B. Harrell

1963

Southport—C. H. Lancaster
Camp—H. A. Phillips
Ocean View—R. R. Knowles

Bethel-Concord—James Starnes,
    James Carroll
Shallotte Charge—W. B. Gregory
Town Creek—Allen Richardson,
    H. B. Harrell, Asso.

1964

Southport—C. H. Lancaster
Shallotte Camp—M. L. DeHart
Ocean View—R. R. Knowles

Bethel-Concord—James A. Starnes
Shallotte Circuit—W. B. Gregory
Town Creek—David D. McKay

1965

Southport—W. S. Davenport
Shallotte Camp—M. L. DeHart
Ocean View—R. R. Knowles

Bethel-Concord—J. P. Pegg
Shallotte Circuit—D. A. Weaver
Town Creek—Thomas R. McKay

1966

Southport—W. S. Davenport
Shallotte Camp—M. L. DeHart
Ocean View—J. S. Huggins

Bethel-Concord—J. P. Pegg
Shallotte Circuit—D. A. Weaver
Town Creek—Thomas R. McKay

1967

Southport—W. A. Davenport
Shallotte Camp—Frank Salmon
Ocean View—J. S. Huggins

Bethel-Concord—J. C. Dunn
Shallotte Circuit—D. A. Weaver
Town Creek—Thomas R. McKay

United Methodist Appointments

1968

Southport—W. A. Davenport
Shallotte Camp—Frank Salmon
Ocean View—J. S. Huggins

Bethel-Concord—J. C. Dunn
Shalotte Circuit—Tracie Varnun
Town Creek—J. A. Williams

1969

Southport—Paul B. Scott, Jr.
Shallotte Camp—Frank Salmon
Ocean View—J. S. Huggins

Bethel-Concord—J. C. Dunn
Shallotte Circuit—Tracie Varnum
Town Creek—J. A. Williams

1970

Southport—Paul B. Scott, Jr.
Shallotte Camp—Frank Salmon
Ocean View—M. W. Warren, Jr.

Bethel-Concord—J. C. Dunn
Shallotte Circuit—Tracie Varnum
Town Creek—J. A. Williams

1971

Southport—Paul B. Scott, Jr.
Shallotte Camp—J. Sidney Epperson
Ocean View—W. W. Warren, Jr.

Bethel-Concord—J. C. Dunn
Shallotte Circuit—Tracie Varnum
Town Creek—Ed C. Batchelor

1972

Southport—Paul B. Scott, Jr.
Shallotte Camp—J. Sidney Epperson
Ocean View—W. W. Warren, Jr.

Bethel-Concord—E. R. Shuller
Shallotte Circuit—Tracie Varnum
Town Creek—Ed C. Batchelor

1973

Southport—J. Earl Richardson
Shallotte Camp—J. Sidney Epperson
Ocean View—W. W. Warren, Jr.

Bethel-Concord—T. H. House
Shallotte Circuit—Tracie Varnum
Town Creek—Ed C. Batchelor

1974

Southport—J. Earl Richardson
Shallotte Camp—J. Sidney Epperson
Ocean View—W. W. Warren, Jr.

Bethel-Concord—T. H. House
Shallotte Circuit—Tracie Varnum
Town Creek—Ed C. Batchelor

1975

Southport—J. Earl Richardson
Shallotte Camp—J. Sidney Epperson
Ocean View—P. D. Midgett, III

Bethel-Concord—Howard Elam
Shallotte Circuit—Tracie Varnum
Town Creek—C. E. Woodruff, Jr.

1976

Southport—J. Earl Richardson
Shallotte Camp—J. Sidney Epperson
Ocean View—P. D. Midgett, III

Bethel-Concord—Howard Elam
Shallotte Circuit—Tracie Varnum
Town Creek—Jimmie Ray Tatum

1977

Southport—J. Earl Robinson
Shallotte Camp—David L. Moe
Ocean View—James L. Hobbs

Bethel-Concord—Howard Elam
Shallotte Circuit—Tracie Varnum
Town Creek—Jimmie Ray Tatum

1978

Southport—J. Claude Chaffin
Shallotte Camp—David L. Moe
Ocean View—James L. Hobbs

Bethel-Concord—Howard A. Elam
Shallotte Circuit—Tracie Varnum
Town Creek—Jimmie Ray Tatum

1979

Southport—J. Claude Chaffin
Shallotte Camp—David L. Moe
Ocean View—James L. Hobbs

Bethel-Concord—David A. Eubank
Shallotte Circuit—E. C. Batchelor
Town Creek—Jimmie Ray Tatum

1980

Southport—J. Claude Chaffin
Shallote Camp—W. W. Wells
Ocean View—James R. Oliver

Bethel-Concord—Robert J. Rudd
Shallotte Circuit—E. C. Batchelor
Town Creek—C. Everett Price, Jr.

1981

Southport—J. Claude Chaffin
Shallotte Camp—W. W. Wells
Ocean View—James R. Oliver

Bethel-Concord—Tracie Varnum
Shallotte Circuit—Robert J. Rudd
Town Creek—C. Everett Price, Jr.

1982

Southport—P. D. Midgett, III
Shallotte Camp—W. W. Wells
Ocean View—James R. Oliver
Sharon—David L. Moe

Bethel-Concord—Tracie Varnum
Shallotte Circuit—Maurice Lancaster
Town Creek—Pearl G. West

1983

Southport—P. D. Midgett, III
Shallotte Camp—Woodrow Wells
Ocean View—James R. Oliver
Sharon—David Moe

Zion—Pearl G. West
Bethel-Concord—Tracie Varnum
Shallotte Charge—Maurice Lancaster
Shiloh—Leon M. Brock

1984

Southport—P. D. Midgett
Shallotte Camp—W. Stanley Smith
Ocean View—Roger E. Thompson
Sharon—Donald Skinner

Zion—Pearl G. West
Bethel-Concord—Ralph M. Hill
Shallotte Charge—Maurice Lancaster
Shiloh—Leon M. Brock

1985

Southport—P. D. Midgett, III
Shallotte Camp—W. Stanley Smith
Ocean View—Roger E. Thompson
Sharon—Donald Skinner

Zion—L. M. Peele
Bethel-Concord—Ralph M. Hill
Shallotte Charge—Maurice Lancaster
Riegelwood-Shiloh—Samuel
  Williams, Jr.

1986

Southport—P. D. Midgett, III
Shallotte Camp—W. Stanley Smith
Ocean View—Roger E. Thompson
Sharon—W. Clark Barfield

Zion—L. M. Peele
Bolivia: Bethel—T. Mike Williamson
Concord—Tracie Varnum
Shallotte Charge—Maurice Lancaster
Riegelwood-Shiloh—Samuel
  Williams, Jr.

1987

Southport: Trinity—P. D.
  Midgett, III
Shallotte Camp—W. Stanely Smith
Ocean View—J. Mark Kasper
Sharon—Robert E. Rattz

Zion—L. M. Peele, Jr.
Bolivia: Bethel—T. Mike Williamson
Concord—Tracie Varnum
Shallotte Charge—Maurice Lancaster
Riegelwood-Shiloh—Samuel
  Williams, Jr.

1988

Southport: Trinity—P. D.
  Midgett, III
Shallotte Camp—George F.
  Blanchard
Ocean View—Mark Kasper
Sharon—Robert Rattz

Zion—L. M. Peele, Jr.
Bolivia: Bethel—Gary Leoffler
Concord—Tracie Varnum
Shallotte Charge—Robert H.
  Hargrove
Riegelwood-Shiloh—David Northcuth

In 1888 the Methodist churches in Brunswick County were one station church and three circuits, with four preachers. In 1988 there were seven station churches, two circuits, and nine preachers.[1]

United Methodists

On April 23, 1968, the Methodist Church and the Evangelical United Brethren were united and became *The United Methodist Church*. The union of these two churches brought together two streams of spiritual life with similar emphases which had their beginnings "in the evangelistic concerns and passions of John Wesley, Francis Asbury, Philip Otterbeim, Jacob Albright, Martin Boehm and others who labored with them." This union brought together two language groups who shared the conviction that Christian faith and experience ought to be expressed in holy living.

On the day of this union, Albert Outler stated in his sermon: "When more of us get accustomed to the notion that this new church of ours can be remade for yet more effective mission, for still more authentic democracy and local initiative, for still more adventurous leadership—and that all this could be done and should be done forthwith!—then the pooled wisdom of our fellowship will surely be enabled to prove that rational, responsible change is a far more faithful pattern of obedience to Christ than the most devoted immobilism can ever be!"[2]

Assuming the new name, the Brunswick County churches became:

Andrews Chapel United Methodist Church
Bethel United Methodist Church
Concord United Methodist Church
Dixon's Chapel United Methodist Church
Ocean View United Methodist Church
Shallotte Camp United Methodist Church

Sharon United Methodist Church
Shiloh United Methodist Church
Southport United Methodist Church
Shallotte Village United Methodist Church
Zion United Methodist Church

Membership Summary
1967-1987

	1967	1972	1977	1982	1987
Bolivia: Bethel	153	129	135	144	140
Concord, at Supply	51	47	55	55	51
Ocean View at Yaupon Beach	231	348	346	366	346
Shiloh at Leland	69	88	102	88	79
Shallotte: Camp	222	248	273	267	407
Shallotte Circuit					
Andrews Chapel, near S.C.	88	90	84	87	88
Dixon Chapel, Varnumtown	110	172	167	138	129
Village Point by Shallotte River	153	143	117	122	108
Sharon, Highway 130	155	167	104	114	147
Southport: Trinity	345	371	412	478	550
Zion, Town Creek	85	186	192	196	216 [3]

Century Summary
for Brunswick County

1878		1 Circuit	1 Preacher	11 Appointments
1881	1 Station Church	3 Circuits	4 Preachers	11 Churches
1908	1 Station Church	2 Circuits	3 Preachers	15 Churches
1988	7 Station Churches	2 Circuits	9 Preachers	11 Churches[4]

Presiding Elders
and District Superintendents

It was John Wesley's desire that a few elders be chosen for work on the American continent, and that the work be divided among them. They would supervise the work, help unordained men, and administer the sacraments. This plan was helpful in many ways while ordained ministers were few in number, especially since it made possible more frequent communion services.

In the elders the bishops had assistants within particular geographic areas, and each elder in his own territory helped solve the problems there.

Bishop Asbury in a letter to Jacob Gruber expressed his view of the importance of his elders: "I must lean on about sixty men . . . The presiding elders are my council of safety, my eyes and ears and mouth everywhere." [5]

Edlers were mentioned in 1787 and 1788 for Bladen Circuit of the South Carolina District and afterwards through 1796. "Presiding elder" came into use in 1797 and until 1850 continued to be used in these districts that at different times included Brunswick County: Camden, Pee Dee, Fayetteville, and Wilmington Districts. [6]

Wilmington District was created by the South Carolina Conference in 1835. Presiding elders that served this district until 1850 are listed with South Carolina Conference appointments for each year. (See list in Chapter XII.)

Most of the original Wilmington District was transferred in 1850 to the North Carolina Conference, which had been set apart from the Virginia Conference. Before the transfer, Wilmington District included Horry County of South Carolina; but afterwards, it was comprised only of North Carolina territory that had been cut off from the Fayetteville District in 1835.

The presiding elder of the Wilmington District of the South Carolina Conference willingly accepted the same position in the North Carolina Conference. After commendable administration in the South Carolina Conference, he became the first presiding elder of the Wilmington District after the transfer to the North Carolina Conference. He and his successors are listed in the following pages with the date and the meeting place of the conference that appointed them. [7]

Presiding Elders,
Wilmington District
North Carolina Conference

William Barringer,
appointed at Warrenton in November, 1850.

James Read,
appointed at Salisbury in November 1851.

Robert J. Carson,
appointed at Louisburg in November 1852;
reappointed at Raleigh in November 1853.

D. B. Nicholson,
appointed at Pittsboro in November 1854;
reappointed at Wilmington in November 1855;
reappointed at Greensboro in November 1856;
reappointed at Goldsboro in December 1857.

C. F. Deems,
appointed at New Bern in December 1858;
reappointed at Beaufort in December 1859;
reappointed at Salisbury in December 1860;
reappointed at Lousburg in December 1861.

David B. Nicholson,
appointed at Raleigh in December 1862;
reappointed at Greensboro in December 1863;
reappointed at Mocksville in December 1864.

L. S. Burkhead,
appointed at Raleigh in December 1865;
reappointed at Fayetteville in November 1866;
reappointed at Wilmington in November 1867;
reappointed at Statesville in December 1868.

William Closs,
appointed at New Bern in November 1869;
reappointed at Greensboro in November 1870;
reappointed at Charlotte in November 1871;
reappointed at Fayetteville in December 1872.

W. S. Black
appointed at Goldsboro in December 1873;
reappointed at Raleigh in December 1874;
reappointed at Wilmington in December 1875;
reappointed at Greensboro in November 1876.

L. S. Burkhead,
  appointed at Salisburg in November 1877;
  reappointed at Charlotte in November 1878;
  reappointed at Wilson in December 1879;
  reappointed at Winston in December 1880;
  reappointed at Durham in December 1881.
R. O. Burton,
  appointed at Raleigh in December 1882.
W. H. Bobbitt,
  appointed at Statesville in December 1883.
P. J. Carraway,
  appointed at Wilmington in December 1884;
  reappointed at Charlotte in December 1885;
  reappointed at Reisdville in December 1886.
T. W. Guthrie,
  appointed at Fayetteville in December 1887.
F. D. Swindell,
  appointed at New Bern in November 1888;
  reappointed at Greensboro in November 1889;
  reappointed at Wilson in December 1890;
  reappointed at Greenville in November 1891.
W. S. Rone,
  appointed at Goldsboro in December 1892;
  reappointed at Wilmington in December 1893;
  reappointed at Durham in December 1894
  reappointed at Elizabeth City in December 1895.
R. C. Beaman,
  appointed at Kinston in December 1896;
  reappointed at Raleigh in Decewmber 1897.
R. F. Bumpass,
  appointed at Elizabeth City in November 1898
  reappointed at Washington in December 1899.
R. B. John,
  appointed at New Bern in December 1900;
  reappointed at Fayetteville in December 1901;
  reappointed at Wilmington in December 1902;
  reappointed at Goldsboro in November 1903.
M. Bradshaw,
  appointed at Henderson in November 1904;
  reappointed at Wilson in November 1905.

W. L. Cunningham,
  appointed at Rocky Mount in December 1906;
  reappointed at New Bern in December 1907;
  reappointed at Durham in December 1908;
  reappointed at Raleigh in November 1909.

N. H. D. Wilson,
  appointed at Elizabeth City in November 1910;
  reappointed at Kinston in November 1911.

L. E. Thompson,
  appointed at Fayetteville in November 1912;
  reappointed at Oxford in December 1913;
  reappointed at Washington in November 1914;
  reappointed at Wilmington in December 1915.

J. H. Shore,
  appointed at Durham in December 1916;
  reappointed at Greenville in December 1917;
  reappointed at Goldsboro in December 1918;
  reappointed at Wilson in November 1919.

J. M. Daniel,
  appointed at Rocky Mount in November 1920;
  reappointed at New Bern in November 1921;
  reappointed at Raleigh in November 1922;
  reappointed at Elizabeth City in November 1923.

H. A. Humble,
  appointed at Wilmington in November 1924;
  reappointed at Fayetteville in November 1925.

H. M. North,
  appointed at Durham in November 1926;
  reappointed at Raleigh in November 1927;
  reappointed at Wilson in October 1928;
  reappointed at Kinston in October 1929.

W. C. Martin,
  appointed at Henderson in November 1930;
  reappointed at Greenville in November 1931;
  reappointed at Rocky Mount in November 1932.

L. B. Jones,
  appointed at Durham in November 1933;
  reappointed at Washington in November 1934.

W. A. Cade,
> appointed at Wilmington in November 1935;
> reappointed at New Bern in November 1936;
> reappointed at Raleigh in November 1937;
> reappointed at Elizabeth City in November 1938;
> reappointed at Fayetteville in November 1939.

At the Kansas City Uniting Conference in May of 1939, the United Methodist Church approved the new term "district superintendent" to replace "presiding elder."

Wilmington District
Superintendents

A. S. Parker,
> appointed at Wilmington in November 1940;
> reappointed at Durham in November 1941;
> reappointed at Wilson in November 1942;
> reappointed at Rocky Mount in November 1943;
> reappointed at Raleigh in November 1944;
> reappointed at Goldsboro in November 1945.

John C. Glenn,
> appointed at Henderson in November 1946.

E. L. Hillman,
> appointed at Elizabeth City in November 1947.

C. D. Barclift,
> appointed at Greenville in November 1948;
> reappointed at Sanford in November 1949;
> reappointed at Kinston in November 1950;
> reappointed at Wilmington in November 1951.

Virgil G. Queen,
> appointed at Burlington in October 1952;
> reappointed at Durham in October 1953;
> reappointed at Raleigh in October 1954.

Jasper E. Garlington,
> appointed at Fayetteville in June 1955;
> reappointed at Greenville in june 1956;
> reappointed at New Bern in June 1957;
> reappointed at Wilson in June 1958;
> reappointed at Wilmington in June 1959;
> reappointed at Rocky Mount in June 1960.

Clyde S. Boggs,
appointed at Durham in June 1961;
reappointed at Kinston in June 1962;
reappointed at Greenville in June 1963;
reappointed at Burlington in June 1964;
reappointed at Raleigh in June 1965.

Clyde G. McCarver,
appointed at Rocky Mount in June 1966;
reappointed at Goldsboro in June 1967;
reappointed at Fayetteville in June 1968;
reappointed at Chapel Hill in June 1969;
reappointed at Greenville in June 1970.

William J. Neese,
appointed at Fayetteville in June 1971;
reappointed at Durham in June 1972;
reappointed at Fayetteville in June 1973;
reappoinetd at Fayetteville in June 1974.

James A. Auman,
appointed at Fayetteville in June 1975;
reappointed at Fayetteville in June 1976;
reappointed at Fayetteville in June 1977;
reappointed at Fayetteville in June 1978;
reappointed at Fayetteville in June 1979;
reappointed at fayettevilel in June 1980.

Vernon C. Tyson,
appointed at Fayetteville in June 1981;
reappointed at Fayetteville in June 1982;
reappointed at Fayetteville in June 1983.

James Bailey,
appointed at Fayetteville in June 1984;
reappointed at Fayetteville in June 1985;
reappointed at Durham in June 1986.

Samuel D. McMillan, Jr.
appointed at Fayetteville in June 1987;
reappointed at Fayetteville in June 1988.

Chapter XVI

Collectanea

Excerpts from Minutes
of Early Methodist Conferences

1780   All traveling preachers take a license imparting they are assistants or helpers in connection with us. It is a shame for preachers to be in bed till six in the morning.

Concerning pay, wives are to receive equivalent with their husbands ''if they stand in need.'' The conference disapproves the practice of distilling grain into liquor; preachers are to disown friends who will not renounce this practice.

1783   ''How shall we conduct ourselves towards any European Methodist should they come to this country?'' Not recommend them without a letter of recommendation which we have no reason to doubt.'' Set two Thanksgiving days for ''public peace, for temporal and spiritual prosperity, and for the glorious work of God.''

1784   The General Conference voted to expunge ''obey'' from the ritual of marriage.

1785   Recognition of necessity to ordain in America. Wesley's blessing: ''They are now at full liberty, simply to follow the scriptures . . .and we judge it best that they should stand fast in that liberty wherewith God has so strangely made them free.''

The church purpose adopted: ''to reform the Nation and spread Scriptural holiness throughout the land.''

1787   ''What shall we do to promote the spiritual welfare of the coloured people?''

''We conjure all our ministers and preachers, by the Love of God, and the salvation of souls, and do require them by the authority that is vested in us, to leave nothing undone for the spiritual benefit and salvation of them, within their respective circuits, or districts; and for this purpose to embrace every opportunity of inquiring into the state of their souls, and to unite in society those who appear to have a real desire of fleeing from the wrath to come, to meet such in class, and to exercise the whole Methodist discipline among them.'' ''Let register books be provided by all the Societies, that the elders and Deacons may enter the marriages and baptisms regularly in them; and let every such Register-Book be kept in the hands of the steward or any other proper person of each society. Let one general Register-Book be also kept in the hands of the General Steward of every circuit, in which the contents of all the private Register-Books in the circuit may be inserted at convenient times.''

1790   Emphasis: Sunday school at all preaching places.

1793   Caution: ''The brethren are requested to be on their guard against imposters—one of this character having made his way through North and South Carolina, collected money, purchased a horse by falsehood, and disappeared.—If a preacher is on the traveling plan he will be sent out from the District Conference; if he is in the local line, he can be recommended from his quarterly meeting.—If doubts arise relative to any person who may appear under the character of a Methodist preacher, refer him to the preacher who is in charge of the circuit, for examination, before he is permitted to preach.

1794   The last Friday in February is set apart in the United States by the Methodist Episcopal Church for solemn fasting and prayer.

1795   The first Friday in March is recommended to be held as a most solemn day of fasting, humiliatic prayer, and supplication.

The last Thursday in October, 1796, is to be a day of holy gratitude and thanksgiving—to take into remembrance the goodness and wisdom of God displayed toward America.

1798   ''Jenkins also preached, and did it as he would have done it in the backwoods. Some said it 'had too much fire in it'—not fox fire or of the sheet lightning sort, you may be assured, but akin to the tongues of fire on the day of Pentecost.''

from Chreitzberg p. 73

1858   *Doctrines and Disciplines of the Methodist Episcopal Church*, page 57:

Question   How shall we try those who profess to be moved by the Holy Ghost to preach?

Answer: Let the following questions be asked, namely:
1.   Do they know God as a pardoning God? Have they the love of God abiding in them? Do they desire nothing but God? And are they holy in all manner of conversation?

2.   Have they gifts (as well as grace) for the work? Have they (in some tolerable degree) a clear sound understanding, a right judgement, in the things of God, a just conception of salvation by faith? Do they speak justly, readily, clearly?

3. Have they fruit? Are any truly convinced of sin and converted to God by their preaching?

As long as these three marks concur in any one, we believe he is called of God to preach. These we receive as sufficient proof that he is moved by the Holy Ghost.

The Story Exchange

Methodism had a hard struggle to get a foothold in Georgetown. The plain points and truths of our preachers stirred opposition. One Sabbath Brother Humphries was to preach. A lady advised him, "Now Brother Humphries, recollect that you are going to preach to town folks: it won't do to be too plain."

He made no reply, but in preaching he brought out this sentence: "If you don't repent you'll be damned."

He jumped back into the pulpit as if terribly alarmed, saying: "I beg your pardon, you are *town* folks."

This he repeated during the sermon, adding that God would cast *them* into hell just as soon as he would a piney-woods sinner; if they did not repent and become converted.

There sat the good sister with her head down. But she never again tried to instruct the preacher as to his sermon preaching.

Joseph Travis *Autobiography* p. 87

Thomas Humphries was on the Bladen Circuit in 1789 and preached many times at Georgetown. James Jenkins was converted by his preaching.

Of two comrades in the episcopacy, William Capers (1790-1855) and J. O. Andrew (1794-1871):

"One day they were together and Capers said to Andrew, 'James, how is it, when you preach my wife gets happy, and when I preach your wife gets happy; but my wife never gets happy when I preach, nor your wife when you preach?'

'Well,' said Andrew, 'it is because they know us so well.' "

Life of J. O. Andrew

James Jenkins of cultured Dr. Capers:

"Brother William Capers and Nicholas Talley were with us at our camp meeting at Beaverdam. Brother Capers got so happy that he sat on the ground, and shouted with all his might for a considerable time. A doctor was present who said that no one but Negroes and weak-minded women would be overcome in that way; but when he saw Dr. Capers so powerfully exercised he said he would give up."

Jonathan Jackson preached to 300 colored people on "putting the hand to the plow and looking back." In the love feast one colored brother testified: "I have put my hand to the gospel plow and I am determined to plow my furrow clean up to glory."

From Henry Boehm's *Reminiscences*

175

Lewis Myers was a full blooded German born in the United States. He continued warning preachers about marriage and did not want the conference to admit men who were contemplating matrimony. At the Conference in 1811, consideration was being given to admitting one such young man. Lewis Myers commented:

"A young brudder comes to us and wishes to breach. We dell him we dry him a year. He goes out and do bretty well; we dell him we will dry him again. Then he comes to us and says: 'Bredren, I must get married.' We say, 'No brudder, go breach.' But he says: 'I must get married'; and marry he does. It is sight enought to make angels weep! And brother G. was not admitted; but was, *later*."

From Dr. G. G. Smith's
*History of Methodism in
Georgia and Florida* p. 99.

Selected Comments of Some Pioneer Preachers

George Whitefield, traveling from Philadelphia to North Carolina, wrote "I am here, hunting in the woods, these ungospelized wilds, for sinners." From Whitefield's *Journal*

When Joseph Pilmoor first saw North Carolina, he wrote: "O that the Great Master of the vineyard would raise up and thrust out laborers unto his field, such as will not hold their peace day or night, but constantly run to and fro, that the knowledge of God may be increased, and poor wandering sinners brought into the fold of Christ!" From Pilmore's *Journal*

As Joseph Pilmoor approached Wilmington in 1772, the town officials gave precautionary orders: "Let the Constables of said Town, do in turn, walk the streets on Sundays, near the place of worship, during the time of Divine Service and take up or disperse all such persons who are noisy, riotous, or whose conduct may tend to disturb those assembled on that Solemn Occasion."

Colonial Records (1772)

Mr. Wesley and I are like Caesar and Pompey: he will bear no equal, and I will bear no superior."

Asbury *Journal and Letters III,* p. 75

Having crossed Broad River, "Fox" was given credit for getting the Bishop "swiftly and safely through the swell of waters: he is a noble beast."

At the next place of lodging, "brandy and the Bible were both handed to me; one was enough—I took but one."

Asbury *Journal,* December 8, 1812

The itinerant preacher of that day carried no heavier luggage than saddlepockets, and it can seem no wonder that Methodism went in a gallop. There was no time to be lost; the nation must be evangelized, the task was big, men must make haste. Twelve years had passed, and until now the southern half of the great commonwealth had not heard the Gospel as preached by the followers of John Wesley. Beverly Allen leaps to the saddle and speeds away toward the mouth of the Cape Fear . . . and sounds the bugle notes of Repentance and Justification by Faith. That was in 1784. But it takes loud blasts of the trumpet to awaken the dead; almost as difficult is it to arouse those who are under the thrall of that fine anaesthetic of the devil, formalism, to the exclusion of spirit. The Established Church had pre-empted the ground, and the inhabitants slept the enchanted sleep. Allen's efforts failed, and his feeble societies crumbled away, so that in 1786 the Wilmington Circuit was discontinued, and the next year Bladen Circuit took its place in this region.

> From Thomas Smoot's Address to the
> North Carolina Conference Historical
> Society at Fayetteville, November 27,
> 1912.

Joseph Travis Comments on His First General Conference:

"Probably the most exciting topic which enlisted the talents of this august body of ministers was the election of local preachers to elders' orders in our church. ••• Those in favor of their election took the ground of both expediency and necessity. But Jesse Lee in his dispassionate, logical and argumentative manner, left but little hope for local deacons ever obtaining elders' orders. Indeed he appeared to make it plain that the bishop could not in good conscience ordain the local deacons to elders' orders, particularly whilst our form of ordination continues as it is: stating that the form requires the person ordained to promise to devote himself entirely to the ministry.

" 'Now,' said Mr. Lee, 'how can a man devote himself entirely to the ministry, when at his plough, his school-room or behind the counter?' That the form is altogether incompatible with the necessary character and situation of the local preacher, he argued at length, and I thought conclusively. Indeed I viewed the case as lost, much to the grief of my own mind.

"But as Mr. Lee sat down, a thin and by no means interesting looking man from the far end of the house arose, and with a squeaking voice commenced:

" 'Mr. President: our worthy delegate from the Virginia Conference had argued the incompatibility of ordaining our local brethren to elders' orders from the printed form of our ordination. Mr. President, I would state but one fact in replay to the long and eloquent argument—namely: the same printed form requires the person to be ordained to promise to rule well his own

177

family. Our worthy delegate made this promise twenty years ago, and had not fulfilled to this day.' (Lee was a bachelor.)

"Mr. Lee shook his big sides with laughter, and the entire Conference was in a risible mood; when the vote was called for, the motion was carried by a considerable majority—making local deacons eligible for elders' orders in four years after their ordination as deacons.

"There was also some little sparring in reference to the election of presiding elders, Mr. Nicholas Snethen boldly declaring that his 'Very soul hated the present plan of presiding elders.' However, their appointment (by the bishop) remained as it originally was, and now is and ever will be."

from Travis Autobiography pp. 77-78

(This sixth General Conference met in John Street Methodist Church, New York City, on May 1, 1812. Nine annual conferences were represented.)

Evolution of the Collection Plate

Methodist class leaders collected dues from members. Later, loose collections were first received in "boxes" with members, one after another, walking to the front and placing their gift in a b.ox.

"Box collections" were later replaced by "bag" collections. The bag was made of plush or other fabric and fastened to the end of a pole; this was extended to members in the pews.

By 1849 the bags were replaced by baskets, and later the plates came into use.

Old St. George's, Philadelphia.

Dr. Francis H. Tees
*The Beginning of
Methodism in England
and in America* p. 213

Dr. Tees was for many years the pastor of old St. George's Methodist Church in Philadelphia. This church is still active and continues to use the oldest Methodist building in America that is still in use.

Of Public Worship

Question 1. What directions shall be given for establishment of uniformity in public worship?

Answer 1. Let the morning service consist of singing, prayer, the reading of a chapter out of the Old Testament, and another out of the New, and preaching.

2. Let the afternoon service consist of singing, prayer, the reading of one or two chapters out of the Bible, and preaching.

3. Let the evening service consist of singing, prayer and preaching.

4. But on the days of administering the Lord's Supper, the two chapters in the morning service may be omitted.

5. In administering the ordinances, and in the burying of the dead, let the form of Discipline invariably be used. Let the Lord's prayer also be used on all occasions of public worship including the first prayer, and the apostolic benediction, 2 Cor. xiii. 14, in dismissing the congregation.

Question 2. How shall we guard against formality in singing?

Answer 1. By choosing such hymns as are proper for the congregation.

2. By not singing too much at once; seldom more than five or six verses.

3. By suiting the tune to the words.

4. By often stopping short, and asking the people, "Now! do you know what you said last ? Did you speak no more than you felt ?"

5. Do not suffer the people to sing too slow. This naturally tends to formality, and is brought in by those who have either very strong or very weak voices.

6. In all our congregations let the people learn to sing.

7. Recommend our tune book. And if you cannot sing yourself, choose a person or two at each place to pitch the tune.

8. Exhort every person in the congregation to sing; not one in ten only.

10. If a preacher be present, let him alone give out the words.

Question 3. Is there not a great indecency sometimes practiced among us, viz. : talking in the congregation before and after service ? How shall this be cured ?

Answer. Let all the ministers and preachers join as one man, and enlarge on the impropriety of talking before or after service; and strongly exhort those that are concerned to do it no more. In three months, if we are in earnest, this vile practice will be banished out of every Methodist congregation. Let none stop until he has carried his point.

Question 4. Is there any exception to the rule, "Let the men and women sit apart"?

Answer. There is no exception. Let them sit apart in all our churches.

(From the *Discipline* of the Methodist Episcopal Church, South, 1858, Section V.)

Two Sermons Here at Home
from Bishop Asbury's *Journal*

February 10, 1799, at Shallotte, N.C.

"My subject was Acts XIV, 22.

I showed first that the souls of the disciples must be confirmed in doctrine, experience, practice and discipline of the Gospel of Christ in the Church of God. It was observed how plainly these were taught in the oracles of God. I offered some arguments in favour of revelation, to induce its continuance in the substance and exercise of faith through life: through such tribulation entering the eternal kingdom of glory: an object so great it is not to be gained without trials from every enemy, in doing and suffering the whole will of God."

February 22, 1801

"We attended a meeting at Lockwood's Folly. I gave a sermon upon 2 Cor. IV, 5.

1. What the apostles of our Lord did "*not*" preach.

2. What they *did* preach.

3. The relation of ministers to Christ and to souls.

The principles of their service. They sought not their own honour, ease or interest—they did not make disciples for themselves—they had not wisdom, righteousness, redemption, for souls; nor grace to convict, convert or regenerate. They preached Christ in his prophetic, priestly, and kingly offices—in his Gospel; in his sacrifice, once offered, of himself—in his Divinity. Ourselves your servants 'for Christ's sake,' his saved, his qualified, his commissioned servants (not slaves) bound to his word, his grace, his love,—not for any worldly consideration, but 'for Christ's sake'; warning sinners, hopocrites, Pharisees and backsliders; comforting mourners, strengthening believers, and urging and inciting to holiness of heart and life. I observed 'servants,' yet their rulers; ascending to scripture testimony."

see Hebrews XIII, 17; I Peter V, 2.

Letter to the Presiding Elder of Wilmington District; it was read to the Conference June 21, 1899.

Dear Bro:

I was anxious to greet you and the District Conference in person, but must be content to greet you and them in this way. My thoughts have turned lovingly toward you all very often for some weeks. Forty years ago I was pastor at Smithville. Some of the best people I ever knew, white and black, were there. Most of them , I trust , are in Heaven. God bless the few remaining ones and ripen them for the Home above. Please ask all to pray for me. I want someone to send me a flower or a leaf from the grave of my little Eddie, buried there in 1861.

What precious names gather about me! Potter, Dozier, LeHew, Curtis, Wescott, Swain, Galloway, Drew, etc. etc. ! Glory to God for the Hope of Heaven!

Yours in Christ,
A. D. Betts

"On the Happy Golden Shore"
"Meet Me There"

Recalling his time in Brunswick County, Dr. Betts mentioned some of the people and his beloved son. He did not mention the hardships of his schedule while serving the Smithville Circuit, which included eleven Methodist classes in Brunswick County. His appointments to this circuit were made by the North Carolina Conference of December 1858 and December 1860.

Unique Methodist Progress

Mrs. Olive DuRant Mercer of Bolivia, North Carolina, was a lifetime working member of Bethel Methodist Church. Her children hold in sacred memory her dedication and sacrificial service. They learned from her that her grandfather, Christopher Columbus Mercer, was a devout Methodist who contributed much of his time as Sunday School leader, volunteer librarian, and provider of religious books for community families. At the Conference of 1853, he was licensed to preach, and he continued to lead the Methodists of Zoar Class, antecedent of Bethel United Methodist Church.

The present Mercer family treasures also the record of Mrs. Olive DuRant Mercer's father, the Reverend Daniel DuRant of South Carolina. He loved and labored many years with concern for unheeding hearers. One of his unique experiences has been preserved in a written record and may interest Methodists of today.

Reverend Daniel DuRant had permission from a Baptist minister to hold a meeting in the Baptist meeting house. The congregation was quiet and cool during the altar call. Reverend DuRant was continuing his prayer and weeping for the lost when the "big shake" came. After the initial small tremor, the floor heaved and the walls jerked; the preacher continued with "Shake 'em again, Lord, shake 'em again." As the meeting house again shook and swayed, the terrified congregation fled through doors and windows. They had never seen such an early answer to prayer.

This was the prelude to a great revival; the altar afterwards had standing room only. Young and old presented themselves for Methodist church membership. A new building was soon constructed for the Methodist church that had its beginning in an earthquake. (Charleston earthquake of August 31, 1886).

181

Methodist Organizations in Brunswick County
1787-1989

Preaching Places	Societies	Classes	United Methodist Churches
Bell's	Benton's		
Bepent's			
Boatwright's	Christian Chapel		
Brunswick Town	Cape Fear Missions		
Brunswick County Courthouse at Lockwood's Folly	Macedonia	Concord	Concord
Green Hill	Governor's Creek		
	Piney Grove	Piney Grove	
	Hood's Creek	Delco	
	Horeb	Lanvale	
Moore's		Leland	
Murrel's	Myrtle Branch		
William Gause's	New Hope (2nd)	New Hope (2nd)	Seaside (1989)
New Home	Harmony		Dixon's Chapel
	Rehoboth	Rehoboth	
Smithville	Smithville	Smithville	Southport: Trinity
Charlotte (Shallotte)	Shallotte Camp	Shallotte Camp	Shallotte: Camp
		Shallotte Village	Shallotte Village
	Hewett's	Sharon	Sharon
Turner's	Summerville	Shiloh	Shiloh
	Patmos	Union	Andrews Chapel
	Waccamaw Mission	Wet Ash	
	Wayman	Wayman	Riegelwood: Wesley (Columbus County)
Wingate's			Ocean View
Town Creek (Daniel's, Rourk's, Charles Gause's, Sullivan's, New Hope No. 1)	Zion	Zion	Zion
	Zoar	Bethel	Bethel

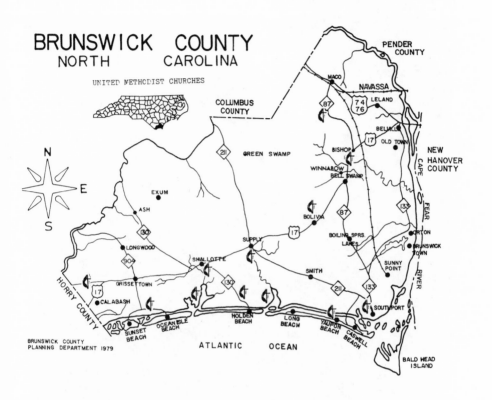

This map shows the location of United Methodist Churches, 1989.

His Spirit, Our Heritage
by V. Gillispie

Author's Musings

As a child in Sunday School I enjoyed singing Jemima Luke's verses set to the tune of an old Irish air:

> I think when I read that story of old,
> When Jesus was here among men,
> How he called little children as lambs to his fold,
> I should like to have been with them then.
>
> I wish that his hands had been placed on my head,
> That his arms had been thrown around me,
> And that I might have seen that kind look when he said,
> 'Let the little ones come unto me.'

To this song I attribute my tendency to delve into the past for meaningful historical gems, and to make a mental list of events which I might have witnessed, enjoyed, and shared. In such musings, the emphasis usually concentrates on people who seemed to be able to do the impossible.

One of these people was Susanna Wesley. With her nineteen children she tried to provide for each of them regular periods for individual instruction, discussion, and guidance.

Susanna's son Charles would have been of interest to me as he composed hundreds of poems, and finally over 6,500 hymns.

John Wesley impressed me with his earnest concern for poor children, and his methodical efforts to reach, teach and feed so many of them. Of particular interest also was his plan to evangelize England and his outreach with twenty-one trips to Ireland and twenty-four trips to Scotland. In these evangelistic efforts he was visiting the island homelands of my ancestors; but at that time my ancestors were emigrating to America. Soon afterwards, Wesley's Methodist missionaries appeared in this New World.

By the time my forebears were making trails in the Blue Ridge Mountains, Joseph Pilmoor was traveling south and north along the Carolina coast, all of them facing the perils of pioneer travel. Both of these areas became parts of the "long road", the 275,000 miles over which the first American Methodist bishop traveled, preached 6,500 sermons, and ordained 4,000 preachers.

Now residing on this Carolina Crescent, I look each day at the Atlantic Ocean over which the early volunteer preachers came to the New World more than two-hundred years ago. Each Sunday while I ride in a car to a little church on Asbury's path, I remember that this first bishop in America "drew the map of his ministry with the hoofs of his horse," as Bishop J. W. Hamilton said. I think of Bishop Asbury and his traveling companion Jesse Lee to whom we are indebted for their journals in which both gave accounts of a special 1799 prayer meeting and revival among the early settlers around the site on which our little white church building now stands.

Beside and beneath the present paved highways are hidden the tracks of many circuit riders. Those who made tracks here before 1800 were each year rewarded with $64.00 and the joy of serving. Most of them were young men, and because of adverse living conditions, half of them died before they reached even thirty years of age.

I cannot forget the young circuit rider who walked when he thought his horse was not able to carry him; the one who preached while wearing a coat that had one sleeve missing after being worn through a thicket; the one who was held under a well spout until he almost drowned; the one who drowned as he tried to cross Brown Marsh; the one who was evicted from the preaching place, followed by pews thrown after him into the road; others who met threatening circumstances and had to seek safety in the woods.

I think especially of those who are not recognized in voluminous records and memorials, but who, like silent embers for rekindling, worked unheralded for the warming of hearts and enlightening of minds. Preserved embers continue to be for us the potential of enduring flames to glow unflickering in face of the challenges of our future.

The rediscovered and reactivated spirit of the pioneer preacher lives on and is becoming a cherished gem from our HEARTENING HERITAGE.

Notes and References

Chapter I: The Coastal Crescent

1. William S. Powell, "Settlement of the Cape Fear," *NEWSLETTER* of Brunswick County Historical Society, XIV, 4 (November 1974) hereinafter cited as Powell "Cape Fear." See also H. C. Chitwood's *A History of Colonial America* and the Vespucci map dated 1526 and showing River Jordan. This map, the earliest with evidence of a known exploration on the Carolina coast, is available at the North Carolina State Archives and is included in W. P. Cumming, *North Carolina in Maps*, p. 1.

2. Hugh Lefler, editor, *North Carolina History Told by Contemporaries*, p. 1, hereinafter cited as Lefler, *North Carolina*.

3. Lawrence Lee, *Indian Wars in North Carolina, 1663-1763*, p. 41, hereinafter cited as Lee, *Indian Wars*.

4. Chicora was the name applied to the Carolina coastal area, probably extending from the present Cape Fear River to the Savannah River. William S. Powell, *The Gazetteer of North Carolina*, p. 105, hereinafter cited as Powell, *Gazetteer*. See also Samuel E. Morison, *The European Discovery of America*; also J. A. Doyle, *The English Colonization of America*; p. 78, hereinafter cited as Doyle, *Colonization*,

5. Hubert E. Bolton and Thomas M. Marshall, *The Colonization of North America, 1492-1783*, p. 40; Morison, *Discovery of America*, p. 332.

6. Dr. Sheath Satterthwaite, "A Brief History of Smith Island" in *NEWSLETTER* of Brunswick County Historical Society, V, 3 (August 1965) hereinafter cited as Satterthwaite, "Smith Island"; Bolton and Maxwell, *Colonization of America*, p. 40; Lawrence Lee, *New Hanover County*, pp. 3-4. (It was customary for Spanish explorers to provide one priest or friar for each passenger vessel.)

7. William S. Powell, *Gazetteer* and "Cape Fear"; Richard Walser, *Literary North Carolina*, p. 3; Charles Joyner, *Down by the Riverside*, p. 4; Paul Quattlebaum, *The Land Called Chicora*; W. P. Cumming, *North Carolina in Maps*, Plate A.

187

8. Gonzalo Fernández de Oviedo was a Spanish historian who received an appointment in the newly discovered island of Hispaniola. His twenty-one-volume *Historia General y Natural de las Indias Occidentales* includes the report of Friar Montessimo concerning Ayllón's settlement.

9. Powell, "Cape Fear"; "Consecions" granted by Proprietors August 5, 1663, in *North Carolina Charters and Constitutions* edited by Mattie E. Parker; Lawrence Lee, *History of Brunswick County*, pp. 13-20.

10. Malcolm Ross, *The Cape Fear*; Lefler and Newsome, *North Carolina*, p. 34; Satterthwaite, "Smith Island"; Powell, "The Cape Fear"; Lee, *Brunswick County*, p. 13.

11. James Sprunt, *Chronicles of the Cape Fear*, pp. 40-43; Ebenezer Hazard, *Journal*, portions in *Georgia Historical Papers* and in the *Wilmington Messenger*, August 22, 1897; Cumming, *North Carolina in Maps*, p. 14.

12. Satterthwaite, "Smith Island"; Meredith, *Account of the Cape Fear*; Powell, "Cape Fear"; Hugh F. Rankin, *The Golden Age of Piracy*, pp. 95-103.

13. Satterthwaite, "Smith Island"; Powell, "Cape Fear"; Hugh F. Rankin, *The Golden Age of Piracy*, pp. 95-103.

14. *Colonial Records*, I, 92; *Collection of State Papers*, VII, 70.

15. John F. Woolverton, *Colonial Anglicanism in North America, 1492-1873*, p. 168, hereinafter cited as Woolverton, *Colonial Anglicanism*.

16. Beth Crabtree, *North Carolina Governors 1585-1974*, pp. 20-21, hereinafter, Crabtree, *North Carolina Governors*.

17. *Colonial Records*, I, 571-572; Lefler and Newsome, *North Carolina*, p. 59; *State Records*, XXV, 151.

18. David T. Morgan, "Scandal in North Carolina," *North Carolina Historical Review*, XLVII, 3, 233-243, hereinafter cited as "Scandal in N.C."

19. Gerald Fethergill, *List of Emigrating Ministers to America 1690-1811*; Woolverton, *Colonial Anglicanism*; *Colonial Records*, I, 601; Charles Frederic Pascoe, *Two Hundred Years of the Society for the Propagation of the Gospel in Foreign Parts, 1700-1900*, Vol. I, hereinafter, Pascoe, *SPG*.

20. Morgan, "Scandal in N.C.," *NCHR*, XLVII, 3, 233-243; *Colonial Records*, I, 572, 715.

21. *State Records*, XXIII, 3-4; Lefler, *North Carolina*, p. 48.

22. Woolverton, *Colonial Anglicanism*, pp. 169-170.

23. Crabtree, *North Carolina Governors*, p. 33. Stanley South, "Some Notes on St. Philip's Anglican Church at Brunswick Town" in *NEWSLETTER* of Brunswick County Historical Society, VIII, 2 (May 1968).

24. Elizabeth Wellborn, "Reverend John LaPierre" in *NEWSLETTER* of Brunswick County Historical Society, IX, 3 (August 1969); Joseph B. Cheshire, Jr., *Sketches of Church History in North Carolina*, p. 66, hereinafter Cheshire, *Church History*.

25. *Sprunt, Chronicles*, pp. 38-40; Stanley South, *Colonial Brunswick*, p. 5.

26. Blackwell Robinson, *Five Royal Governors of North Carolina*, p. 7, hereinafter cited as Robinson, *Royal Governors*.

27. Sprunt, *Chronicles*, 38-40; Lee, *Lower Cape Fear*; Samuel A. Ashe, "Early Times on the Cape Fear," *North Carolina Booklet*, XIII, p. 152.

Chapter II: The Anglican Church Parish of St. James

1. *Colonial Records*, IV, 509-510.

2. Stanley South, *Colonial Brunswick*, p. 5; *Colonial Records*, IV, 510.

3. Lefler and Newsome, *North Carolina*, pp. 143-144; Beth Crabtree, *North Carolina Governors*, pp.32-33.

4. *Colonial Records*, III, 90-118.

5. *State Records*, XXIII, 3-4; 173, 174.

6. *Colonial Records*, IV, 529-553; Elizabeth Wellborn, "Reverend John LaPierre"; Cheshire, *Church History*, p. 36; Stanley South, "St. Philip's" in *NEWSLETTER*, VIII, 2.

7. This author was present at the unveiling of the LaPierre Historical Marker November 24, 1968.

8. Robinson, *Five Royal Governors*, p. 16; Lefler, *North Carolina*, pp. 33-34.

9. Robinson, *Five Royal Governors*, pp. 16-18; Morgan, "Scandal in N.C." *NCHR*, 1970, p. 237; "St. James Parish," Anniversary Booklet, 1939; Lefler, *North Carolina*, pp. 32-34.

10. *Colonial Records*, IV, 245; *NCHR*, 1950, 440; Morgan, *"Scandal in N.C.,"* *NCHR*, XLVII, 3 (July 1970).

11. *State Records*, XXIII, 146-148; Robinson, *Five Royal Governors*, pp. 12-14.

12. *State Records*, XXIII, 146-147.

13. Crabtree, *North Carolina Governors*, p. 34.

14. *Colonial Records*, IV, 606.

15. Fred A. Olds, "The Parishes of North Carolina," *North Carolina Booklet*, XXI, 81-89.

Chapter III: Saint Philip's Parish, 1741

1. *Colonial Records*, IV, 606-607; *State Records*, XXIII, 146-147.

2. Malcolm Ross, *The Cape Fear*, p. 43; *Colonial Records*, IV, 605-606; *State Records*, XXIII, 535-537.

3. *Colonial Records*, IV, 606-608, 621, 876-877; Sarah Lemmon, "Genesis of the Diocese of North Carolina," *NCHR*, 28 (1951) p. 441.

4. *Colonial Records*, VI, 710.

5. *Colonial Records*, IV, 877.

6. Crabtree, *North Carolina Governors*, pp. 35-38; *Colonial Records*, V, 3; Cheshire, *Sketches of Church History*, pp. 112-113.

7. *Colonial Records of North Carolina*; *Correspondence of Governor William Tryon*, Vol. I, 83; Desmond Clark, *Arthur Dobbs, Esquire*; Crabtree, *North Carolina Governors, 1585-1974*; Lawrence Lee, *History of Brunswick County*; Lefler and Newsome, *North Carolina*; Robinson, *Five Royal Governors*; Stanley South, *Colonial Brunswick*; "Russelboro: Two Royal Governors' Mansion," *NCHR*, XLIV, 4 (Autumn, 1967) pp. 360-372.

8. *Colonial Records*, VI, 32-33; South, "St. Philip's Anglican Church at Brunswick Town," *NEWSLETTER* of Brunswick County Historical Society, VIII, 2, hereinafter, South "St. Philip's Anglican Church."

9. *Colonial Records*, VI, 236.

10. Reverend John McDowell's letter to SPG, *Colonial Records*, VI, 236-237.

11. St. Philip's Church Wardens' letter to SPG, *Colonial Records*, VI, 232-233; South, "St. Philip's Church," *NEWSLETTER* of Brunswick County Historical Society, VII, 1 (February 1967).

12. Letter of John McDowell June 15, 1762, *Colonial Records*, VI, 729-730.

13. Malcolm Ross, *The Cape Fear*; South, "St. Philip's"; Lawrence Lee, "Old Brunswick," *NCHR*, 1952, p. 241.

14. Secretary of State Papers # 837; Legislative Papers 11.1 at North Carolina Archives.

15. Robinson, *Five Royal Governors*, pp. 47-51; South, "St. Philip's."

16. South, "Crisis at Brunswick Town", *NEWSLETTER*, V, 4; Robinson, *Five Royal Governors*, pp. 52-53.

17. *Correspondence of Governor William Tryon*, Vol. II, 364.

18. *Colonial Records*, VII, 103, 164, 515, 789.

19. *Correspondence of Governor William Tryon*, Vol. I, 83-85. For lack of ministers, justices of the peace married and buried people. There was no minister within a hundred miles when Governor Dobbs was buried.

20. Addison, *The Episcopal Church in the United States, 1789-1936*, p. 38.

21. *Correspondence of Governor William Tryon*, Vol. I, 228-229.

22. *Colonial Records*, VII, 161, 164.

23. *Colonial Records*, VII, 789-790.

24. Letter of John Barnett Aug. 22, 1767, to SPG.

25. *Colonial Records*, VII, 103; *SR*, IX, 21; Fred Olds, "The Parishes of North Carolina," *North Carolina Booklet*, Vol. 21, pp. 81-89.

26. South, "St. Philip's Church" in *NEWSLETTER* of Brunswick County Historical Society, VII, 1; Olds, "Parishes of North Carolina," *North Carolina Booklet*, Vol. 21, pp. 81-89.

27. Crabtree, *North Carolina Governors*, p. 42.

28. Letter of July 27, 1774, by Nicholas Christian; C. C. Crittenden, "Overland Travel and Transportation in North Carolina 1763-1789," *NCHR*, VIII (1931).

29. Robinson, *Five Royal Governors*, p. 63-74.

30. Crabtree, *North Carolina Governors*, p. 43.

31. Hugh Rankin, *North Carolina Continentals*, p. 9.

32. Robinson, *Five Royal Governors*, p. 70; Hugh Rankin *North Carolina Continentals*, pp. 9, 15.

33. *Colonial Records*, X, 335-336; *Virginia Gazette*, April 5, 1776.

34. Robinson, *Five Royal Governors*, p. 73; Crabtree; *North Carolina Governors*, p. 44.

35. Alonzo Dill, *Governor Tryon and His Palace*, p. 10; South, "St. Philip's at Brunswick," *NEWSLETTER*, VII, 1.

36. Crabtree, *Royal Governors*, p. 62.

37. Samuel Morison, *Oxford History of the American People*, p. 293; Cheshire, *Church History*, p. 88.

38. Addison, *Episcopal Church*, p. 38.

39. W. W. Sweet, *Religion on the American Frontier*, p. 9; George Troxler's review of Sarah Lemmon's "Parson Pettigrew of the Old Church," *NCHR*, 1971, 194-195.

40. Malcolm Ross, *Cape Fear*, p. 64.

41. *Colonial Records*, VI, 730; VII, 164.

42. Woolverton, *Colonial Anglicanism*, p. 190.

43. Frank Mead, *Handbook of Denominations*, p. 7.

44. Paschal, *History of North Carolina Baptists*, Vol. I, p. 323; M. A. Huggins, *History of North Carolina Baptists*, p. 408; Frederick Wees, *Colonial Clergy of Virginia, North Carolina, and South Carolina*, p. 64.

Chapter IV: Birth of Methodism in England; Advance to America

1. Maldwyn L. Edwards, *John Wesley*, pp. 3-5; E. T. Clark, *Charles Wesley*, pp. 1-10; Luke Tyerman, *Life and Times of John Wesley*; Frederick Maser, *Susanna Wesley*, p. 15.

2. Paul F. Douglas, "Methodism" in *Encyclopedia Americana* Vol. 18, 721-727; Edwards, *John Wesley*, p. 6; A. D. Betts, *Methodism in South Carolina*, pp. 11-41.

3. Clark, *Charles Wesley*, pp. 8-9.

4. Douglas, "Methodism"; W. W. Sweet, *Methodism in American History*; Nolan B. Harmon, *Organization of the Methodist Church*, pp. 13-15; Clark, *Charles Wesley*, p. 9.

5. Douglas, "Methodism"; Clark, *Charles Wesley*, p. 9; John R. Tyson, "Charles Wesley and Edward Young," *Methodist History*, Vol. 27, 2 (January 1989).

6. James M. Dudley, *History of Methodism*, p. 96.

7. Douglas, "Methodism."

8. M. Edwards, *John Wesley*, p. 10.

9. Francis Tees, *Beginning of Methodism*, pp. 50, 213, 214.

10. Warren Thomas Smith, *Thomas Coke*, p. 7.

11. Ibid., pp. 10-17.

12. Ibid., p. 18.

13. Rudolph, *Francis Asbury*, pp. 6-36; Francis Tees, *The Beginning of Methodism*, pp. 101-114. A few other writers have stated that the first society was in New York; A. D. Betts, in *Methodism*, p. 18, places the first American Methodist Society on the island of Antigua in the West Indies.

14. A. D. Betts, p. 33.

15. W. W. Sweet, *Religion on the American Frontier*, p. 6; Lee, *New Hanover County*, p. 21; Pilmore, *Journal*, January 1793.

16. Pilmore, *Journal*, February 1773. At Brusnwick the church was St. Philip's; "chief shepherd" was William Hill.

17. David Lovejoy, *Religious Enthusiasm and the Great Awakening*, p. 34; Wesley Gewehr, *The Great Awakening in Virginia 1740-1790*, p. 8; Betts, *History of South Carolina Methodism*, pp. 23-26; James McGraw, *Great Evangelistic Preachers of Yesteryear*, p. 61; Joseph Travis, *Autobiography*. Travis, the first Brunswick Circuit preacher, mentioned "New Lights" as disciples of the "great and good Mr. Whitefield."

18. Woolverton, *Colonial Anglicanism*, p. 190.

19. James M. Buckley, *History of Methodism*, p. 250; George Whitefield, *Journal*, p. 387.

20. Elmer Clark, *Francis Asbury*, p. 5; L. C. Rudolph, *Francis Asbury*, p. 26; Asbury, *Journal*, I, p. 3.

21. Introduction to the Asbury *Journal*, I, xi; Douglas, "Francis Asbury."

22. Clark, *Francis Asbury*, p. 4; Introduction to the Asbury *Journal*, I, xii; Asbury, *Journal*, September-October 1771.

23. Clark, *Francis Asbury*, pp. 4-5; Asbury, *Journal*, September-October 1771.

24. Letter dated April 27, 1988, to this author from David Eichelberger, Research Assistant, General Archives, Madison, N.J.

25. Asbury, *Journal*, I, pp. 6-7; Clark, *Francis Asbury*, p. 6.

Chapter V: The New Denomination, 1784; Southward, 1785

1. *Minutes of the Annual Conference of the Methodist Episcopal Church from 1773-1828.*

2. Asbury, *Journal*, March 1785; Reverend Thomas A. Smoot, "Early Methodism in the Lower Cape Fear," address to the North Carolina Conference Historical Society November 27, 1912.

3. Asbury, *Journal*, II, p. 494; A. M. Chreitzberg, *Early Methodism in the Carolinas*, pp. 216-217; Smoot, "Lower Cape Fear."

4. Lefler and Newsome, *North Carolina*, p. 244.

5. Malcolm Ross, *Cape Fear*, p. 64.

6. Stephen Daniel was a son of John Daniel, resident of Charleston, S.C. and benefactor of the Anglican Church there. In 1763 each son was bequeathed a plantation; Stephen's land was located at upper Town Creek.

7. Asbury, *Journal*, I, pp. 486-487 (March 1785).

8. W. L. Grissom, *History of Methodism in North Carolina*, pp. 219, 224; Jesse Lee, *History of Methodism*; Asbury, *Journal*, I, p. 486, (note).

Chapter VI: South Carolina District, Bladen Circuit, 1787

1. A. D. Betts, *History of South Carolina Methodism*, pp. 10, 70; E. O. Watson, *Methodism in South Carolina*.

2. *Minutes of the Methodist Conferences held in America 1773-1813*; Chreitzberg, *Early Methodism in the Carolinas*, p. 219; A. Deems, *Annals of Southern Methodism*, hereinafter, Deems, *Annals*.

3. A. D. Betts, *South Carolina Methodism*, p. 61.

4. *South Carolina Annual Conference Minutes*, 1788.

5. Ibid., 1789.

6. A. D. Betts, *South Carolina Methodism*, p. 63.

7. Chreitzberg, *Early Methodism*, p. 218.

8. Asbury, *Journal*, February 13, 1791. Charlotte River was later called Shallotte River.

9. Ibid., February 23, 1791.

10. *Minutes of the South Carolina Conference*, 1792; Chreitzberg, p. 219.

11. Grissom, *Methodism in North Carolina*, p. 219; D. K. Bennett, *Chronology of N.C.*, p. 97; Asbury in North Carolina, p. 230; Richard N. Price, *History of Holston Methodism*; E. T. Clark, *Methodism in Western North Carolina*, p. 41.

12. Asbury, *Journal*, December 30, 1793; the sick were Philip Bruce and Bishop Asbury.

13. Asbury, *Journal*, note on entry of December 30, 1793.

14. *Minutes of South Carolina Conference of 1794*.

15. The conferences of 1794 and 1795 convened on New Year's Day; also other conferences through 1803.

16. Asbury, *Journal*, December 19-21, 1795.

17. *South Carolina Conference Minutes*, 1796; Grissom, p. 221.

18. *South Carolina Conference Minutes*, 1796.

19. Asbury, *Journal*, December 22, 1796.

20. Ibid., February 8, 1803.

21. Ibid., February 15, 16, 1803.

22. Annette Reesnor, "History of the First United Methodist Church, Conway, South Carolina."

23. Journals of Asbury, Norman, and Lee, 1787-1850.

24. *South Carolina Conference Minutes*, 1801-1805; Jenkins, *Autobiography*; Grissom, *Methodism*; Chreitzberg, *Methodism*.

25. Chreitzberg, p. 222.

26. Asbury, *Journal*, January 1799.

27. Jesse Lee, *Journal*, January 1799, quoted in Minton Thrift's *Memoirs of the Reverend Jesse Lee*. This Courthouse was the earliest regular appointment in Brunswick County.

28. The name of the tavern owner appears in official records most frequently as "Bellune," but sometimes Belloon and Belon.

29. Jesse Lee, *Journal*, quoted in Thrift's *Memoirs of the Reverend Jesse Lee*, p. 247.

30. Asbury, *Journal*, January 1800.

31. *South Carolina Conference Minutes*, 1800.

32. Asbury, *Journal*, January 1800.

33. Chreitzberg, *Methodism*; Norman, *Journal*, January 1800.

34. *South Carolina Conference Minutes*, January 1800.

35. Jesse Lee *Journal*; Norman, *Journal*, February 1800.

36. Asbury, *Journal*, February and March 1801.

37. Ibid., II, p. 494.

38. Norman, *Journal*, Asbury, *Journal*, January 1800-1801.

39. *South Carolina Conference Minutes*, 1802; Asbury, *Journal*, January 1802.

40. This location is now Shallotte, Camp United Methodist Church.

41. Asbury, *Journal*, January and February 1802.

42. Ibid., February 1803.

43. *Minutes of the Conferences Held in America 1773-1813*.

44. *South Carolina Conference Minutes*, January 1804 and 1805; Asbury, *Journal*, II, 424; Betts, pp. 483, 484.

45. Asbury, *Journal*, February 6-10, 1804.

46. Ibid., February 12-15, 1804.

47. *South Carolina Conference Minutes of 1805*; Asbury, *Journal*, January 14, 1805. Fayetteville was then the meeting place of the North Carolina Legislature.

48. Asbury, *Journal*, January 17, 1805.

49. *South Carolina Conference Minutes*, December 1805 to January 1806; Asbury, *Journal*, December 1805 and January 1806.

50. *South Carolina Conference Minutes*, 1806, 1807.

Chapter VII: South Carolina Conference; Camden and Pee Dee Districts; Brunswick Circuit

1. Asbury, *Journal*, 1807; *South Carolina Conference Minutes*, 1807.

. Chreitzberg, *Early Methodism*; Betts, *Methodism*, pp. 133, 172.

3. Travis, *Autobiography*, pp. 33, 40, 41.

4. Chreitzberg, *Early Methodism*; Travis, *Autobiography*, pp. 41, 247; Betts, *South Carolina Methodism*.

5. Chreitzberg, "Early Methodism in Wilmington," *Historical Papers of Trinity College*, Series 1-8, p. 67.

6. Travis, *Autobiography*, p. 43.

7. Ibid., p. 44.

8. *South Carolina Conference Minutes*, 1807-1811.

9. Rudolph, *Francis Asbury*, p. 84.

10. Matthew H. Moore, *Sketches of Pioneers in Methodism*, p. 167.

11. *South Carolina Conference Minutes*, 1812-1815.

12. Asbury, *Journal*, January 18-20, 1815. (Asbury's final trip to Brunswick County, N.C.).

13. E. T. Clark, "Asbury's Last Journey" in *Journal*, II, pp. 804-807.

Chapter VIII: Bishop Asbury's Efforts on the Crescent

1. Asbury, *Journal*, 1785-1815.

2. Ibid., September 12, 1771.

3. Ibid., August 3, 1775.

4. Ibid., January 27, 1787.

5. Ibid., March 21, 1795.

6. Ibid., October 3, 1775.

7. Ibid., November 20, 1814.

8. Clark, "Asbury's Last Journey," *Journal*, II, p. 806.

9. *Methodist History*, IV, No. 1 (October 1965).

10. Frank Baker, *From Wesley to Asbury*, pp. 139-140.

11. Asbury, *Journal and Letters*, III, letter of July 3, 1793.

12. Clark, *Francis Asbury*, pp. 15-16.

13. Asbury, *Journal*, September 2, 1805.

14. *The First Discipline*, quoted in John O. Gross, *Beginning of American Methodism.*

15. James McGraw, *Great Evangelistic Preachers of Yesterday*, p. 74.

16. The Bible, I Timothy 1:15-16.

17. Asbury, *Journal and Letters*, III, pp. 472-473.

18. Ibid., III, p. 514.

19. President Calvin Coolidge, address at the Dedication of the Asbury Statue in Washington, D.C.

20. E. T. Clark, *Francis Asbury*, p. 19.

Chapter IX: Years after Bishop Asbury

1. Betts, pp. 158-169.

2. Travis, *Autobiography*; Betts, p. 175.

3. *South Carolina Conference Minutes*, 1818-1824.

4. *North Carolina Directory*, 1822-1823.

5. *South Carolina Conference Minutes*, 1812-1824.

6. Ibid.

7. Ibid.

8. *Life and Letters of James O. Andrew*, quoted in Betts' *History of South Carolina Methodism*, p. 142.

9. *South Carolina Conference Minutes*, 1825-1834.

10. Ibid.

11. Betts, pp. 174, 233; *South Carolina Conference Minutes*, 1873.

Chapter X: South Carolina Conference, Wilmington District Formed

1. *South Carolina Conference Minutes*, 1835-1842.

2. Ibid., 1842-1850.

3. Asbury, *Journal*, March 1785; Chreitzberg, p. 95; Will of John Daniel, 1763, Brunswick County Deeds Registry.

4. Joseph Travis, *Autobiography*; Asbury, *Journal.*

5. Short, *United Methodism in Theory and Practice*, p. 192.

6. Knox, "History of Zion Methodist Church."

7. *Smithville Circuit Record for 1847.*

8. *South Carolina Conference Minutes*, 1849.

9. Ibid.

Chapter XI: The Transfer Debate and Decision 1850

1. *General Conference, Methodist Episcopal Church, South, Minutes*, May 1850.

2. *South Carolina Conference Minutes*, December 1850.

3. Ibid.

Chapter XII: Recapitulatory Records to Reconstruction

1. *South Carolina Conference Minutes*, 1803-1850.

2. *South Carolina Conference Minutes*, 1787-1850.

3. *South Carolina Conference Minutes*, 1787-1850.

4. *South Carolina Conference Minutes*, 1788-1850.

5. *South Carolina Conference Minutes*, 1843.

6. Miscellaneous selections from the manifold sources listed in the Bibliography.

Chapter XIII: North Carolina Conference, Wilmington District

1. *North Carolina Conference Minutes*, 1850-1851.

2. *Smithville Circuit Record 1851*; Sallie Betts Knox, "History of Zion Methodist Church"; Chreizberg, p. 293.

3. *U. S. Census, North Carolina, Brunswick County, 1850*.

4. *North Carolina Conference Minutes*, 1850 through 1860.

5. *Smithville Circuit Record*, 1858.

6. *Smithville Circuit Record*, 1859.

7. Memoirs of Dr. A. D. Betts, *North Carolina Conference Journal*; William A. Betts, ed., *Rev. A. D. Betts, Experiences of a Confederate Chaplain.*

8. *North Carolina Conference Minutes*, 1861 through 1865.

9. Knox, "History of Zion Methodist Church."

10. *Wilmington District Conference Record Book*, 1866.

11. *North Carolina Conference Minutes*, 1866-1867.

12. *Wilmington District Record Book*, 1868.

13. *North Carolina Conference Minutes*, 1868 through 1878.

14. *North Carolina Conference Minutes*, 1872.

15. *Wilmington District Conference Minutes*, 1876.

16. Ibid., 1876, 1878, 1879.

17. Ormand, *The Country Churches in North Carolina.*

18. *North Carolina Conference Minutes*, 1879, 1881, 1908; Wilmington District Record for 1881 (unpublished manuscript).

19. Ibid., 1890.

20. Ibid., 1891.

21. Knox, "History of Zion Methodist Church"; Report of R. W. Bailey to Wilmington District Conference August 7, 1901.

197

22. *North Carolina Conference Minutes*, 1879 through 1898.

23. *North Carolina Legislative Record*, March 4, 1887.

24. *North Carolina Conference Minutes*, 1889, 1898, 1899.

25. *North Carolina Conference Minutes*, 1899, 1900, 1901.

26. *South Carolina Conference Minutes*, 1812-1850.

27. *North Carolina Conference Minutes*, 1851-1865.

28. *North Carolina Conference Minutes*, 1874-1894.

29. *North Carolina Conference Minutes*, 1887-1894; "History of New Hope Methodist Church" in the Manuscript Room, Perkins Library, Duke University.

30. Charles Force Deems was presiding elder of Wilmington District 1858 through 1861. He had organized the mission Church of the Strangers for regional expatriates in New York.

31. Roy Short, *United Methodism in Theory and Practice*, p. 194.

32. *Wilmington District Conference Minutes*, 1875; W. W. Sweet and Umphrey Lee, *Short History of Methodism*.

33. A. D. Betts, *History of South Carolina Methodism*, pp. 160-161.

34. James Jenkins, *Autobiography*, pp. 146-147.

35. Joseph Travis, *Autobiography*, pp. 280-281.

Chapter XIV: Brunswick County's Methodist Classes, Local Preachers, Churches, Ministers to 1950.

1. Wilmington District Conference Records, 1838-1950; *North Carolina Conference Minutes*, 1901-1951.

2. Brunswick County Registry of Deeds, 1897.

3. *North Carolina Business Directory, 1914*

4. *North Carolina Conference Minutes*, 1910, 1920, 1930.

5. *Wilmington District Conference Minutes*, 1901.

6. Ibid.

7. Ibid.

8. Ibid.

9. *North Carolina Conference Minutes*, 1859, 1944.

10. Ibid., 1954-1973.

11. Ibid., 1901-1950.

12. *North Carolina Conference Journals*, 1947-1988.

Chapter XV: Churches and Ministers after 1950.

1. All appointments are listed from the *North Carolina Conference Journal* for each year. *Quarterly Conference Records*, 1888-1988, give supplementary information.

2. *The Book of Discipline*, 1984, pp. 16-18; Armstrong, *United Methodist Primer*, p. 26.

3. *Wilmington District Directory*, 1988.

4. *North Carolina Conference Journals*, 1878, 1881, 1908, 1988.

5. Asbury letter of January 29, 1813, *Journal and Letters*, III, 469.

6. *South Carolina Conference Minutes*, 1787-1850.

7. *North Carolina Conference Journals*, 1850-1988.

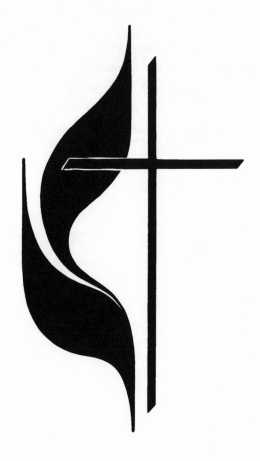

Bibliography

I. **Manuscripts, Unpublished Papers and Records**

Chreitzburg, A. M. "Early Methodism in Wilmington" in *Historical Papers* collected by the Historical Society of Trinity College, Series 1-8.

Davidson, Elizabeth H. "The Establishment of the English Church in the Continental American Colonies" in *Historical Papers* collected by the Trinity College Historical Society, Series XX.

Boyd, William K. "Methodist Expansion in North Carolina after the Revolution," an address to the North Carolina Conference Historical Society meeting at Wilmington, N.C., November 30, 1915. Treasure Room, Perkins Library, Duke University.

Brunswick County Grants and Deeds Registry 1764-1800. Brunswick County Government Complex, Bolivia, N.C.

Grissom, W. L. "Some First Things in North Carolina Methodism." *Duke University Historical Papers*, Vol. 9, p. 22-32.

Kirby, Samuel. "History of Sharon Methodist Church," Manuscript in collection of local church histories, Manuscript Room, Perkins Library, Duke University.

Lee, Lawrence E. "The History of Brunswick, North Carolina, the Political and Economic Development of a Colonial Town." Thesis (M.A.) University of North Carolina, Chapel Hill, N.C. 1951.

Legislative Papers #11.1, State Archives, Raleigh, N.C.

Minutes Book of the Brunswick Circuit, 1879.

New Hanover Grants and Deeds Registry to 1764. New Hanover Courthouse, Wilmington, N.C.

Norman, Jeremiah. *Diary*, Section 18. Manuscript in Stephen B. Weeks Papers 1748-1913, Southern Historical Collection, University of North Carolina, Chapel Hill, N.C.

North Carolina Secretary of State Papers #837, North Carolina State Archives, Raleigh, N.C.

North Carolina Secretary of State Land Grant Records for the Cape Fear Area 1728-1800. Raleigh, N.C.

Norton, J. A. "The Narrative of Horry County." Typescript located in Horry County Library, Conway, South Carolina.

Reesnor, Annette E. "A History of the First United Methodist Church of Conway." Typescript of notes of Carl Sessions, Conway, South Carolina. Library of the First United Methodist Church, in Conway, South Carolina.

Smithville Circuit *Quarterly Conference Record Book*, 1851-1890. Original record at Zion United Methodist Church, Leland, N.C.

Smithville *Circuit Record* 1858-1859 in Betts Papers No. 3173, Southern Historical Collection, UNC, Chapel Hill, N.C.

Wilmington District Conference *Records of Minutes* 1866-1897. Manuscript Room. Perkins Library, Duke University.

Wilmington District Conference *Record of Minutes* 1898-1950. Manuscript, N.C. Conference Archives, Raleigh.

II.   Published Official Records

Clark, Walter, ed. *The State Records of North Carolina*, 16 vols. Goldsboro, N.C., Winston, N.C. 1895-1914. Vol. 23, Vol. 25.

Minutes of the Methodist Conferences Held in America 1773-1813, Inclusive. Philadelphia, Tuckniss, 1795.

Minutes of the Anuual Conferences of the Methodist Episcopal Church from 1773-1828. New York, Mason and Love, 1840.

Minutes of the General Conference of the Methodist Episcopal Church, South, at St. Louis 1850.

Minutes of the South Carolina Conferences of the Methodist Episcopal Church 1787-1844.

Minutes of the South Carolina Conferences of the Methodist Episcopal Church, South, 1844-1851.

Minutes of the North Carolina Conferences of the Methodist Episcopal Church, South, 1850-1939.

Minutes of the North Carolina Conferences of the Methodist Church 1939-1967.

Minutes of the North Carolina Conference of the United Methodist Church 1968-1988.

Parker, Mattie Erma, ed. *North Carolina Charters and Constitutions*1578-1698. Raleigh: Carolina Charter Tercentenary Commission, 1963.

Saunders, William L. ed. *The Colonial Records of North Carolina*, 10 Vols. Raleigh: Hale, 1886. Vols. I, VII, X.

Thompson, Doris L., compiler. *Federal Census of Brunswick County, North Carolina, for 1850*. New Bern: Owen Dunn, 1977.

Wilmington District Directory 1988-1989 Compiled by Dr. Samuel D. McMillan.

III. Articles in Journals and Periodicals

Asbury, R. V. "Belvedere Plantation." *NEWSLETTER* of Brunswick County Historical Society Vol VI. No. 1 (February 1966).

Ashe, Samuel A. "Early Times on the Cape Fear." Address to North Carolina Society of Colonial Dames at Brunswick Town. *North Carolina Booklet XIII.*

Baker, Frank. "Early American Methodism: a Key Document." *Methodist History*, Vol. VIII, No. 2. (January 1965) pp. 3-15.

Bull, Robert J. "John Wesley Bond's Reminscences of Francis Asbury." *Methodist History IV*, No. 1. (October 1965) pp. 3-33.

Crittendon, C. C. "Overland Travel and Transportation in North Carolina 1763-1789." *North Carolina Historical Review*, Vol. 8 (July 1931) 239-257.
----"Means of Communications in North Carolina 1763-1789." *North Carolina Historical Review* Vol. 8 (October 1931) 373-383.

Douglas, Paul F. "Methodism." *Encyclopedic Americana* Vol. 18, 721-727.

Galloway, Frank. "Courthouse at Lockwood's Folly." *NEWSLETTER* of Brunswick County Historical Society XXVII, No. 3 (May 1986).

Keever, Homer M. "The Methodist Church of 1866 in North Carolina." *Methodist History XX*, No. 4 (July 1982).

Knox, Sallie Betts. "History of Zion Methodist Church." *NEWSLETTER* of Brunswick County Historical Society IV, No. 2 (May 1964).

Lee, Lawrence E. "Old Brunswick, the Story of a Colonial Town." *North Carolina Historical Review* XXIX, No. 2 (April 1952) 230-245.

Lower Cape Fear Historical Society Bulletins, I, XVI, XIX.

McIver, Colin. *North Carolina Directory and U.S. Calendar,* "Brunswick County Local Methodist Preachers" quoted in *NEWSLETTER* of Brunswick County Historical Society XV, No. 3. (October 1975).

Martin, Mrs. M. "The New Church in Wilmington." In *Methodism, Christianity in Earnest*, bound volume, 1855. Manuscript Room, Perkins Library, Duke University.

Mintz, Rudolph I. "Court Houses—Brunswick County." *Bicentennial Brunswick County, North Carolina.* Brunswick County Historical Society, 1964.

Mitchell, Joseph. "Southern Newspapers During the Civil War." *Methodist History* II, No. 2, p. 20.

Morgan, David T. Jr. "The Great Awakening in North Carolina 1740-1775: The Baptist Phase." *North Carolina Historical Review* XLV, No. 3 (July 1968) 264-283.

Olds, Fred A. "The Parishes of North Carolina." *North Carolina Booklet,* Vol. 21, 81-89.

Powell, William S. "Settlement of the Cape Fear." *NEWSLETTER* of Brunswick County Historical Society XIV, No. 4 (November 1974).

"Saint James Parish." *Program Booklet,* Saint James Parish Anniversary, 1939, New Hanover Public Library, North Carolina Room.

Satterthwaite, Dr. Sheaf. "A Brief History of Smith Island." *NEWSLETTER* of Brunswick County Historical Society V, No. 3 (August 1965).

Schell, Edwin, Comp. "Methodist Traveling Preachers in America 1773-1799." *Methodist History* II, 2 (January 1964).

Smoot, Thomas A. "Early Methodism on the Lower Cape Fear." Address to the North Carolina Conference Historical Society at Fayetteville, November 27, 1912. *Historical Papers* of the North Carolina Conference Historical Society, Duke University.

South Carolina Gazette article "Brunswick in North Carolina," September 23, 1748; quoted in *NEWSLETTER* of Brunswick County Historical Society III, No. 3 (August 1963).

South, Stanley A. " 'Russelboro: Two Royal Governors' Mansion at Brunswick Town." *North Carolina Historical Review* XLIV, No. 4 (Autumn 1967) 360-372.

South, Stanley A. for Brunswick County Historical Society *NEWS-LETTER:* "A Crisis in Brunswick Town" (Vol. V, No. 4); "Excavating the Royal Governors' Mansion at Brunswick Town" (Vol. VI, No. 2, No. 3); "Saint Philip's at Brunswick Town" (Vol. VII, No. 1); "Some Notes on Saint Philip's Anglican Church at Brunswick Town" (Vol. VIII, No. 2).

Troxler, George, reviewer, Sarah M. Lemmon's "Parson Pettigrew of the Old Church." *North Carolina Historical Review XLVIII,* 194-195.

Tyson, John R. "Charles Wesley and Edward Young." *Methodist History* 27:2 (January 1989.)

Vigneras, L. A. "A Spanish Discovery of North Carolina." *North Carolina Historical Review* XLVI, 398-414.

Wilborn, Elizabeth. "Reverend John LaPierre." *NEWSLETTER* of Brunswick County Historical Society IX, No. 3. August 1969.

Wright, J. Leitch, Jr. "Spanish Reaction to North Carolina." *North Carolina Historical Review* XLI, No. 4.

IV. Books

Addison, James Thayer. *The Episcopal Church in the United States 1789-1936.* New York: Charles Scribner's Sons, 1951.

Armstrong, James Edward. *History of the Old Baltimore Conference from the Planting of Methodism in 1773 to the Division of the Conference in 1857.* Baltimore: King Brothers, 1907.

Armstrong, James. *The United Methodist Primer.* Nashville: Tidings, 1972.

Asbury, Francis. *The Journal and Letters.* 3 vols. Editors Elmer T. Clark, J. Manning Potts, Jacob S. Payton. Nashville: Abington, 1958.

Asbury, Francis. *Francis Asbury in North Carolina.* Portions of I and II of Clark Edition of the *Journal.* Introductory notes by Grady L. E. Carrol. Nashville: Parthenon Press, 1964.

Ashe, Samuel A. *Biographical History of North Carolina.* 8 vols. Greensboro: C. L. Van Noppen, 1905-1917.

-----*History of North Carolina*, 2 volumes, Vol. I. Greensboro: Charles L. Van Noppen, 1908-1925.

Ayers, Samuel G. *Methodist Heroes of Other Days.* New York: Methodist Book Concern, 1916.

Baker, Frank. *From Wesley to Asbury: Studies in Early American Methodism.* Durham: Duke University Press, 1976.

Bangs, Nathan. *A History of the Methodist Episcopal Church.* 3 Vols. Vol. I. New York: Mason and Lane, 1839, 1840. In Special Collection, Wofford College.

Barclay, Wade C. *Early American Methodism*, 1769-1844, 2 vols. New York: Board of Missions, Methodist Episcopal Church, 1949-50.

Beckley, James M. *History of Methodism*, 2 Vols. Vol. I. New York: Harper, 1898.

Belden, Albert D. *George Whitefield, the Awakener.* London: Rockliff, 1930.

Betts, Albert Deems. *History of South Carolina Methodism,* Columbia: The Advocate Press, 1952.

Betts, W. A., ed. *Experiences of a Confederate Chaplain, 1961-65.* Greenville, S.C.

Billingsby, A. S. *Life of George Whitefield.* New York: John Balden, 1889.

Biographical Directory of Methodist Ministers. New York: Scarecrow Press, 1965.

Bolton, Herbert E. and Thomas M. Marshall *The Colonization of North America, 1492-1783.* New York: McMillan, 1936.

Boykin, James H. *North Carolina in 1861.* New York: Bookman Association, 1961.

Branscom, Levi. *North Carolina Business Directory,* 1867-68. Raleigh: J. A. Jones, 1968.

Brickell, John. *The Natural History of North Carolina.* Dublin, 1743. Edited by J. B. Grimes and reprinted, Raleigh, 1911.

Buckley, James M. *History of Methodism,* 2 Vols. New York: Harper, 1898.

Burkhead, L. S., ed. *Centennial of Methodism in North Carolina.* Raleigh: Nichols, 1876.

Calhoon, Robert M. *Religion and the American Revolution in North Carolina.* Raleigh: N. C. Department of Cultural Resources, Division of Archives and History, 1976.

Cameron, Richard M. *The Rise of Methodism: A Sourcebook.* New York: Philosophical Library, 1954.

Carter, Henry. *The Methodist Heritage.* New York: Abington, 1951.

Cheshire, Joseph B. Jr. *Sketches of Church History in North Carolina.* Wilmington, N.C.: W. L. DeRosset, Jr., 1892.

Chitwood, H. C. *A History of Colonial America.* New York: Harper and Brothers, 1948.

Clark, Desmond. *Arthur Dobbs, Esquire.* Chapel Hill: UNC Press, 1951.

Clark, Elmer T. *Charles Wesley.* Lake Junaluska: Commission on Archives and History of the United Methodist Church, 1976.

------*Methodism in Western North Carolina,* Historical Society of the Western North Carolina Conference, 1966.

------*Francis Asbury.* Madison, New Jersey: Commission on Archives and History of the United Methodist Church, 1984.

Cliffe, Albert W. *The Glory of Our Methodist Heritage*. Nashville: General Board of Evangelism of the Methodist Church, 1956.

Coke, Thomas. *Extracts from the Journal of the Late Thomas Coke*. Dublin: Methodist Book Room, 1816.

Corbett, David L. *The Formation of North Carolina Counties, 1663-1943*. Raleigh: State Department of Archives and History, 1950.

Crabtree, Beth G. *North Carolina Governors 1585-1974*. Raleigh: Division of Archives and history, Department of Cultural Resources, 1974.

Dallimore, Arnold A. *Life and Times of the Great George Whitefield*. London: Banner of Truth Trust, 1970.

Daniels, W. H. *The Illustrated History of Methodism*. New York: Methodist Book Concern, 1879.

Deems, Albert. *Annals of Southern Methodism for 1857*. Nashville: J. B. McFerrin, Agent, 1858.

DePuy, W. H., ed. *The Methodist Centennial year Book for 1884*. New York: Phillips and Hunt, 1883.

Dill, Alonzo Thomas. *Governor Tryon and His Palace*. Chapel Hill: UNC Press, 1955.

Doyle, J. A. *English Colonization in America*. New York: Holt, 1889.

Dubose, Horace M. *Francis Asbury: A Biographical Study*. Nashville: Publishing House of the Methodist Episcopal Church, South, 1909.

Duncan, Norman C. *Pictorial History of the Episcopal Church in North Carolina*. Asheville, N.C.: Miller Printing Co., 1965.

Duncan, Watson B. *Twentieth Century Sketches*. Columbia, S.C.: The State Co., 1901.

Dunn, Gordon E. and B. I. Miller. *Atlantic Hurricanes*. Baton Rouge, La.: LSU Press, 1960.

Edwards, Maldwyn L. *John Wesley*. Lake Junaluska, N.C.: Commission on Archives and History of the United Methodist Church, 1976.

Eure, Thad. *North Carolina Manual, 1955*. Winston-Salem: Winston Printing Co. (n.d.)

Fethergill, Gerald. *List of Emigrant Minsiters to America 1690-1811*. London: E. Stock, 1904.

Finley, Hugh. *Journal Kept by Hugh Finley*. Brooklyn: F. H. Norton, 1867.

Flood, Theodore. *Lives of Methodist Bishops*. New York: Phillips and Hunt, 1882.

Freeman, Harlon L. *Francis Asbury's Silver Trumpet: Nicholas Snethen*. Nashville: Parthenon Press, 1950.

Gewehr, Wesley M. *The Great Awakening in Virginia, 1740-1790*, Gloucester, Mass.: Peter Smith, 1965.

Godbald, Albea. *Forever Beginning: 1766-1966*. Lake Junaluska, N.C.: Association of Methodist Historical Societies, 1967.

Gorrie, Peter D. *The Lives of Eminent Methodist Ministers*. New York: Miller, Orton, and Mulligan, 1856.

Grill, C. F. *Methodism in the Upper Cape Fear Valley*. Nashville: Parthenon, 1966.

Grissom, W. L. *History of Methodism in North Carolina*, Vol. I. Nashville: Publishing House of the Methodist Episcopal Church, South. 1905.

Gross, John O. *The Beginning of American Methodism*. Nashville: Abington Press, 1961.

Harmon, Nolan B. ed. *Encyclopedia of World Methodism*. Nashville: United Methodist Publishing House, 1974.

Harmon, Nolan B. *The Organization of the Methodist Church*. Nashville: Abington, 1953.

Hawks, Francis L. *History of North Carolina*, Vol. I. Fayetteville, N.C.: n.p., 1859.

Hazard, Ebenezer. *Journal*. Extracts in *North Carolina Historical Review* Vol. LIX (1959) pp. 359-381.

Hedges, John W. *Crowned Victors: The Memoirs of over 400 Methodist Preachers*. Baltimore: Methodist Episcopal Book Depository, 1878.

Henry, Stuart C. *George Whitefield, Wayfaring Witness*. Nashville: Abington, 1957.

Holy Bible, King James Version. Philadelphia: The John C. Winston Co. (n.d.)

Huff, Archie Vernon, Jr. *United Methodist Ministers of South Carolina*. Columbia, S.C.: Annual Conference, 1984.

Howell, C. T. *Prominent Personalities in American Methodism* Birmingham, Ala.: Lowry Press, 1945.

Huggins, M. A. *A History of North Carolina Baptists*. Raleigh: General Board of Baptist State Convention, 1967.

Hyde, A. *The Story of Methodism*. Springfield, Mass.: Willey and Co., 1888.

Jackson, Thomas. *The Lives of Early Methodist Preachers*, Vol. I. London: Wesleyan Conference Office, 1865-66.

Jenkins, James. *Experiences, Labours, and Sufferings of Reverend James Jenkins*. Printed for the author, 1842 (n.p.)

Joyner, Charles. *Down by the Riverside*. Urbana and Chicago: University of Illinois Press, 1984.

Lawson, John. *A History of North Carolina*. London, 1709, 1714. Reprinted, Charlotte Observer Printing House, 1903.

Lee, Jesse. *A Short History of Methodists in the United States of America, 1766-1809*. Baltimore: Magill and Cline, 1810.

Lee, Lawrence, *A History of Brunswick County North Carolina*. Brunswick County Bicentennial Commission, 1978.

------*Indian Wars in North Carolina*. Raleigh: The Carolina Charter. Tercentenary Commission, 1963.

------*Lower Cape Fear in Colonial Days*. Chapel Hill: UNC Press, 1965.

------*New Hanover County: A Brief History*. Raleigh: State Department of Archives and History, 1971.

Lee, Leroy M. *The Life and Times of Reverend Jesse Lee*. Louisville: John Early for Methodist Episcopal Church, South, 1848.

Lefler, Hugh T., ed. *North Carolina History: Told by Contemporaries*. Chapel Hill: University of North Carolina Press, 1965.

Lefler, Hugh T. and Albert Newsome. *North Carolina: The History of a Southern State*. Chapel Hill: University of North Carolina Press, 1954-1973.

Lennon, Donald R. and Ida Brooks Kellam, eds. *The Wilmington Town Book*, 1743-1778. Raleigh: Division of Archives and History, N.C. Department of Cultural Resources, 1973.

Lovejoy, David S. *Religious Enthusiasm and the Great Awakening*. Englewood Cliffs, N.J.: Prentice Hall, 1969.

McCrady, Edward. *History of South Carolina under the Royal Government*. New York: McMillan, 1899.

McCutchan, Robert G. *Our Hymnody*, 2nd edition. Nashville: Abington, 1937.

McGraw, James. *Great Evangelical Preachers of Yesterday*. Nashville: Abington, 1961.

McIntyre, Holland. *A History of Methodism*. Nashville: Barbee and Smith, 1892.

Manross, William W. *A History of the American Episcopal Church*. New York: Morehouse-Gorham, 1959.

Maser, Frederick E. *Susanna Wesley*. Lake Junaluska, N.C. Commission on Archives and History, United Methodist Church, 1976.

Mead, Frank S. *Handbook of Denominations*, 6th ed. Nashville: Abington, 1979.

Meredith, Hugh. *An Account of the Cape Fear Country, 1731*. Perth Amboy, N.J.: Charles Heartman, 1912.

Mood, F. A. *Methodism in Charleston*. Nashville: Stevenson, 1856.

Moore, Matthew H. *Sketches of the Pioneers in Methodism in North Carolina and Virginia*. Nashville: Southern Methodist Publishing House, 1884.

Morison, Samuel E. *The European Discovery of America*. New York: Oxford Press, 1971.

------*The Oxford History of the American People*. New York: Oxford Press, 1965.

Norwood, Frederick A. *The Story of American Methodism*. Nashville: Abington Press, 1974.

Nunez, Alvar. *Relation of Nunez Cobeza de Vaca*, Translation of the Spanish record published in 1542. Ann Arbor, Michigan: University Microfilms, Inc. 1966.

Ormond, Jesse M. *The Country Church in North Carolina*. Durham: Duke University Press, 1931.

Oviedo y Valde, Gonzalo Fernandes de (historian of the Indies) *Historia General y Natural de las Indias Occidentales*. Spain 1535; republished by Academy of History 1851-1855.

Paine, Robert. *Life and Times of William McKendree, Bishop of the Methodist Episcopal Church*, 2 vols. Nashville: Southern Methodist Publishing House, 1869.

Parker, Mattie Erma. *Money Problems of Early Tar Heels*, 3rd ed. Raleigh: State Department of Archives and History, 1951.

------, ed. *North Carolina Charters and Constitutions*. Raleigh: Carolina Charter Tercentenary Commission, 1963.

Paschal, George W. *History of North Carolina Baptists*, Vol 1. Raleigh: General Board of North Carolina Baptist State Convention, 1930.

Pascoe, Charles Frederick. *Two Hundred Years of the Society for the Propagation of the Gospel in Foreign Parts* 1701-1900, Vol. 1, London, SPG Offices, 1901.

Phoebus, William. *Beams of Light on Early Methodism*. New York, 1887.

210

------*Memoirs of the Reverend Richard Whatcoat*. New York: Joseph Allen, 1828.

Pilmore, Joseph. *Journal*, Editors F. E. Maser and H. T. Maag. Philadelphia: Message Publishing Company, 1969, for the Historical Society of Philadelphia Annual Conference.

Pollock, John. *George Whitefield and the Great Awakening*. Garden City: Doubleday, 1972.

Price, Richard N. *History of Holston Methodism*, 5 Vols. Nashville, 1912.

Porter, Reverend James. *A Compendium of Methodism*. Boston: Rand, 1853.

Powell, William S. *The North Carolina Colony*. New York: Crowell-Collier Press, 1969.

Quattlebaum, Paul. *The Land Called Chicora: Carolinas under Spanish Rule 1520-1670*. Gainesville: University of Florida, 1956.

Rankin, Hugh F. *The North Carolina Continentals*. Chapel Hill: U.N.C. Press, 1971.

------*The Golden Age of Piracy*. Colonial Williamsburg, 1969. Distributed by Holt, Rinehart & Winston, New York.

Robinson, Blackwell P. *Five Royal Governors of North Carolina 1729-1775*. Raleigh: Carolina Charter Tercentenary Commission, 1963.

Rogers, George C., Jr. *The History of Georgetown County, South Carolina*. Columbia: USC Press, 1970.

Rose, Harold W. *The Colonial Houses of Worship*. New York: Hastings House, 1964.

Ross, Malcolm. *The Cape Fear*. New York: Holt, Rinehart, and Winston, 1965.

Rouse, Jordan K. *Some Interesting Colonial Churches in North Carolina*. Kannapolis, N.C.: 1961.

Rudolph, L. C. *Francis Asbury*. Nashville: Abington, 1966.

Sauer, Carl O. *Sixteenth Century North America*. University of California, 1971.

Semmel, Bernard. *The Methodist Revolution*. New York: Basic Books, 1973.

Shipp, Albert M. *The History of Methodism in South Carolina*. Nashville: Southern Methodist Publishing House, 1884.

Short, Roy H. *United Methodism in Theory and Practice*. Nashville: Abington, 1974

211

Shuler, Frank E. *The Methodist Fact Book*. Evanston, Ill.: Council on World Service, 1962-64.

Simpson, Matthew, ed. *Cyclopedia of Methodism*, Philadelphia: Everts, 1881.

Smith, G. G. *History of Methodism in Georgia and Florida*. Macon, Georgia: J. W. Burke and Co., 1877.

Smith, John A. *Cross and Flame*. Nashville: Parthenon, 1984.

Smith, K. L. *The Church and the Churches*. London: SCM Press, 1948.

Smith, Warren T. *Thomas Coke*. Lake Junaluska, N.C.: Commission on Archives and History of the United Methodist Church, 1976.

South, Stanley. *Colonial Brunswick*. Raleigh: State Department of Archives and History, 1960.

Sprague, William B. *Annals of the American Methodist Pulpit*. New York: Robert Carter and Brothers, 1861.

Sprunt, James. *Chronicles of the Cape Fear River*. Raleigh: Edwards and Broughton, 1914.

------Ed. *James Sprunt Historical Publications*, Vol. 9. Raleigh: *North Carolina Historical Review*, 1910.

Stevens, A. *Memorials of the Introduction of Methodism in the United States*. New York: Scott and Lane, 1849.

Stephens, Emory, ed. *The History of American Methodism*. New York: Abington Press, 1964.

Summers, Thomas O. *Biographical Sketches of Eminent Itinerant Ministers*. Nashville: Southern Methodist Publishing House, 1859.

Sweet, W. W. "Methodism's Debt to the Church of England" in *Methdoism* edited by William Anderson. Nashville: Methodist Publishing House.

------*Methodism in American History*. Nashville: Abington Press, 1954 revised edition.

------*Religion on the American Frontier* 1783-1840, Vol. II. New York: Cooper Square Publishers, 1964.

Tees, Francis H. *The Beginnings of Methodism in England and in America*. Nashville: Parthenon, 1940.

Thrift, Minton. *Memoirs of the Reverend Jesse Lee, with Extracts from His Journals*. New York: Bangs and Mason, 1823.

Tigert, John J. *A Constitutional History of American Episcopal Methodism*. Nashville: Publishing House of the Methodist Episcopal Church, South, 1904

Tipple, Ezra S. *Francis Asbury, the Prophet of the Long Road.* New York: Methodist Book Concern, 1916.

Travis, Joseph. *Autobiography.* Nashville: E. Stevenson and J. E. Evans, agents for the Methodist Episcopal Church, South, 1856.

Tryon, William. *Correspondence of Governor William Tryon,* Vols. 1 & 2 Raleigh: Division of Archives and History, Department of Cultural Resources, 1980.

Tyerman, Luke. *Life and Times of John Wesley.* New York, 1870.

United Methodist Church. *Lost Chapters Recovered from the Early History of American Methodists.* New York: Carlton and Porter, 1858.

------*The Book of Discipline 1984.* Nashville: United Methodist Publishing House, 1984.

Vickers, John. *Thomas Coke, Apostle of Methodism.* Nashville: Abington Press, 1969.

Waddell, Alfred M. *History of New Hanover County* 1725-1800. Wilmington, N.C.: Privately printed, 1909.

Walser, Richard. *Literary North Carolina,* Raleigh: Department of Archives and History, 1970, pp. 1-6.

Watson, E. O. *Methodism in South Carolina,* 1785-1935. Columbia, S.C.: 1936.

Wesley, John. *A Collection of Hymns for the Use of the People Called Methodists.* London: Wesleyan Conference Office, 1780.

------*Sunday Service of the Methodists in North America.* London, 1784. Rare Book Room, Duke University.

Wees, Frederick L. *Colonial Clergy of Virginia, North Carolina, South Carolina.* Baltimore: Genealogical Publishing Co., 1976.

Who's Who in American Methodism, Elmer T. Clark, Editor in Charge for Association of Methodist Historical Societies U.S.A.

Woolverton, John Frederick. *Colonial Anglicanism in North America.* Detroit: Wayne State University, 1984.

V. Atlases, Maps, Gazetteers

Cumming, W. P. *North Carolina in Maps*. Raleigh, N.C.: State Department of Archives and History, 1966.

Fite, Esmond D. and Archibald Freeman, compilers and editors. *A Book of Old Maps Delineating American History*. New York: Dover Publications, 1969.

Powell, William S. *The North Carolina Gazetteer*. Chapel Hill: UNC Press, 1968.

United States Coast and Geodetic Survey by U.S. Corps of Engineers 1934-1936. Shoreline of North Carolina and South Carolina.

Miscellaneous Maps of Brunswick County and of North Carolina.

Index

216

217

218

222

New Hope Circuit, 54
New Lights, 31, 37
New Town, Newton, 15, 19, 124
Newell, Joshua, 93
Newton, Joseph, 28
Newton, J. A., 141
Newton, J. R., 141
Newton, W. J., 141
Nicholson, David B., 103, 168
Norman, Aquila, 93
Norman, Jeremiah, 68, 69, 73
Norris, Kermit, 162
North, H. M., 170
North, W. B., 138
North Carolina Anti-Saloon League, 155, 156
North Carolina Conference, 97, 103, 104, 105, 135, 139, 142
North Carolina Christian Advocate, 139
North Carolina Province, 84
North Carolina University, 127
Northcuth, David, 165
Northeast Cape Fear River, 72
Norton, James, 79, 80, 108
Norton, John W., 92, 93

Ocean View, 166, 182
O'Kelly, James, 55, 59
Old Brunswick County Courthouse, 137
Old Forge, 51
Oliver, James R., 151, 164
Onslow Circuit, 136, 140
Ormand, J. M., 137
Orton Plantation, 101
Otterbeim, Philip, 165
Outler, Albert, 165
Oviedo, Gonzalo, 3
Owen, Travis, 95, 161
Oxford University, 40, 41, 44, 124

Paine, John, 28
Parker, A. S., 171
Parker, E. M., 141
Parker J., 100
Parsons, James, 92
Paschal, George, 37
Pastoral Letter, 117

Patmos, 132, 182
Pavy, Walter, 159
Pee Dee Circuit, 97
Pee Dee Mission, 100
Pee Dee River, 3, 25, 59
Peele, L. M., 164, 165
Peele, W. W., 155
Pegg, J. P., 162
Pegues, W. L., 105
Pennsylvania, 59
Pepper, E. M., 133
Perisan, Thomas, 28
Perkins, N. A., 139
Peurifoy, Archibald, 95
Pfister, John, 161
Philadelphia, 52
Philadelphia Conference, 63
Phillips, C. H., 105
Phillips, C. N., 59
Phillips, H. A. Jr., 162
Phoebus, William, 107
Pickett, H. T., 162
Pickett, John R., 98
Pierce, Lovick, 107, 108
Pierce, Riddick, 77
Pilmoor, Joseph, 39, 46, 49, 64, 126, 176
Piney Grove, 137, 148, 157, 182
Plantations, Brunswick County, 101
Pleasant Oaks Plantation, 101
Plyles, Calvin, 133
Plymouth Colony, 122
Point Repose Plantation, 101
Porter, Edwards, 28
Porter, Hugh, 71, 73, 142
Porter, John, 71
Porter, J. J., 139, 141
Porter, Robert, 73
Potter, James, 133
Potter, Miles, 28, 99
Potter, Captain S., 142
Potter, Samuel, 99
Potter, Whitefield, 99
Potter, William Henry, 99
Potter, William T., 99
Price, C. Everette, Jr., 164
Price, W. F., 147
Primitive Methodists, 55
Prince, Nicholas, 93

225

226

South Carolina, 85, 91
South Carolina Conference of
  American Methodism, 61, 63, 69,
  92, 94, 96, 97, 99,. 100, 103,
  104, 105, 107, 130
Southport, 137, 138, 139, 148
Southport: Trinity, 148, 157, 161,
  166, 182
Spanish attack, 20, 36
Spain, Hartwell, 108
Spence, F. M., 153, 159
Spears, William, 28
Spring Garden Plantation, 101
Stacy, J., 103, 104, 108
Stamp Act, 30
Stanaland, John B., 133
Stanaland, plantation, 101
Starnes, James A., 162
Starnes, W. B., 161
State House, 64, 72, 127
Stevens, Simeon L., 95
Strawbridge, Robert, 46
Sturges, Jonathan, 28
Suburb, N.C., 148
Sullivan, Edward, 78, 93, 99, 182
Sullivan, Richard, 99
Sullivan's, 64
Summerville, 137, 182
Sumter, S.C., 84
Supply, N.C., 147
Swain, David, 28
Swain, James H. 41
Swain, Jonathan, 28
Swain, S. P., 141
Swain, plantation, 101
Swannanoa, N.C., 62
Swansboro, 56, 57
Swindell, F. D., 169

Talley, Alexander, 108
Talley, Nicholas, 95, 96, 98, 100,
  103, 104, 108
Tar River Circuit, 54
Tarpley, Joseph, 107, 108
Tart, J. H., 137, 138, 143
Tatum, Jimmie Ray, 163, 164
Taylor, E. W., 141
Taylor, Marble N., 132, 142
Taylor, R. F., 139

Taylor, R. T., 151
Tees, Francis, 178
Temperance Society, 129
Thanksgiving Days, 173
The Forks Plantation, 101
Thomas, John, 28
Thomas Gore, plantation, 101
Thompson, Emerson, 151
Thompson, J. B., 139
Thompson, John E., 135
Thompson, L. E., 170
Thompson, Leo, 151
Thompson, Roger E., 164
Tinkers Creek, 94
Topsail Charge, 131, 134, 136
Town Creek, 20, 54, 56, 57, 64,
  71, 80, 99, 101, 145, 147, 182
Town Creek Charge, 147, 148,
  157, 161
Townsend, Joel W., 93
Travis, Joseph, 76, 77, 78, 92, 93,
  95, 107, 108, 145, 177
Traynham, D. D., 158
Tripp, J. F., 141
Tryon, Lady Mary, 29
Tryon, William, 19, 29-31, 34, 35,
  36
Tucker, Epps, 107
Tucker, Reuben, 95, 108
Tunnell, John, 61
Turner, James B., 95
Turner's, preaching place, 61, 182
Turrentine, Morgan C., 97, 142
Tuttle, D. H., 138
Tyson, Vernon C., 172

Underwood, W. J., 158
Union Chapel, 70
Union Church, 147, 157, 182
Union Class, 132, 182
United Brethren, 128, 165
Usry, J. F., 152

Vaiden, Gerald, Jr., 162
Vanderbilt, Cornelius, 143
Varnum, Tracie, 159, 162, 164, 165
Varnum, Clementine, 159
Vernon, Nancy, 28
Verrazzano, Giovanni de, 1

227